A tour de force. From education to euthanasia, from intellectual debate to culture, Shortt presents a compelling case for a Christian vision of what it means to live well.

Peter Sedgwick, academic and ethicist

A persuasive and elegantly written analysis of one of the most important cultural shifts of recent times – the erosion of Christian faith in the West and the inability to replace it with anything remotely capable of providing coherence and cohesion.

Graham Tomlin, Director, Centre for Cultural Witness

Compulsory reading for all who claim Christianity is dead, irrelevant or over. A lively and rigorous argument for the centrality of the Christian faith for the West and for humanity and for the gap left by its decline. To lose Christianity is to lose grounds for believing in human dignity, human rights and human equality: this is a strong case for a return to our sources.

Angela Tilby, author and theologian

Building on extensive research, Shortt presents a brave and splendidly ambitious case both for Christians and secularists to take Christianity seriously, in a Western world more desperate than it acknowledges for soundly based principles and hopes. He shows we have them, though we are mostly too lazy or complacent or defeatist to acknowledge what they are and on what they depend. Never strident, never obvious, never over-simplified, this very readable book, informed by considerable philosophical and theological learning, is an attack on the carelessness and ignorance of negative secular assumptions about Christianity and all faith in God. It is also an attack on Christian betrayal of the strangeness and definiteness of Christian truth. Its title is well chosen: an eclipse casts a shadow over the brightness of the sun or the moon; it does not extinguish it.

Lucy Beckett, author of *In the Light of Christ:*
Writings in the Western Tradition

The nature of the decline of formal forms of Christianity in the West is hard to discern accurately. Rupert Shortt's careful research and analysis of the religious and spiritual yearnings of a secular age, and his thoughts about the way churches are responding and why Christianity still matters, provide rich food for thought. His central question, of how we might recover sight of the transcendent in a time that feels adrift, is, I have no doubt, of fundamental importance.

Mark Vernon, psychotherapist and author

A brilliant survey of Christianity's decline in Britain – how it's happened, and why it matters – by one of our most learned and stimulating apologists.
Tom Holland, author of *Dominion*

Lucid, brilliant, accessible. A must read! **Ayaan Hirsi Ali, author of *Infidel***

Rupert Shortt is always clear, cogent, compassionate, flawlessly reasonable and perfectly informed. He makes religion intelligible, its predicament plain and its future reassuring. This combined 'celebration and lament' distils his thought and work. The Church, subverted and persecuted, still mobilises goodness, sanctifies lives, saves souls and challenges and changes the world. The eclipse is partial: a bright ring surrounds the passing darkness. Whether you feel tempted to dismiss Christianity or called to defend it, you must read this book.
Felipe Fernandez Armesto, academic and author

Referring to a curious donut-like phenomenon, Rupert Shortt explores the ways in which Christianity is increasingly scorned in public life while finding multiple forms of less visible but important expression. Wide-ranging, readable, and forthright, his study offers an acute analysis of the problems and prospects facing Christian faith today.
David Fergusson, Regius Professor of Divinity, University of Cambridge

In this fluent and engaging guide to the contemporary cultural landscape, Shortt marshals a remarkably diverse range of evidence to support his case that the eclipse of Christianity is profoundly to be regretted.
John Cottingham, Professor Emeritus of Philosophy, University of Reading

Rupert Shortt has not only given us an electric encomium to the intellectual resilience of Christianity but also recalled us to its enduring power both to relieve our existential restlessness and to remedy the maladies of modernity through social and cultural renewal. I couldn't recommend it more highly.
James Orr, Associate Professor of Philosophy of Religion,
University of Cambridge

The Eclipse of Christianity

and why it matters

Rupert Shortt

HODDER &
STOUGHTON

First published in Great Britain in 2024 by Hodder & Stoughton
An Hachette UK Company

1

Copyright © Rupert Shortt 2024

The right of Rupert Shortt to be identified as the Author of the Work has been
asserted by him in accordance with the Copyright, Designs and Patents Act 1988.

Unless indicated otherwise, Scripture quotations are taken from the Holy
Bible, New International Version (Anglicised edition). Copyright © 1979,
1984, 2011 by Biblica Inc.® Used by permission. All rights reserved.

A CIP catalogue record for this title is available from the British Library

Hardback ISBN 978 1 399 80274 1
ebook ISBN 978 1 399 80276 5

Typeset in Sabon MT by Hewer Text UK Ltd, Edinburgh
Printed and bound in Great Britain by Clays Ltd, Elcograf S.p.A.

Hodder & Stoughton policy is to use papers that are natural, renewable
and recyclable products and made from wood grown in sustainable
forests. The logging and manufacturing processes are expected to
conform to the environmental regulations of the country of origin.

Hodder & Stoughton Ltd
Carmelite House
50 Victoria Embankment
London EC4Y 0DZ

www.hodderfaith.com

For David and Susan Warnes

Contents

"No symbolic system in history has been able to rival religious faith, which forges a bond between the routine behaviour of billions of individuals and ultimate, imperishable truths. It's the most enduring, deep-rooted universal form of popular culture that history has ever witnessed, yet you won't find it on a single cultural studies course from Sydney to San Diego."

Terry Eagleton

"Christian faith is . . . the substantiating principle of all true wisdom, the satisfactory solution of all the contradictions of human nature, of the whole riddle of the world. This alone belongs to and speaks intelligibly to all alike, the learned and the ignorant, if but the heart listens."

Samuel Taylor Coleridge

Preface

Forecasts of the West's imminent demise have a long history. How tumultuous the time ahead will be politically and economically compared with other postwar generations is in my view harder to predict than often supposed. Less contentious are two claims endorsed by legions of religious believers and secularists alike: that the mainstream Churches are declining at speed not only throughout Europe but also in North America; and that our Judeo-Christian cultural foundations are denied or denounced with greater confidence in the twenty-first century than ever before.

There is thus a measure of agreement between pro- and anti-Christian camps. Differences simply hinge on whether the evidence is a source of relief or regret. Has secularisation made us better and freer than our grandparents and great-grandparents? Or is liberty unsustainable unless grounded in practices more associated with a spiritually active past, including the cultivation of virtue?

In supporting the second option (among other points it seems ominous for a society to know what it believes, but not why), I am also acutely aware of the Church's failings. No part of my argument rests on a denial of institutional flaws. That Christianity has faltered in some of its historic heartlands must be the responsibility of its representatives to a marked degree. But this awareness in turn does not undermine suggestions that we are losing something vital. Shoots without roots easily perish.

Several further factors deserve emphasis at the outset. One is that eclipses are not irreversible. Since the Christian presence continues to grow strongly at a global level, it would be rash to conclude that shadows across Europe, especially, will never give way to fresh shafts of light. There are further reasons why what follows is in part a celebration as well as a lament. Having set out to chart an apparently sobering situation, I again and again encountered what from a Christian standpoint are seeds of hope. These, too, needed recording. Conscious that many academic chronicles of church decline have already been published, I opted to concentrate more on the consequences of secularisation than its causes. I have also drawn a good deal on other people's writings and views, including those of Rowan Williams and Joseph Ratzinger, my two biographical subjects. Needless to say, the judgements of these and other major figures carry a good deal more weight than my own.

As well as being far from comprehensive, *The Eclipse of Christianity and Why It Matters* does not purport to be a historical work. I have only attempted to sink a probe at various points in a large landscape. (Full coverage of the ecclesiastical scene could easily fill more than one stout volume.) There are no chapters on the Free Churches or on Ireland, for example. Though ranging beyond the UK, I glance at Europe more widely through a series of vignettes and thumbnail sketches, rather than detailed studies. That is not just a function of space constraints. Countries such as Spain, France and Poland clearly differ greatly from each other, as well as from Britain. But history in one society after another around the continent rhymes enough to make certain generalisations viable.

Finally, my third chapter – asking what Christian belief amounts to, and whether it holds water in the first place – may require explanation. The historian Keith Thomas speaks for a large cohort of intellectuals and opinion formers in making a sweeping claim. Christianity has more substantial rituals than humanism (as he puts it in his interview with Alan Macfarlane, available on YouTube); but the comforts it offers are spurious, because atheism is true. In challenging what strikes me as secular dogmatism, I felt a need to revisit material in my quartet of recent books – *God Is No Thing, Does Religion Do More Harm Than Good?, Outgrowing Dawkins* and *The Hardest Problem* – broadly concerned with the coherence of religious belief. Readers already familiar with my arguments may wish to skip this section. I hope others will judge it to be useful groundwork. Early on I describe Christianity as the foremost expression of human culture in existence – though you are unlikely to find it mentioned on many a Cultural Studies course today. There is little point in commending it as a transformative global presence unless it is credible – or at least shown to be worthy of respect.

For agreeing to be interviewed or for offering advice and other forms of support, I am very grateful to Andrew Allen, Jimmy Anderson, Mark Arena, Jonathan Ashley-Norman, David Bagnall, Victoria Barrett, John Barton, Tina Beattie, Lucy Beckett, Jonathan Benthall, Russell Blacker, Alan Bookbinder, John Booth, Philip Booth, Nicholas Boyle, Rosemary Boyle, Gina Buijs, Leon Cane, J. Kameron Carter, Steve Chalke, David Challender, Madeline Cohen, Richard Collyer-Hamlin, John Cornwell, the late Peter Cornwell, John Cottingham, Serena Cox, Tim Crane, Andrew Davison, Bernard Dive, Ben Dowell, Edward Dowler, Adrian Dyer, Jonathan Elijah, Mark Elsdon-Dew, Maria Exall, Felipe Fernández-Armesto, Clive Field, James Francis, Paul de Fritaes, Claire Gilbert, Mo Glackin, Jan Gould, Brigid Graff, Thomas Graff, Chris Green, Brian Griffiths, Tudor Griffiths, Brian Grim, Enrico Grube, Nicky Gumbel, Hattie Haines, Christopher Harrington, Katie Harrison, David Bentley Hart, Usama Hasan, Jack Haughton, Jane Haughton, Diana Healey, Ian Helps, Linda Helps, Ayaan Hirsi Ali, Johannes Hoff, Sheila Hollins, Margaret Holness, Joshua Hordern, Arnold Hunt, David Albert Jones, Robert Jones, Blake Joseph, Oliver Keenan, John Keown, John Kennedy, Lizelke Klindt, Jane Leek, Toby Lees OP, Chieh Lin, Tim Livesey, Tim Llewellyn-Jones, Steve Lukito, Jonathan Luxmoore, Ángel Maldonado, Marc Manera, Jean-Luc Marion, Bernice Martin, Philip McCosker, Alban McCoy, Iain McGilchrist, Neil McKenna, Maren Meinhardt, Alison Milbank, John Milbank, Vittorio Montemaggi, Len Moore, Jeremy Morris, Fitzroy Morrissey, Mark Oakley, Oliver O'Donovan, Chris

Oldfield, Elizabeth Oldfield, Helen Orr, James Orr, Glyn Paflin, Martin Palmer, Robin Parry, Richard Peaver, Jacob Phillips, Trevor Phillips, John Plender, the late Christa Pongratz-Lippitt, John Pontifex, José Prado, Gareth Rayner-Williams, Ernie Rea, Callum Roberts, John Roberts, Dominic Robinson SJ, Daniel Rowlands OP, Nicholas Sagovsky, the late Christoph Schwöbel, Peter Sedgwick, Jane Shaw, Alison Shell, John Sherrington, Tom Shortt, Janet Soskice, Nick Spencer, Edward Stourton, Vincent Strudwick, Simon Sylvester, Wojciech Szczerba, Adrian Tahourdin, Angela Tilby, Maxine Valensky, Teresa Vallès, Rosa María Valverde, Anna Vaux, Robert Verrill OP, Miroslav Volf, Michael Wakelin, Justin Walford, Marcus Walker, Brendan Walsh, Luke Walton, Christoph Warrack, Albert Weale, Anthony Weale, Kate Weale, George Weigel, Dominic White OP, Joshua White, Taylor Wilton-Morgan, Russell Winfield, Justin Wise, Tom Wright, Martin Wroe and Engin Yildirim.

I am most indebted of all to David and Susan Warnes, the dedicatees of this book; and to Andy Lyon, Abigail Chatterjee and their colleagues at Hodder. It has been an abiding delight to work with publishers of their calibre.

Rupert Shortt
St Edmund's College, Cambridge, Eastertide 2024

Part I
Faltering Faith

I

A Flight from Enchantment

A while back I came across a stimulating essay by Arnold Hunt on Charles Maurice Davies, the Victorian cleric and journalist once famous for his accounts of London's spiritual scene.[1] Hunt mainly writes about the early modern era. Departing from his core area of research, he spotlighted a large social mosaic by quoting one of Davies's contemporaries to rich effect: 'At no period of history, probably since the schools of religion and philosophy jostled one another in the streets of Alexandria, have the forms of religious life been more exuberant and diversified than in London at the present time.'[2]

These words ring true. Britain's capital city in 1870 was the largest on earth. Its population would surpass four million over the following twenty years. Growth on this scale made it not just home to many hundreds of churches, but also a seedbed for new kinds of faith and belief. Even then, the religious variety of mid-Victorian London was seen as unprecedented. Hunt's outline of his subject's quest is highly instructive against this backdrop. The voyage only started within established boundaries. Davies moved successively from Christianity to freethought, secularism and atheism, before settling on the wilder shores of spiritualism and magic. His four books *Unorthodox London* (1873), *Orthodox London* (1873), *Heterodox London* (1874) and *Mystic London* (1875) cover the gamut of Victorian religion and irreligion. With Davies as a guide, Hunt adds, we can see how the city's religious past is still visible now: 'Just as London in the 1870s carried the seeds of modernity, so its religious landscape today, 150 years later, offers clues to the future of religion at another moment of radical change.'

In other words, Davies's world is our world – with 'our' referring far beyond London to a great number of twenty-first-century urban settings. Yes, Europe's (and perhaps the world's) most cosmopolitan city retains a Victorian shape in many respects. Its Victorian suburbs are linked by a Victorian transport system, its districts dotted with Victorian parks and cemeteries, its skyline heavily marked by the spires of Victorian churches. But Hunt also draws out deeper similarities between Davies's setting and the present:

> The process of religious change that he witnessed was one of simultaneous growth and fragmentation, as the established churches found themselves competing with new expressions of religious faith. This is very similar to the situation in London today, where it is estimated that the number of churches has grown by 50 per cent since 1979, largely owing to the emergence of new Pentecostal and black-majority congregations. London has once again become the seedbed for religious transformation, as it was 150 years ago, and Davies can give us the historical perspective to help understand why.[3]

This book offers an overview of traditional – and for now, still mainstream – Christianity's fading profile in the present. It is anything but exhaustive: there are plenty of more detailed studies available in the academic literature. My goal is partly to turn the soil at various points in a broad field and gauge its quality for a general audience. At the same time, I consider it vital to qualify talk of decline at the outset. In many parts of our world the Christian canopy grows ever broader, in others the saplings bloom, and even in Western Europe any assessment of the plants' health cannot only be negative. The Church is young as well as old. An analogy from the arts offers another sidelight on things. Predictions of the imminent death of classical music were common during much of the twentieth century. While this once central component of civilisation has certainly dwindled in importance, it has also recast itself. Fewer people go to concert halls in person, but a platform such as Spotify gives users access to vast libraries of previously hidden material. And orchestral scores (often of the highest quality) are central to a genre such as film.

So the many heralds of a godless new dawn from the Enlightenment onwards have not been vindicated in any straightforward sense. If you locate all fundamental urges in the will to power (Nietzsche) or economic drives (Marx) or sex (Freud), then spirituality will of course appear redundant. Yet sociologists of religion rarely take theories as crude as these with any seriousness today. More plausibly, we have witnessed a doughnut effect of sorts: though coined by American demographers to describe middle-class flight towards the suburbs, it could also be applied in a religious context. The traditional Christian centre has certainly languished. Far from dying out, however, expressions of faith have simply moved to the edges of society in the form of Muslim, Hindu and Jewish renaissances – and 'fresh expressions' of church. That is why the life and times of Charles Maurice Davies do not only subvert stories told by believers of a uniformly devout past, but also the claims by some campaigners of a non-religious present. Especially notable is Christianity's capacity to survive its obituarists.

The pages ahead therefore pivot on a paradox. Given its historical profile and geographical reach, Christianity counts as the foremost expression of human culture. The faith continues to expand: at a global level tens of thousands of fresh converts are registered every day across Africa alone. Pentecostalism, the Christian counterpart to Islamic revivalism, has long been spreading at exponential speed across the Global South and in East Asia. A trend on this scale confirms claims that secularisation has gone into reverse in many places. As I have noted in my book *Christianophobia*,[4] a record of faith-based political groups would include Vishwa Hindu Parishad in India (which sowed the seeds of Hindu nationalism reaped by the BJP during the 1990s), the Muslim Brotherhood in Egypt and Jordan, Hamas in the Palestinian territories, Hezbollah in Lebanon, the Nahdlatul Ulama in Indonesia, Pentecostals across the regions already noted; and, in the Catholic world, an array of forces including European Christian Democrats, Opus Dei and the newer religious movements. Faith communities are also forging remarkable transnational capabilities, appealing to foreign governments and international bodies judged supportive of their aims. Whether one views these phenomena with gladness or unease (or with mixed feelings), a conclusion reached by two prominent American sociologists, Timothy Samuel Shah and Monica Duffy Toft, is fair:

> The belief that outbreaks of politicized religion are temporary detours on the road to secularization was plausible in 1976, 1986, or even 1996. Today, the argument is untenable. As a framework for explaining and predicting the course of global politics, secularism is increasingly unsound. God is winning in global politics. And modernization, democratization and globalization have only made him stronger.[5]

Although these points should serve to qualify my main pitch, none discredits claims of a Christian recession. Whatever is happening on other continents, the faith overall falters in its Middle Eastern and European heartlands. Ancient communities with roots in the apostolic era across some Arab societies are being crushed through active persecution. Europe's path is plainly very different. The older generations are often residually attached to beliefs imprinted in childhood. But residues are apt to fade away by definition. The middle aged are usually far less connected to the Church than their parents, having long since cast aside the fairy story (as they see it) taught at Sunday school without exploring it further. The young, accordingly, do not even have something to kick against. Christianity is thus a blank slate to a high proportion of millennials and members of Generation Z.

Britain's most recent census bears this out. In November 2022 the Office for National Statistics released figures confirming that the proportion of people identifying as Christian in England and Wales had fallen below half for the first time.[6] The figure was 71.7

per cent (37.3 million people) in 2001, 59.3 per cent in 2011, and 46 per cent in 2021. Nearly four-fifths of senior citizens tick the box marked 'Christian'; among twentysomethings only 30 per cent do. The census also shows that 10.8 per cent of people in the same territory adhere to other faiths, up from 8.4 per cent in 2011. The proportion of Muslims rose from 4.8 per cent of the population to 6.5 per cent (3.9 million people). Scotland's position broadly matches that of its southern neighbours.[7]

No one in the UK has processed the data more meticulously than Clive Field of the University of Birmingham. Among much else, his indispensable book *Counting Religion in Britain, 1970–2020*[8] records the scale of decline across the denominations. In 1924, 3.5 million people were registered on the Church of England's electoral rolls. There were only 900,000 by 2019. Catholic candidates for confirmation fell from 72,000 in 1971 to 24,000 in 2019. The Methodist Church had 617,000 members in 1970, but only 164,000 half a century later. Looking over the same time frame, Field records a fair estimate that church membership declined from 7.7 million to 3.9 million. The figure is especially telling given that the population almost doubled during this period. Side by side with all this, a further finding of the census seems significant – and curious by comparison with the figures just listed. Of those who ticked the 'No Religion' box, only half said they didn't believe in God at all, and a fifth of non-believers expressed confidence in some form of afterlife. The reality is thus perhaps messier than we might suppose.

Beyond statistical information, one principal corollary I draw from clear evidence of decline is that Britain and other parts of Europe are impaired by a neglect of their church roots. How so? A credible answer concerns the sobering implications of believing (say) that we are just animals wired up to the struggle for survival, or that meaning, mattering and the quest for transcendence – a higher dimension of reality embodying more exalted values – are illusions. A related reply would be that secular liberalism lacks secure philosophical underpinnings. As an alternative to the solid nourishment offered by grown-up, self-critical Christianity, a creed such as humanism presents an imperative to be kind. The grounds for all this appear shaky: when humanists are asked to show without recourse to metaphysics *why* we should be kind, the answers they give often lack coherence. And we live in far from kind times anyway. Quite apart from the climate crisis, ours is an era of infotainment, an obsession with celebrity and blaming, complaining and shaming, colossal cynicism encapsulated by the term 'post-truth', unprecedented family breakdown, moral relativism, scientific as well as religious fundamentalism, and a polarised public conversation.

The New Testament scholar Tom Wright transposes this awareness into a related key. Noting that nature abhors a vacuum (philosophical as much as physical), he argues that three pagan deities from antiquity – Mars the god of war, Mammon the god of money, and Aphrodite, goddess of erotic love – are still venerated in fresh guises: '. . . our society, claiming to have got rid of God upstairs so that we can live our lives the way we want . . . has in fact fallen back into the clutches of forces . . . that are bigger than ourselves, more powerful than the sum total of people who give them allegiance – forces we might as well recognise as gods.'[9] His analysis is shared by Mary Eberstadt in her important book *How the West Really Lost God*.[10]

My second main corollary is that organised religion in the West is undergoing a profound transformation. For reasons already sketched (and elaborated later), I do not believe the Churches are dying or collapsing. But it seems undeniable that they are changing in very dramatic and sometimes disorienting ways. This book does not just entail a critique of the secularisation thesis and of secularising impulses across contemporary British culture; it also seeks to map aspects of that religious development.

***

From a Christian standpoint, of course, the main reason for paying serious attention to church teaching is that it purports to disclose the truth of our being with special authority. The 'greatest story ever told' is about love's mending of wounded hearts. Core parts of this perceived revelation could be summed up as follows. God's outreach is mediated in creation, which, over time, our Creator patiently allows to yield its own true character. This process operates through worldly agencies, including human beings, who are all made in the divine image. And in and through everything, the Holy Spirit is seeking to re-create and transform, a process realised crucially in God's identification with the world in Christ. Wherever Christians look, whether inside or outside the visible Church, they are likely to find evidence of divine gift, and should thus identify the 'other', especially the outsider, as bearing God to them. The creed therefore provides the strongest available foundations for values including the sanctity of life, the dignity of the individual, and human responsibility for the environment. Moving from the province of faith to more empirical factors, Christians could also say that the Church is the world's single largest source of social capital, mainly in unsung ways. They might re-emphasise that while our culture draws on *some* aspects of a secularised theology, it too often overlooks the deepest strands of all in the Christian repertoire: grace, forgiveness, solidarity and reconciliation. To sum up: Europe's historic faith deserves a more serious hearing than it usually receives from the mainstream.

In saying all this I am not seeking to score cheap points against unbelievers. The institutional Churches' record of past intolerance is deplorable; such chauvinism persists today in pockets of the Protestant, Eastern Orthodox and Roman Catholic worlds. (Jesus himself was the first to warn of wolves in sheep's clothing.) I am also conscious that secularism comes in different forms. It is the 'exclusionary' kind which I find problematic, especially when it insists that faith is a purely private and personal matter for consenting adults in the privacy of their own homes, or possibly the privacy of their own pews, but that it should not have any role in education or wider society. Such a stance has become much stronger in recent decades. Its cloudiness about ethics poses an

abiding problem for reasons I have just hinted at. To claim that
the world would be a better place if we were all kind to each other
is just Pelagianism (the ancient heresy springing from false optimism about unaided human resources) without God. It is based
on a naive assumption that when things go wrong, the culprit
must be ideology. And religion is just another form of ideology. If
you want to see this mindset writ large, just consult the website
of Humanists UK.

The sources of such thinking in the work of Rousseau and other
Enlightenment figures are easy to track. Christians, by contrast,
have far more to say about the reality of human nature: its flaws,
its brokenness, its need of healing. The same is true of ethics,
because the Church can offer imperatives based on a conviction that the material world is an expression of God's nature,
sustained by God's nature, and a gift from God's nature. Those
beliefs mean that ultimately a Christian should not be a utilitarian. When a secularist is pushed into a corner, she or he generally
does turn out in terms of ethical thinking to be some kind of
utilitarian. I hope to show why that is unsustainable.*

---

* Medical ethics – especially involving unavoidable decisions about how
to prioritise care – forms a case in point. The secularist tends to say that
we should save patients in their twenties, say, because they can be offered
decades of quality of life, end of discussion. 'That's an important point,'
the Christian may reply. 'But there is also much to be said about patients
not as individuals, but as part of a network of relationships.' The secularist may well push back and point out that hospitals have limited resources,
and that young people, unlike their grandparents, have their whole lives
ahead of them. Christians need not discount this manner of reasoning in
the least. They may indeed acknowledge that there are certain situations in
which perhaps the utilitarian argument should win out. Secularists on the
other hand are likely to say that the calculus entails nothing but utilitarian
considerations – and in my view there are clear instances where utilitarian
arguments shouldn't win. For example, you could make quite a strong utilitarian argument for the death penalty on the grounds that it costs more to
keep somebody in jail than to send a pupil to Eton. And if they have done
something which necessitates their exclusion from society for the rest of

The arc just traced – namely Christian decline leading to a spiritual void, rather than viable substitutes – was powerfully illustrated for me by a chance encounter early on in my researches. While attending a conference at Maynooth near Dublin, I met a fifty-year-old non-stipendiary Anglican priest who has worked in teaching, publishing and other areas for several decades largely in the west and north-west of England. His words deserve to be recorded.

'I wasn't brought up in the Church,' he explained. 'My parents occasionally took me and my siblings at Christmas, but that was more or less all. So I do have memories of occasionally being in a church service, which I hated. But what we *did* have – and I never thought about it at the time – was school assemblies where we would sing hymns and hear prayers and Bible readings. In the 1970s and 1980s, Bible lessons had a prominent place in primary schools. None of my schools was a church school.'

His family uprooted themselves from the Liverpool area to Wales in the early 1980s, when he was ten.

In time I moved from a village primary school to a comprehensive in Wrexham, the local town. Though it wasn't a Christian foundation, we had daily assemblies involving Christian worship and hymn-singing. From my time on Merseyside I recall that there were seven or eight functioning churches within a short walk of my home. They were very much part of the landscape. Christianity was in the culture. You didn't have to watch religious content on TV. But programmes like *Songs of Praise* were

---

their lives, why should we spend so much money when it could be devoted to far better causes? As an opponent of the death penalty, I feel that this argument should be resisted.

More broadly, I don't discount the appeal of utilitarian movements such as Effective Altruism (EA) and 80,000 Hours as channels for the energies of idealistic young people. But the philosophy behind such endeavours is thin compared with a Christian account of the world.

there in the background, at least getting in the way of things you *did* want to watch!

And of course the vicar or priest was a common figure in dramas. He naturally wasn't the main character, but a cleric was still part of the social fabric. Perhaps the key point is this. I didn't think of myself as a Christian, but I didn't think of myself as *not* a Christian. And while not really thinking about God, I wasn't an active disbeliever either. So when I started to meet Christian friends, it suddenly felt as though there was something implicit to draw on. I realised that I knew a whole lot about Christianity that I didn't know that I knew. We'd all seen [the stage musical] *Godspell*, for example. So I knew the Jesus story. And we'd all been given a Gideon Bible at secondary school, which I'd dipped into. In other words, there was a whole bunch of stuff that I'd absorbed without being aware of it.

When I asked why he judges the situation to be so different in the 2020s, his response was unhesitating.

Because the public spaces have been much more evacuated of Christian material in terms of what we find on radio and television. Regarding what you might call the sociology of knowledge, there's so much less now to *reinforce* the belief. If you go to church, then of course you'll be presented with the narrative. But you're not going to find it in the public spaces, partly from a wish to accommodate non-believers. And of course push and pull factors can be mutually reinforcing. It's also obviously true that very large numbers of people with Christian backgrounds just aren't interested anyway.

He went on to supply some vital historical perspective. Church attendance rates in eighteenth-century England were often patchy, and yet because basic Christian ideas were widely shared and underpinned by community events such as harvest festival, people's worldview was shaped by doctrine in a loose sense.

They hoped for a heavenly future and wanted their children to be baptised. Their views weren't terribly well thought out, but were nevertheless in the bloodstream. So when the Evangelical Revival took off later in the eighteenth century, there was something for preachers to work with. I suspect that a figure like Jonathan Edwards [the renowned American theologian, 1703–58] coming along today would be far more likely to face derision.

One obvious response to all this is that people were suggestible or superstitious in the past and have grown out of all that folk Christianity now. My interviewee rejected this theory out of hand.

Is our deracinated public space really so superior? Vast numbers of people now have little or no sense of who Jesus was or what's in the Bible. They think Easter's about the Easter Bunny. Look at Advent calendars today and there's often nothing to indicate that they mark the build-up to a major Christian festival. Even as recently as my childhood, I remember that such calendars at least had nativity scenes.

Christmas proper begins on Christmas Day of course. But like many people in the UK, most members of my family spend the month of December celebrating, and then think it's all over on the 25th. My sister even removes her decorations then, because the idea of keeping them up for longer strikes her as depressing. From the 26th onwards, the focus is on the sales. As a priest I've also noticed a large decline in congregations at Christmas, especially for Midnight Mass.

He then observed that habituating congregations – a challenge at the best of times – had become vastly harder because of the Covid-19 pandemic.

Work with children was especially impacted of course, because they weren't allowed to touch anything. Habituation is so important, because in general Christianity is a *slow* spirituality, which tends to deepen over the years. As it happens, I eventually came to faith through a charismatic evangelical experience. There was instant pizazz. But maintaining that level of intensity can be pretty exhausting. More traditional forms of Christianity naturally work by building practices and habits. The effect is cumulative, rather like learning a musical instrument. And like an instrument, part of the process can be pretty focused on the mechanics. For a while you may not feel you're reaping much benefit, but over time the investment can pay off.

Those who immerse themselves in the story are likely to know what to say to God, because words and gestures are in their bones and bodies. Now, by contrast, you're constantly having to compete with other activities. I accept that, in the past, clergy had more of a captive audience and could take more for granted. But now what you might call brand loyalty has fallen off a cliff. As a devout member of the Church of England, my grandmother wouldn't have dreamt of attending a non-Anglican church. Her sister, who belonged to the Salvation Army, had similar attitudes. That whole culture has died away now. In the same way that people no longer feel loyalty to anything from shops to the utility providers, pastors now often feel under pressure to provide novelty value to people who feel no source of special commitment to them. So long as it gives people what they want to feel, they'll go. And if it doesn't, they won't.

He also judged that places of worship – especially, perhaps, in the Anglican, Methodist, Baptist and United Reformed communities – have been reframed as clubs.

Members of the clergy feel they have to constantly market themselves, sell themselves and entertain people. And it's difficult to compete. So we lower the threshold as far as possible to be welcoming, which in a way is good of course. But then there's no challenge. A familiar point could be added: that it's congregations making more demands of their members – conservative evangelicals, Pentecostals, some Orthodox and traditionalist Catholics, especially – which are growing.

He felt that his arguments apply with equal force in education.

People would say to me, 'All I want is for you to teach our children ethics.' But *which* ethics, I wondered! If I taught *my* ethics, these parents would have got cross with me, because they'd have seen them as too Christian. If you look at what ethics used to be, it was an induction into ways of life and patterns of behaviour, including virtues and the formation of character and so forth. But the point is that you can only pursue that project in the context of a tradition. So how do you do it in a society where there are fewer and fewer shared customs? A sign of the times is that an Ethics teacher will now typically say, 'Let's look at such and such a moral problem. Here's what *x* says. Here's what *y* says. What do *you* think? Just decide for yourself.'

This is the prevailing mentality. So long as you make an authentic choice, all's fine. But in that climate a teacher is not inculcating virtues or practices or anything like that. You're not forming people. You're just helping them weigh up pros and cons of various moral issues. And how else can you do it in a society that doesn't have a shared framework or tradition? Without such scales, as [the Marxist-turned-Christian philosopher] Alasdair MacIntyre reminds us, you can be reduced to a free-for-all. This forms the huge cultural change, which has made it so much harder to teach ethics.

The same applies to worship. It's all very well, when you can assume that everyone in the village has been baptised, but nowadays they're not. And since they're not being brought up as Christian believers, they may find at school, for example, that the teacher says, 'We're going to be quiet for a bit now. And if you believe in God you can pray, but otherwise we'll be neutral.' This is analogous to the blankness of the multifaith chapel. Of course I understand the reasoning behind all this. It's good to be inclusive and to strive not to offend. But a common language is important as well. Why do we find certain things obvious at an intuitive level? It's not just because we may think we have robust intellectual arguments, or because someone has shown us evidence. It's because we inhabit structures of belief, which are implicit as much as explicit. And in days gone by important areas of society – schools, hospitals and so forth – would have had Christian symbols, Christian prayers, Christian ceremonies, which all subtly supported this belief system. When you evacuate these things from the public arena, the only place they're being reinforced is in church. That can leave even committed Christians feeling rather disoriented.

The slump mapped in these reflections clearly has many causes. They include self-induced wounds in the Churches ranging from corruption to poor communication, as well as the effects of attacks – fair as well as unmerited – of secularists. There are also trends behind falling church attendance that have little to do with ideology. During the nineteenth and first half of the twenti-eth centuries, the Churches offered a rich social environment. But they were trumped by the cultural menu provided by television from the 1950s onwards. It strikes me as interesting that church attendance does not seem to have suffered from the rise of cinema in the 1920s and 1930s, perhaps because going to the pictures involved making the effort to get out of your house and was, like church, a shared group experience involving compelling imagery and emotion and also a place where romantic relationships could begin. The rise of television in the 1950s and 1960s undoubtedly led to a decline in cinema attendance and was surely also a factor in the decline of churchgoing.

Just as I'm sceptical as to whether intellectual ideas have been a *primary* cause of decline, I think it's clear that scandals about clerical abuse have become *ex post facto* justifications for a lack of interest and involvement in church which already existed and turned some people hostile towards organised religion who were previously merely indifferent to it. A major message to emerge from a recent study such as *Tracing the Cultural Legacy of Irish Catholicism*[11] is that the various scandals regarding paedophile priests, and the harsh treatment of unmarried mothers by nuns, were accelerants to a downward trajectory that had already set in for other reasons, not a primary cause of decline.

Notwithstanding the force of these factors, I do not think that ideology in its various guises is insignificant. Take feminism. The mainstream Churches were very patriarchal before the 1980s. While Methodism moved to ordaining women from 1974, the Church of England took another eighteen years to pass the canon paving the way for women priests. Many educated women now of retirement age, informed by the ideas of feminist writers, were both baffled and repelled by the delay.

As already hinted, one way of trying to reconcile the very different pictures painted so far (vibrancy in much of the world, alongside enfeeblement in Europe leading to confusion or apathy, rather than carefully considered secularism) involves the gap between opinion-formers and ordinary people. While seeing feminism as a major blessing – and much feminist theology as solidly rooted in the Gospels – I wouldn't hesitate to describe the hostility to Christianity displayed by many educators and journalists as a blind spot. A decade ago I wrote *God Is No Thing*,[12] a brief defence of Christian belief beginning with a focus on this point. My argument was backed up by an elaboration of the lament already outlined, especially with reference to an array of cultural figures. Among those cited was the painter and printmaker Anthony Green. He said in a BBC interview that attention to religious themes can be the kiss of death to an artist's career.[13] Other examples I gave bear repetition. Discussing Marilynne Robinson's acclaimed novels *Gilead*, *Home* and *Lila*, the journalist Bryan Appleyard has written that these works will seem curious to a high number of readers, 'because what is going on here is religion'.[14] He went on to argue that 'many, probably most, British people – artists, writers, audiences – will find this exotic because to them, religion has been embarrassed out of existence.' Robinson stands out as a considerable Christian thinker, as well as a novelist. By contrast, an ample company of established British writers have little or nothing to say about transcendence. When religion is broached in their works (think Julian Barnes or Ian McEwan or Alan Hollinghurst or Martin Amis, as well as a gallery of younger writers), it is regularly in terms of a simplistic opposition between faith and reason. Genuine rationality can become the first casualty of this attitude. Novelists who address religious themes – my random sample would include Jill Paton Walsh, Anita Mason and Lucy Beckett – have consciously operated out of left field. A figure such as Robert Skidelsky speaks for squadrons of intellectuals in stating dogmatically that there is no longer any alternative to a disenchanted take on reality. 'We cannot imagine a different paradigm because we can no longer imagine a God who cares for us.'[15]

In an area of non-fiction such as memoir, misery trumps mirth for understandable reasons. In the same way that a volcanic eruption counts as news while underground streams supplying stability of life to generations are widely ignored, tales about bad religion sell. Think of examples including Matt Rowland Hill's *Original Sins* (on fundamentalism of a Baptist stripe), Edmund Gosse's *Father and Son* (the Plymouth Brethren), Jeanette Winterson's *Why Be Happy When You Could Be Normal?* (Pentecostalism) or Patricia Lockwood's *Priestdaddy* (Catholicism). I don't decry such publications for a moment. On the contrary, their authors have my admiration. It is because I am myself a Catholic that I have so much to say about dysfunctionality, as well as great good, in my own Church. I am simply making an observation about human nature and how it can relate to commercial imperatives. The point was once crisply summed up by a Fleet Street editor. When asked why there were so few good-news stories in his paper about the Church of England, he replied that creditable material wasn't eye-catching: 'Our readers want to hear about vicars with their hands in the till or their trousers round their ankles.'

I added that Brian Cox's high reputations as a physicist and a broadcaster are secure, but in suggesting an equivalence between reflecting on the existence of God and that of witches,[16] he strayed well beyond his spheres of competence. And I drew attention to a blind spot uniting commentators of Left and Right alike. A decade on, they continue to bang the same drums. The year I began this book, 2022, was bookended by tin-eared attacks on Christianity by Polly Toynbee[17] and Matthew Parris.[18] Numerous similar articles by less famous journalists could be cited.

In revisiting such material I do not mean to imply that the direction of travel is all uniform. Religious Studies is now treated more seriously in English-speaking countries than two generations ago, when sociologists and others tended to see the study of faith communities as akin to examining dead civilisations. Philosophers with Christian allegiances such as Charles Taylor, Jean-Luc Marion and Alasdair MacIntyre are internationally renowned. So, too, are theologians including John Milbank, Sarah Coakley and Rowan Williams, to cite just three names from the ranks of my own teachers. In Britain, political opinion-formers such as Adrian Pabst (Blue Labour) and Phillip Blond (Red Tory) have notably strong theological backgrounds. Pabst's writings in the *New Statesman* form an especially valuable resource for appreciating deeper cultural currents. Their prescriptions are in turn shadowed by the rich intellectual genealogies found in the work of figures including Larry Siedentop, or by social-market theorising in Germany, itself a rich expression of Catholic Social Teaching.

One of my aims in *God Is No Thing* was to commend a self-aware, unstrident form of Christianity to sceptics and outright scoffers. Yes, religion – like all forms of kinship bond, including patriotism and family life – can go terribly wrong at times. Expressions of faith come in multiple forms. But those whose default assumption is that the Churches and other communities of conviction should be relegated to the margins are themselves taking sides.

I also realised that my protests about the deliberate sidelining of faith would draw a swift protest from some. Public religious voices in North America and parts of Europe are often robust and sometimes shrill. In the UK, of course, Church and state are still officially connected, even if the cords that bind them have been slackening for over 150 years. Perhaps it is precisely these factors which render dislike of Christianity among religion's cultured despisers all the more pointed. From the other side of the fence, though, rising levels of hardline secularism look just as doctrinaire as some expressions of Christian faith. To cite the journalist Will Lloyd's bracing indictment of groupthink of a related kind (this time among student activists at Oxford), 'A hermetic monoculture that, in rejecting views that did not conform to its own advanced ethical standards, had returned to the overbearing orthodoxies of its medieval founding.'[19]

This is noteworthy because of the gap already traced above between opinion-formers and ordinary people. The secularist claim that we are ceasing to be a population of religious believers should be qualified by the observation that a country like the UK has ceased to be one of church attenders. The ONS figures cited above appear conclusive on the face of it. As I have suggested, though, they need placing in a broader context. A priest of great experience sums things up like this.

> Almost all clerics in the C of E would say to you on the basis of funeral preparation, particularly, that the number of unchurched people who nevertheless have some sort of belief in God, and some sort of belief in an afterlife – and some sort of sense of the importance of ritual in marking transitions – is enormous. Some of that may count as superstition. Much of it is perhaps hazily thought through. But it's immensely strong. The secularist suggestion that we have ceased to be a religious society is based on a narrow sample of secularists talking to other secularists.

The point is epitomised by that famous retort, 'We don't do religion', once given by Tony Blair's chief spin doctor Alastair

Campbell. Many observers will have asked why he said that, working for a man who at that stage was a practising Anglican on the verge of becoming a Catholic, and married to a devout Catholic. Whence that embarrassment? I do not think it has anything whatsoever to do with what the great mass of the population might have thought. It has far more to do with the assumptions of a small metropolitan coterie. Having partly grown up in Spain before travelling a good deal around the northern Mediterranean, I know that this insight applies far more broadly than the UK.

God Is No Thing is not a work of sociology probing the sources of secularisation. A more broadly based study might have elaborated upon the ecclesiastical failings to which I have already alluded. When it comes to poor communication, I see fault in ecclesiastical and mainstream media ranks alike in the perpetuating of false stereotypes about a supposed clash between Christianity and science, among other matters. The creed is far more intellectually seaworthy than appreciated even by regular worshippers, but one would never think so to judge by BBC output or most daily newspapers.

More of this later. Meanwhile, any bid to establish co-ordinates on unstable terrain needs to say more about what has happened, and a good deal more about the two major follow-up questions already signposted. First, why should we care? And second, why are belief in God and in Christianity's historical foundations credible in the first place? Many who are not actively hostile to faith readily grant the positive role played by Europe's Christian heritage in raising us to the branches on which we now perch, but still think that the ladder can be kicked away for the simple reason that atheism is true. Given this, I doubt whether a study concentrating only on the Churches' role as sources of good works will hold much sway without some deeper conceptual discussion first. An already large menu cannot avoid some philosophical ingredients as well.

***

Let us start by amplifying the comments made by my conversation partner at Maynooth. Several different discourses must be disentangled. When sociologists talk about secularisation today, they mean not just the retreat of religion from the public square or the decline in attendance, but also the thinning out of religion itself. A hard-edged secularisation theorist like Bryan Wilson, for example, author of *Religion and Secular Society* (1964),[20] exemplified this trend. His work is regularly quoted as confirmation of a process whereby religion loses its grip. As an intellectual system a faith like Christianity is represented as marginalised, but also as diluting its own metaphysical claims. Wilson used this paradigm to argue that even in the United States – where churchgoing as a proportion of the population had risen – secularisation was still advancing because the Churches were becoming worldlier. So very broad-brush assumptions about the cultural retreat of religion took root.

The two phenomena often get confused as a consequence of this approach, particularly by historians themselves, because they assume secularisation to have occurred seamlessly. A. J. P. Taylor is a notable exemplar of this fallacy. His bestselling *English History 1914–1945*[21] contains the fanciful (albeit perhaps tongue-in-cheek) suggestion that the Rector of Stiffkey in Norfolk – a defrocked clergyman found guilty of conduct unbecoming in 1932 – had more impact on church affairs than Cosmo Gordon Lang, then Archbishop of Canterbury. The claim reflects Taylor's own conviction about secularisation and his habit of weaving it into his work. Similar instances of bias are widespread, not only among Marxist or Marxist-influenced scholars who shaped the emergence of social history in the 1960s and 1970s, but also in liberal and conservative ranks. I wrote above of tunnel vision among well-known novelists. The same charge could be brought against many of Taylor's younger colleagues.[22]

Broadly, there is a pair of positions in the historiography of secularisation, as well as numerous further subdivisions. One reflects this anti-religious pattern of thought; the other forms a reaction against it. The classic negative view holds that modern society is becoming intrinsically inimical to religion. It dates back to figures including Max Weber and Ferdinand Tönnies (author of the classic study *Gemeinschaft und Gesellschaft (Community and Society)*, 1887). At root, religion, a cultural feature of the organic, tradition-bound past, is pictured as giving way to a much more rational and instrumental account of reality. Among contemporary sociologists, a figure such as Steve Bruce stands strongly in this line of interpretation.[23] So does Callum Brown, author of *The Death of Christian Britain*,[24] but in a more nuanced way. Practitioners who start by assuming that religion is in a downward spiral are apt to adopt the tools and methods that back up their thesis.

The revisionists – figures including David Martin, Bernice Martin, Hugh McLeod, Mark Smith and Jeffrey Cox – have done much to lay bare the pessimists' presuppositions. This has led in the hands of some people to the opposite problem, which is almost a denial of the reality of church decline. The approach is exemplified by David Goodhew, a historian and cleric who has forged a literature around church growth purporting to be based on empirical evidence. Drawing especially on trends in London, he suggests that desecularisation is even happening in England. Churchgoing may not necessarily be under threat at all.

The reason historiography and historical research should be disentangled is that it seems to me incontestable, for the reasons already spelt out, that the Churches are struggling. The retreat is particularly evident in the traditional denominations, but that should be distinguished from arguments about sociological theory. Much anglophone sociology does indeed operate with a secularising paradigm. Better forms of historiography are now trying to find a way of describing the vicissitudes of religion in modern Britain that do not assume the inevitability of secularisation on the one hand, or, on the other, ignore clear evidence of ebbing numbers, falling income and so forth.

Francophone and British methodologies differ substantially. Sociologists in the UK tend to shun theological assumptions, basing their work on a mixture of economics, politics and social observation. In France, the term *sociologie* as applied to religion relates to understandings of the social appeal of Catholicism in particular. It was pioneered not by Marxist-influenced social historians, but by scholars of Christian allegiance – people like Gérard Cholvy or Yves-Marie Hilaire, who were particularly interested in the post-revolutionary situation of the French Church – and in studying its impact on the ground. Various measurements were devised, including figures for Easter communicants or for numbers of regular weekly communicants (*pascalisants* and *messalisants* respectively): massive accumulations of statistics ensued. Debate has also been greatly influenced by post-revolutionary Church–state conflict and the implementation of *laïcité*. The Anglican–Roman Catholic state secondary school in Cambridge near where I work is steeped in Christian symbolism. There are crucifixes in many classrooms. That would of course be impossible in France. So the different national cultures and their different national histories undoubtedly make a synthesised account of the trajectory of religion in the West more difficult.

The German situation is different again, being profoundly affected by catastrophe and renewal during the twentieth century, and above all by church involvement in politics for both good and ill. So national histories have shaped methodologies. Scandinavia forms a further point of contrast. While levels of regular attendance are extremely low, the Lutheran state Churches are still sources of great social capital through the running of care homes and other institutions. It was only in 1991 that Sweden instituted civil registration of births, marriages and deaths. Before that, responsibility for such information-gathering had rested with the Church. In Britain, the move to state control had been ushered in as far back as 1837.

Spain's evolution matches that of neighbouring countries in major respects, but is also influenced by local causes such as the legacy of civil war. Though the conflict is still widely misconstrued as a dress rehearsal for the Allies' confrontation with Hitler, many of its causes were distinctively Spanish. The saga of colonisation by the Moors and subsequent *Reconquista* was a precursor to two polarised views captured by the term 'two Spains': one Catholic and traditionalist; the other more cosmopolitan and relaxed about porous boundaries. Napoleon's invasion served to intensify these divisions, in the process discrediting liberalism as an import of the French oppressor. By the 1930s, Spain was riven with extremists of Left and Right alike. While having nothing positive to say about Franco's dictatorship, a historian such as Antony Beevor is correct in also excoriating anti-democratic elements on the far Left – forces content to goad the other side by burning churches and banning the religious orders during the lead-up to the nationalist uprising. (Beevor took the trouble to rewrite his history of the civil war after the opening up of KGB archives during the 1990s revealed the full extent of Stalin's plan to subjugate Spain.) The secular Left still tends to see the Church as tainted by association with Franco, and a brake on progressive social reforms. Conservative attitudes are shaped by a conviction that the dictatorship saved the country from communism, and thus from evisceration by Hitler. The tenacity with which these attitudes are held renders moves towards consensus and reconciliation extremely hard.

Ultimately, however – and despite the huge growth in the Pentecostal and house church movements across Europe already registered – we are all still talking about convergence in a group of historically very different societies: a situation in which the traditional Churches are struggling in terms of numbers, recruitment and so forth. A generation ago the idea that Catholicism in southern Europe was a firewall against secularisation in the continent's northern tier would have seemed fair. Grace Davie, another leading sociologist in the field, could popularise the term 'believing without belonging' to make sense of paradoxical attitudes to Christianity in northern Europe. The term is less used today. It is therefore very difficult to escape a straightforward conclusion that even if we resist the prognoses of hard-edge pessimists, there are aspects of today's culture which make it hard for traditional Christianity to flourish. External hostility to the Church, and a less than robust response from ecclesiastical ranks, are mutually reinforcing. Historians need to find a way of describing a social reality – namely the decline of religion in institutional terms – without relying on a teleological account that builds in its own predetermined conclusions.

In Britain Clive Field is much associated with the avoidance of agenda, partly through his website British Religion In Numbers,[25] based on highly detailed accumulations of evidence across many eras. His work is about as close as one could get to a thorough-going statistical description; it also challenges oversimplifications on either side of the religion–secularism debate. I have reported his clear demonstration of decline since the 1960s and 1970s. But the 1950s was not the golden age of churchgoing it is often supposed to have been. Nor was it true that religious observance had become irrelevant by then. Furthermore, Field has shown that the nineteenth century was an era of expansion. Practically the whole of the main period of industrialisation and urbanisation in Britain was accompanied by rising attendance and the streamlining of structures to match. He is not alone in demonstrating this point: it is supported in the work of Jeremy Morris, among other experts.[26]

The Churches' effective response to change extended at least until the 1870s and 1880s, when population growth began to outpace church growth. This led to relative but not absolute decline. Absolute decline did not take root seriously until after the First World War. We can certainly see a growth in civil weddings in the mid-twentieth century, but not the very sharp fall in religious ceremonies witnessed since the 1960s. When people started being able to marry on football pitches or in hotels and so on, the figures for church weddings shrank dramatically. As reported, numbers preparing for confirmation also tell an important story.

Self-inflicted aspects of the problem are plainly very varied. The fall in Anglican baptisms, for example, is likely a result in some measure of a rigorist insistence that parents should be active believers or undertake a course. This in turn maps onto a surge in Anglican Evangelical confidence since the 1960s. But baptism had previously been a classic way for the clergy to connect with the surrounding population. On one level this belongs to the essence of a Constantinian Christianity: that most people get baptised, and then in due course the Church tries to get them to recognise that the rite means something – they will need to act on it later in life. It is the rationale for establishment, and for Catholicism in the broadest sense. That is how the whole of Europe became Christianised in the first place. Once a church stops baptising all (or almost all) comers, it loses one of its principal levers.

And there are extraneous or adventitious factors to be borne in mind alongside a disaster such as the Covid-19 pandemic, which still keeps worshippers (especially the elderly) away from church. Consider the extreme winter of 1962–3. Several weeks after Christmas a two-day blizzard virtually cut off Scotland from England. It was not just the north which suffered. The south-east of England was severely affected by similar conditions: cars were strewn across roads, trains became trapped in snowdrifts, ferries had to steer through waters teeming with ice floes. People stopped attending services through worry over the effects of frost: the concern lasted for months. More than one older friend has told me that congregations failed to return to their previous sizes afterwards.

***

So much, in broad outline, for *what* has happened. How about *why*? We have seen that the reasons are both social and intellectual. In the second of these areas stands distrust of agencies said to lie beyond the tangible in a notionally rational universe. There is also (and here head and heart overlap) a sense that widespread undeserved suffering makes talk of an all-powerful, all-loving God incoherent at best. Senseless slaughter on an unmatched scale between 1914 and 1918 proved a strong spur to unbelief. These objections are substantial enough to merit separate discussion in a later chapter.

At a level unconnected to theology or preaching, one of the most convincing explanations for secularisation to my mind is also one of the least discussed. Sometimes called the welfarist theory, it identifies an inverse correlation between the extent to which the state takes on responsibilities for welfare provision and the size of the Church. It is one of the reasons why the United States has withstood the huge secularisation trend in the past fifty or sixty years across Western countries. There are other reasons, one related to the separation of Church and state in America, which means that atheism has always found it very difficult to get off the ground compared to various countries where throne and altar were once much more closely aligned. But sticking to the main point: in industrial and post-industrial societies people tend to come into contact with the love of God *through the love of the godly*, rather than first and foremost through theological argument, let alone any scientific reasoning. And if the love of the godly is severely circumscribed by the ability of the state to meet people's material needs, then many may ask what the point of the Church is any more. That is one of the reasons why Victorian Britain, while becoming the first major industrialised nation on earth, did not simultaneously secularise. In any simple reading of secularisation theory, the world's richest state modernised, industrialised and became better educated. All of these should be markers for a steep and rapid decline of religion. But claims that Britain was a less religious place in 1900 than in 1830 are hard to back up. The country plainly had less of the ancien régime culture about it, but that did not necessarily make it less religious. And in the twentieth century church attendance grew in the 1930s, partly because religious affiliation can increase in periods of economic malaise.

Churchgoing fell after the Second World War when much of the social provision previously emanating from the Churches was picked up by the state, and the Church was left asking what it still had to talk about. Some (both believers and non-believers) may say wryly that this was the moment at which preachers started to focus more on what people do in their bedrooms. A caricature of course, but not wholly inaccurate. By the 1970s and 1980s people with very little cultural memory of Christianity began to ask, 'What exactly is the point of all this? There are some rituals around when I die perhaps, but in terms of a living faith that's actively changing the public square, what's the purpose of it?'

Other important currents need flagging up – particularly the eruption of social, and then economic, liberalism in the 1960s and 1980s by turn. These changes altered the underlying preconception of what the good is in the first instance. As is widely recognised, the 1960s and 1980s revolutions shifted the idea of the good towards sovereign autonomy. That has always been *part* of Christianity, as a major essay in intellectual history such as Siedentop's *Inventing the Individual: The Origins of Western Liberalism*[27] shows. But for the Church, liberalism has generally been tempered by a deep-rooted communitarianism. The private autonomous self is not thought of as sole arbiter of meaning and value. From the standpoint of a contemporary secular liberal, there are bits of Christianity that pass muster, but many aspects that do not, because the Church has so much to say about duty, virtue and the renunciation of our freedom for the sake of a greater good.

Despite the strong Methodist and subsequent Anglican allegiances of Margaret Thatcher (and the residual tag in her day that the Church of England was the Tory Party at prayer), many free-market economists have a big problem with Christianity. Equally clearly, social liberals often harbour strong reservations about the faith as well. We can thus note a pincer movement. I have observed that many people's contact with the love of God was once funnelled through the love of the godly; and whereas vast companies of volunteers were once doing all kinds of things for more or less explicitly Christian reasons, today a place of worship is not always the right port of call for such activity. Nor should it be. Churches cannot run hospitals in the way they were able to do a hundred years ago; in a pluralist society they must adapt significantly in their approach to education. So I am certainly not suggesting that we should revert to pre-1945 patterns of life in order that the Church can enhance its role. But if we want to understand why the Christian footprint is smaller, I think welfare provision stands near the top of the list.

The changing size of the public square needs particular emphasis. In Britain during the 1930s there was a saying that it was only the opinions of three people which really mattered: the Prime Minister, the Editor of *The Times* and the Archbishop of Canterbury. This was naturally a joke. Largely false then, it became less and less true after the Second World War. And in the 2020s much of the world has clearly been democratised via social media to an extent inconceivable even thirty years ago. The public square has mushroomed just as the Church has grown smaller. There are different dynamics at work in different European countries, but the family resemblances are substantial.

A convincing answer to our third question – namely why it all matters – is given by Nick Spencer in his book *Freedom and Order: History, Politics and the English Bible*.[28] It builds on some of the judgements I have already aired by citing the maxim that a person travelling along a road scarcely thinks of those who first dug the ditches and levelled the way. Here is a powerful image deriving from John Locke showing how we have reached our present state because of the heavy lifting performed by earlier generations. Spencer rightly adds a caveat about this point. People who make it can be heard as saying that society will collapse without Christianity. That sounds too apocalyptic and, in any case, it is very important to emphasise that even *with* Christianity, things have sometimes gone profoundly awry. We only have to look at how many millions of churchgoers in Germany made an easy peace with the Nazis.

Yet the secularist still cuts corners in inferring that the Church has done its job and can now fade away. First, because we are metaphysical animals. We are unlikely to abandon age-old quests for a fundamental and inclusive context of meaning. (A Christian may go further by adding that secular reason is not reasonable enough, because it fails to give an account of this deeper context.) Second, because human beings are also naturally rapacious. We display a dangerous thirst for unreality, which is another way of saying that we are sinners. Often misconstrued as a spurious notion based on moralising dogma, sin is the basic empirical reality that Christian teaching responds to and makes sense of. That is why the correct definition of a Christian is not a good person, but someone who acknowledges their *failure* to be good. The most authentic strands in a Christian worldview have infiltrated societies without necessarily changing them at root. We should not be surprised by this. The Church regards itself as both a divine society instituted by Christ, and a human fellowship with a sometimes terrible history. According to Jesus in Matthew 13, the sifting of the wheat and the tares will be carried out by God alone in the fullness of time.

Among the upshots of this awareness are a sober model of the human person and an avoidance of false optimism. It is a fantasy to suppose that we are rationally capable of discerning our good and then able to achieve it smoothly. I do not see how anybody who has ever studied history can really believe that. It is no more convincing now than during the Enlightenment. In Spencer's image, societies are a combination of centrifugal and centripetal factors, and a good society is one that gets the centrifugal and centripetal impulses in rough balance. Money – and energy – are very powerful centrifugal forces. They pull us apart by creating the impression that we have no need of one another. They allow us to achieve our sovereign moral autonomy. Liberalism in that regard is heavily connected to late capitalism. In headline terms, it is probably fair to say that liberal ideology finds a very fertile soil in rich (especially energy-rich) societies. The problem is that things *do* fall apart. There are always countervailing pressures in society – namely centripetal forces. Totalitarian China and Russia are centripetal societies par excellence. Theocratic regimes are centripetal; nationalistic ones are also essentially centripetal. And if you live in one such society, life is as dehumanising as it would be under unlimited centrifugal conditions.

The title of Spencer's book reflects an awareness that there are centrifugal and centripetal forces at work in the Bible and church history. Christianity accentuates both human freedom and social order. There were naturally multiple missteps as the faith spread across many disparate mission fields. Yet in due course it achieved a relatively humanising balance of centrifugal and centripetal forces in Western Europe. There is a danger that society flies apart when only centrifugal forces are in play. To remedy this, we are already importing other centripetal forces (usually based on the state) that can be less conducive to human welfare.

I have already argued that society, like metaphysics, abhors a vacuum. My inference is that if we deny Christianity some kind of anchor-like role, we either risk a form of very slow social disintegration or, as indicated, a situation in which the state increasingly feels that it needs to impose its norms on citizens. If you support Burke's appeal to society's 'little platoons', then you will cherish a space where public morality, local loyalty and a sense of community used to hold sway. Tellingly, Spencer notices how the British rediscovered religion as a socialising force in the face of the French Revolution. Faith was acknowledged as the most secure vehicle through which humanity's passions have been tamed. The statement can sound oppressive from one angle; from another vantage point, it is profoundly wise. Sin can be controlled either externally, by the state, or by the invisible police of one's conscience. Notwithstanding abuses, Christianity has on the whole done a creditable job on that front. We lack something crucial without it.

I am all too conscious that the necessarily impressionistic thoughts set out in this chapter may raise almost as many questions as they answer. My aim at this point has simply been to outline a paradoxical mixture of decline and renewal in British Christianity, supplemented by glances at other parts of Western

Europe; then to note a deposit of ethical assumptions deriving from church teaching but now floating around secular society detached from their theological moorings. For this and other reasons we will not make secure progress without first moving backwards in time to excavate traditions long pre-dating Charles Maurice Davies – and, for that matter, Enlightenment pioneers such as Locke.

2

What Have the Roman Catholics and Other Christians Ever Given Us?

One of my main claims will already be apparent in embryo. Mainstream European culture is hurtling forward largely without the fuel that Christianity has historically supplied. What are this fuel's main ingredients? A much-analysed sample emerges in the American Declaration of Independence: 'We hold these truths to be self-evident: that all men are created equal; that they are endowed by their Creator with certain unalienable rights, that among these are Life, Liberty and the pursuit of Happiness.' A high proportion of the Founding Fathers didn't practise what they preached. Two-thirds of them owned slaves. The truly self-evident point, always and across all cultures, is that people are not at all equal in any ordinary human sense. Lucy Beckett makes the point forcefully:

> From the cradle to the grave, in virtue, in brains, in looks, in health and strength, in evenness of temper, in kindness and patience, in short in value to others, they are far from equal. Only in the eyes of God are they equal: the statement that all . . . are equal is meaningless unless it is given meaning by belief in the existence of God and belief that all human beings are created in the divine image.[1]

Beckett's range is broad: she is a historian and literary critic, as well as a novelist. *In the Light of Christ*,[2] her outstanding survey of the Western literary canon read through a Christian lens, deserves a larger audience. And she is hardly a lone voice. Related expressions of the message can be found throughout the writings of Samuel Moyn, the Yale historian, and Tom Holland, among others. In *Dominion*,[3] Holland argues that the Founding Fathers were 'garbing in the robes of the Enlightenment' the Christian teachings they had been brought up on, but which they no longer accepted in an orthodox form. This, he adds, is what secular humanists frequently do if they haven't dispensed with morality altogether. His message in brief is that the Christian gospel not only subverted the thirst for power and status taken for granted across the Roman Empire and elsewhere in the world, but also moulded much of subsequent history. The ideal has of course been very imperfectly observed on the ground. A high standard is not discredited by people's failure to observe it, however.

Holland is also celebrated for his studies of civilisations further east, especially *Persian Fire*.[4] He makes a revealing statement in *Dominion*: that when feeling horror at the blood-soaked eras covered in his early work he was presupposing Christian standards of morality almost universal in the West, but not often recognised as such by a high proportion of teachers and commentators. Holland means that it is because we swim through Christian waters that we have no awareness of the surrounding sea.

This claim will be tested as well as restated later on. Meanwhile, the outline already sketched needs to be filled in further. The extraordinary assertion that the crucifixion and resurrection – the death by a form of torture commonly inflicted on slaves, and its miraculous overcoming – of Jesus of Nazareth had changed everything for flawed, suffering humankind was the heart of the Good News. The ground for such an apparently far-fetched claim might be defended as follows. Over and again in his ministry, Jesus had indicated that the question of how people relate to him will govern how they relate to the God he called Father. In effect, he was re-embodying and radicalising God's call to Israel at the dawn of the biblical drama. The early Church announced that a new phase of history had dawned. Through an act of faith in Christ, human agency, so often seen simply as a plaything of stars, gods or fate, could become a medium for God's love. What was more, by 'speaking' to us in the person of Christ, God was inviting humanity to share in the divine life – as daughters and sons by adoption. The Church is the community on earth representing this 'new creation'. Its calling is to implement God's will for universal reconciliation.

Good roads enabled St Paul to spread this message: he travelled around ten thousand miles before being martyred in Rome. A decent infrastructure facilitated intellectual as well as physical commerce. He drew on the Stoic notion of conscience to elaborate his message. Later the Church played an indispensable part in transmitting the achievements of classical civilisation after the Western Roman Empire fell apart in the fifth century. The thought of earlier thinkers such as Cicero (especially his belief that the only fulfilling model for life rests on altruistic endeavour) was Christianised through emphasis on love of God and neighbour. As a previously robust education system crumbled, core pagan texts and the work of outstanding Christian thinkers such as St Augustine were preserved.

The debunkers' complaints are familiar, especially at a time of hostility towards traditional institutions. Prominent among commentators with a strident agenda was Christopher Hitchens, author of *God Is Not Great*,[5] whose claim that religion lies at the heart of all conflict rests on a widely accepted story. It runs like this: people were for the most part ignorant and superstitious during the periods of church ascendancy. Heretics were hounded while the achievements of classical civilisation lay discarded. The Reformation was a positive move in so far as it served as unwitting midwife to the Enlightenment.

Hitchens's case is not trifling. Elements of it would be endorsed by close observers, including Jonathan Israel. The Crusades, Inquisition and Thirty Years' War, to cite just three examples, naturally form huge stains on the Christian record. But the charge is nevertheless deeply partial. The vista looks very different when viewed from a wider angle. Though parts of the Church grew corrupt over time, its radically egalitarian impulses were on plain view from the start. Pre-Christian religion regularly mandated self-mutilation and human sacrifice. The poor and weak were shunned. Gospel teaching on the radical equality of all, and the founding of hospitals, schools and other philanthropic institutions, marked a profound revolution. Laws introduced under Roman emperors such as Theodosius II and Constantine raised the status of women. Even slavery (common to all pre-modern societies) was described as blasphemous as early as the fourth century by Gregory, Bishop of Nyssa. Though the blasphemy persisted for a further 1,500 years, it was finally curtailed on the initiative of Western Christians.

Hitchens was of course a well-known controversialist. Like many members of his guild, he could cut corners in pursuit of an arresting line. But although vastly better informed figures, including Peter Heather,[6] have also unsettled some traditional assumptions by stressing factors including the role of force and chance in Christendom's rise, I do not think they succeed in undermining the basic story told by David Bentley Hart in an award-winning study such as *Atheist Delusions: The Christian Revolution and Its Fashionable Enemies*.[7]

Modernity's pre-medieval foundations were consolidated during the Middle Ages. For example, St Thomas Aquinas's *Summa Theologiae* contains a far more detailed treatise on justice than anything produced in antiquity by figures of comparable stature. It addresses a host of topics including homicide, unjust enrichment, injuries against the person, slander, fraud and professional misconduct. What is true of social developments also applies in other areas. Charles Taylor's *A Secular Age*[8] is among the most important works of revisionist scholarship to overturn religion-versus-science clichés. For all the obduracy of certain theologians and clerics, modern physics and biology did not arise in opposition to religion: on the contrary, they developed in a godly crucible.

The myth that science and faith are and always have been in conflict is vital to sustain trench warfare between the two kinds of fundamentalist – creationists and supporters of intelligent design on the one hand, and, on the other, the polemicists who dismiss all religion as fundamentally irrational. Yet Copernicus, Galileo, Descartes, Newton, Leibniz, Michael Faraday, James Clerk Maxwell and other builders of the modern world were men of deep religious conviction as well as scientific geniuses. Moreover, their work was preceded by that of medieval pioneers – Muslims and Jews, as well as Christians – often working in productive dialogue. Of course there has been tension between science and theology at times, a classic example being the Oxford debate between T. H. Huxley and Samuel Wilberforce in 1860 (although much of the reporting of this encounter is skewed). Look more closely, however, and you may be struck by how flexible many Christians and others have been in absorbing developments in knowledge.

As is often noted, before castigating Galileo – a saga more due to the clash of confrontational individuals than to scientific matters as such – the Catholic Church jettisoned biblical cosmology in favour of a Greek model, based on the movement of the spheres. Understanding the geological record and its implications for biblical timelines was a task undertaken within a predominantly Christian culture. Among scholars of this field, it is widely accepted that two works in particular encapsulate the warfare narrative: John William Draper's *History of the Conflict between Religion and Science* (1875) and Andrew Dickson White's *A History of the Warfare of Science with Theology in Christendom* (1896). No professional historian now considers these authors remotely reliable. Although many of the 'facts' listed in their work were made up, the damage endures. As the biologist Denis Alexander has observed, researchers are still correcting the 'factual mutants'[9] created by Draper and Dickson White.

A much more objective survey of the terrain can be found in *Galileo Goes to Jail: And Other Myths About Science and Religion*,[10] edited by Ronald Numbers. This book shows that multiple features of contemporary science were nurtured in theological soil, among them trust in the intelligibility of the world, the concept of physical laws, and empiricism itself. The founders of the Royal Society in seventeenth-century England wrote of how their Christian faith impelled them to explore the world. The father of natural history, John Ray, was a Puritan. Christians in the twentieth century such as the Anglican R. A. Fisher and the Orthodox Theodosius Dobzhansky did much to develop the neo-Darwinian consensus. In our own day it is not just figures of no religious allegiance, but also the mathematician Martin Nowak, a Harvard-based Catholic, and the paleobiologist Simon Conway Morris, another Anglican, who are contributing significantly to evolutionary theory. The picture is traced by Nicholas Spencer in his book *Magisteria*.[11]

To sum up, it is no accident that developments including the progress of modern technology, the rule of law, the market economy, democracy and the welfare state have flourished most strongly in traditionally Christian societies. Within the past few generations, the UN Declaration of Human Rights emerged substantially from the hands of Catholics, Protestants, Jews and Hindus working in tandem, while subsequently faith-based conviction – especially among Christians – has mobilised millions of people to oppose authoritarian regimes, inaugurate democratic transitions, and relieve suffering on a grand scale.

These considerations may help shift attitudes to our own era, especially given Holland's resonant comment quoted earlier. By the 1970s a major figure in the areas of law and government such as John Rawls could explicitly leave metaphysics at the door in his writings on justice. Framed as reflecting a wish to be as inclusive as possible in a multicultural society, Rawls's theories carried conviction in a setting where a strong set of residual Christian assumptions held sway. To a Rawlsian in the 1970s and 1980s, say, a principle such as egalitarianism would have been taken for granted. For Rawls and a whole body of thought that has come in his wake, we should see egalitarianism as the apex virtue (even though it still isn't at all taken for granted in many other cultures) yet remain agnostic as to what could possibly *ground* the conviction that human worth does not come in degrees – because to be more explicit would involve trafficking in metaphysics at the frontier between philosophy and faith.

As I have said, that mattered less as long as the West could motor along using the left-over fuel of cultural memory. Rawls himself had a churchgoing background and wrote an undergraduate thesis on theology. But some have always questioned the merit of that approach. Why would you want to bracket your deepest convictions when it comes to delineating the common good and the ingredients for a flourishing public square?

To my mind these observers have been vindicated. The Rawlsian paradigm is now unravelling. One sobering verdict holds that we have reached a point comparable to the intellectual dynamics of fourth-century Rome. Then a reflexive residue of cultural paganism faced a new kid on the block in the form of self-confident Christianity, especially after the conversion of Constantine. On this analogy (and looking a millennium-and-a-half into the future), it is the mainstream Churches that appear enfeebled in the face of creeds – diversity, equity and inclusion (DEI), hardline identitarianism, wokeism, call them what you will – which are organised around a highly self-confident vision and increasingly dominate the commanding heights of the establishment.

Christians (myself included) may say that they are liberal enough to welcome aspects of the new order, and even to accept its Christian roots. I write as a member of Generation X and grandson of Irish immigrants. My grandfather fought against the British in the Irish War of Independence, but later in the British army during the Second World War. I therefore see my own country as an outsider as well as an insider. I can recall a time when gender-based prejudice, homophobia and anti-Catholic bigotry were still widespread in Britain; there is therefore much for Christians to welcome about the evolution of European society since the 1990s. The #MeToo movement, for example, plainly derives in part from traditional Christianity's refusal to trivialise sex. On the other hand, many people of faith are sufficiently concerned about the militant sectionalism of identity politics to sound the alarm over its wilder fringes, including strands such as critical race theory, and the urge to transcend our biological givens reflected in the transgender movement. (There are now surgeons in the United States who are prepared not only to change the gender of children, but also to render patients 'gender-neutral'.) And needless to say, countless Christians who don't fit into simplistic liberal or conservative grooves may straddle what ought to be more porous battlelines.

Let us concentrate on philosophy rather than policy for now, before returning to the question of equality in due course. We have already seen that no two people are descriptive equals in any sense. As it happens, one and the same person is not even descriptively equal from month to month (I myself gained weight while on holiday recently). So a purely descriptive, 'scientific' account of a person is never going to make any sense of the idea that equality is a virtue. The prescription needs to be metaphysical: it cannot be bootstrapping. To draw out the force of Lucy Beckett's insight, what confers equal worth on all human beings as such has to be something that comes from beyond us. No human being can become the ultimate authority on what the source of equal worth is, without implicitly ascribing to themselves an unequal status in being the authoritative source of what counts as equal worth. It must come from beyond.

Our present situation resembles the thought experiment famously proposed by Alasdair MacIntyre at the start of his classic work *After Virtue*.[12] He asks us to imagine an apocalyptic event which shatters almost all we know about the natural sciences. In the aftermath of this catastrophe, survivors try to piece lost bodies of knowledge back together. Shards of earlier wisdom are still on view: such and such a laboratory wasn't totally destroyed; part of a major library is still standing, meaning that some classics still survive. The process of reconstruction will be messy, MacIntyre says – rather like trying to put the bits of a shattered vase back together. He adds that this story represents the state of moral philosophy since the eighteenth century, because the Enlightenment blew apart an earlier set of powerful and internally coherent moral traditions.

Sometimes hailed as the most important work of its kind produced in several generations, Elizabeth Anscombe's 1958 essay 'Modern Moral Philosophy'[13] anticipates MacIntyre's argument by over two decades. Anscombe in effect says that society is still using the language of criminality or the legal process, when judges and courts have been abolished. In denying God, we deny the existence of an absolute authority with respect to ethics. We are instead reduced to talking about fragments as though the apocalypse had not happened. My inference can easily be guessed at. Moving forward to the present, all our talk about DEI is a form of phantom limb syndrome. And maybe our emphasis in the West on quantitative equality is partly a way of concealing our inarticulacy on the subject of qualitative equality.

To repeat one of my main claims in Chapter 1: for a host of reasons, both conceptual and practical, Christianity is worth a second look. Many of us have a deep memory of the revolutionary principle that all people have equal worth. The principle derives from the Bible. Yes, ancient philosophies such as Stoicism do offer some hopeful proposals regarding a kind of divine spark within. But it is an abstract, aristocratic and politically disengaged vision. Young Stoics didn't rescue plague victims; Seneca didn't preach to the poor. Christianity is the first moral revolution to articulate and follow through on claims about the radical equality of all.

And what of Christianity's role today? Adapting its message into a contemporary idiom, believers will insist that no form of Christianity worth its salt will fail to make outreach to the vulnerable a top priority. Jesus loved the poor, comforted the afflicted and afflicted the comfortable. But that stance should be distinguished from loose talk along the lines of 'This group ticks *a* and *b* identity boxes and is therefore right, while others only tick *c* or *d* and therefore have far less claim to be taken seriously.' All are under judgement; the gospel has plenty to say about checking your pride, as well as your privilege. Fashionable hierarchies of victimhood can in any case conceal as much as they reveal. The highest-performing demographic in British schools are girls of East Asian heritage from wealthy backgrounds. In second place stand East Asian girls from poorer households. At the bottom of the heap stand white working-class boys. A complaint regularly made on the traditional Left is that gender and race have displaced class in the taxonomy of social need. While broadly agreeing with this cavil, I would also qualify it with reference to factors that can fall even further off the radar. What of geography, for example? Growing up in a large city can provide access to all sorts of opportunities denied to country-dwellers, especially those in decaying coastal towns. Then there are matters of the spirit. An old line has it that the most important advice any person can receive is 'choose your parents wisely'. It ought to go without saying that countless apparently privileged people were in fact raised in grotesquely dysfunctional homes. More fundamentally, the problem with identity politics of the more bloodthirsty kind is that its obsession with status and recognition involves a betrayal of any notion of a negotiated common good.

***

Moving beyond conflict over identity, I recall that seemingly apocalyptic episodes towards the end of the Cold War were followed by further periods of despair during the Bosnian conflagration of 1992–5, to say nothing of 9/11 and its aftermath, the financial crisis, and many later disasters. Yet latter-day Cassandras of many stripes may feel especially confident of their bearings in reviewing the twenty-first century's first quarter. Fighting climate change plainly constitutes a relatively novel challenge. In other respects, our current discontents map onto horrors witnessed a century ago. The naivety of thinkers who proclaimed the end of history after communism's demise in the Soviet Union – and the indestructability of Pax Americana – has long been exposed. Look at the unspeakable disaster that is Syria. Soon after mass pro-democracy demonstrations began in 2010, the Assad dictatorship tottered. Then government henchmen started barrel-bombing the country into submission. In turn Raqqa, a previously unimportant provincial city, would become capital for the ISIS terror group and a byword for a jihadist campaign of mass murder and beheadings.

Why flag this up when history abounds in evidence of man's inhumanity to man? Augustine faced an allied situation 1,500 years ago as he lay dying and invaders threatened to overwhelm lands under Rome's control. I mention Syria partly because we can be remarkably slow to absorb the lessons of history. The horrors unfolding there during the second decade of the twenty-first century have marked a major turning point for the rest of the world. In particular, it is not Syria which has become more like the West (as reformers hoped), but the West which has imported major strands of the Syrian conflict: its terrorist attacks, polarised politics, toxic religion, and mud-slinging on social media. In Europe and North America, the rise of populism has been boosted by the sight of millions of refugees fleeing west and north. Disputes over the use of chemical weapons has fed the concept of fake news. And the failure of Syria's uprising fuelled distrust in the idea of democracy itself, strengthening Russia (which buttressed the regime) and China (whose authoritarian government started to be viewed more favourably). In brief, Syria, crystallising the new world disorder, makes a mockery of hope and echoes the reaction against shallow optimism seen in politics a century ago. Faith in liberal progress – especially across the Protestant world – was also shattered by the First World War. Lenin's rise prefigured those of Stalin, Hitler and Mao; W. B. Yeats's complaint that the 'best lack all conviction while the worst are full of passionate intensity', or Hannah Arendt's observation about the banality of evil, or Theodor Adorno's on the impossibility of poetry after

Auschwitz, are becoming so familiar again that their currency risks being debased.

My previous paragraph alluded to the taking up of cultural cudgels, as well as real theatres of war. The Left often shoots at an open goal when it castigates far-right extremism. Donald Trump is a stranger to truth; QAnon conspiracy theorists are the streptococci worsening an already putrid wound. The Right's protest against the Left is at least as serious, given that soi-disant progressives wield so much power in education and other institutions of culture.

The drift towards intolerance in academia has been memorably summed up by John Gray, who spent much of his career as a university lecturer. His critique carries additional weight given his lack of religious convictions. Writing in 2018, he recalled that social democrats, conservatives, liberals and Marxists once worked alongside each other in a spirit of free enquiry, despite their deep differences of outlook. Cherished orthodoxies were not unknown; sometimes dissenters had trouble getting heard. 'But visiting lecturers were rarely disinvited because their views were deemed unspeakable, course readings were not routinely screened in case they contained material that students might find discomforting, and faculty members who departed from the prevailing consensus did not face attempts to . . . end their careers. An inquisitorial culture had not yet taken over.'[14]

The conservative backlash represented by a figure such as Douglas Murray is also worthy of note. His thesis is that a relentless campaign is being waged against the West and its traditions not only by home-grown zealots or online trolls in the pay of Vladimir Putin and other dictators, but within the citadels of Western culture itself. Healthy self-criticism has given way to a level of self-laceration shading into self-hatred. Debate on slavery forms a paradigmatic instance of this trend. Justified horror over this trade has issued in two blind spots especially: one regarding the complicity of almost all other imperial cultures from the Greeks and the Romans to the Aztecs, the Mongols, the Ottomans, the Swahili, the kingdom of Benin, the Chinese and many others in a global crime; the other relating to the British Empire's often creditable efforts to stamp out slavery during the nineteenth century. The new Savonarolas who see Western civilisation as irredeemably tainted – so this thesis runs – are not only one-sided. The irony is that they are reinscribing a Eurocentric view of the world. A still greater irony haunts much of the discourse, because it is precisely on the basis of Western values – Judeo-Christian legacy above all – that the West is singled out for excoriation in the first place. Locke and other Enlightenment pioneers in England, Scotland and the United States drank from theological wells. As I have emphasised, the sweetest water they imbibed was biblical.

Murray naturally has vocal critics on the Left. Their complaints are readily guessed at. Especially interesting to my mind is the response of a centrist such as Tom Wright, who challenged Murray on an oversight common, as we have seen, across the political spectrum. Published in *The Spectator*[15] after Murray had attacked the Church of England for its supposed embrace of secular identity politics, Wright's response is worth relaying in full. The letter grants that a citadel is under attack, but its main thrust concerns how little Murray apparently has to say about what that citadel's foundations actually consist in.

Sir — Douglas Murray complains that the C of E has embraced the 'new religion' of anti-racism . . . But the truth, which neither he nor the church seems to have realised, is that the 'anti-racist' agenda is a secular attempt to plug a long-standing gap in western Christianity. The answer is to recover the full message, not to bolt on new ideologies. The earliest Christian writings insist that in the Messiah 'there is neither Jew nor Greek'. The book of Revelation envisages Jesus' followers as an uncountable family from every nation, tribe, people and language. At the climax of his greatest letter, St Paul urges Christians to 'welcome one another' across all social and ethnic barriers, insisting that the church will thereby function as the advance sign of God's coming renewal of all creation.

This is the three-dimensional meaning of 'justification by faith': all those who believe in Jesus, rescued by his cross and resurrection and enlivened by his Spirit, are part of the new family. This was and is central, not peripheral. The church was the original multicultural project, with Jesus as its only point of identity. It was known, and was for this reason seen as both attractive and dangerous, as a worship-based, spiritually renewed, multi-ethnic, polychrome, mutually supportive, outward-facing, culturally creative, chastity-celebrating, socially responsible fictive kinship group, gender-blind in leadership, generous to the poor and courageous in speaking up for the voiceless.

If this had been celebrated, taught and practised, the church would early on have recognised ecclesial racism for what it is: the ugly side-effect of splitting the church into language-groups and thence into national 'churches', preparing the way for, and disarming the church against, the self-serving 'racial' theories of social Darwinism. If it has taken modern secular movements to jolt the church into recognising a long-standing problem, shame on us. But the answer is not to capitulate to the current 'identity agenda', and then to enforce it with breast-beating, finger-wagging neo-moralism. Douglas Murray doesn't like that and neither do I. The answer is teaching and practising the whole biblical gospel.

The Rt Revd Professor N. T. Wright

How might Wright's points be developed? No sane observer can deny that the record of Christ's followers is patchy at best. The Catholic Church had an Index of Prohibited Books within living memory. Protestant fundamentalists have shown intellectual neurosis and authoritarianism of a comparable form. For a self-critical Christian, the point would be that parts of secular society are reproducing some of Christianity's past mistakes without being able to draw on the balm of grace and forgiveness that have always been present in the theological repertoire.

My follow-up thought can be readily guessed at. A culture that pushed historic religion out of the front door has ushered in a quasi-theology of dubious lineage through the back. It is all the more questionable for not being acknowledged as such. The point is well summed up by David Martin, the sociologist and priest who spent decades fighting his corner as a professor in the highly secular environment of the London School of Economics: 'That [Christians and other believers] are accused of illegitimate commitments, in academic milieux riven with them from end to end, nicely indicates where inclusivity fails to include.'[16]

Ignorance of the past explains our plight to a significant degree. Only a fifth of teenagers in the UK now study history after the age of fourteen. A journalist such as Jenni Russell has drawn out the melancholy consequences of this: 'One twentysomething tells me no one in her social groups knows much about history except for the Tudors (long ago, remote, entertaining) or the Nazis, the British Empire and slavery (all monstrous, depressing and bad).' A recently retired schoolteacher developed this awareness in conversation with me by emphasising the extent to which his former pupils from Generation Z tend to campaign on specific issues, rather than committing themselves to institutions.

> Some of those issues – LGBT rights, safeguarding – are ones on which some Churches have questionable records. But rights-based campaigning tends towards factionalism and intolerance – the Trans rights versus Women's rights is an obvious example. At some point, I hope, people will come to see the futility of this approach and be open to the attractions of the Church, because at its best it transcends differences of that kind. 'Love, like death, hath all destroyed / Rendered all distinctions void / Names and sects and parties fall / Thou O Christ art all in all,' as Charles Wesley memorably expresses that thought.

***

What Wright's letter above says about Christianity is perhaps more on target than its verdict on Murray, who understands defences of faith (and whose private peregrinations defy a simple tag). His book *The Strange Death of Europe*[17] shares a crucial premise with another, very different, bestseller: Yuval Noah Harari's *Sapiens: A Brief History of Humankind*.[18] While neither writer professes a religious commitment – Harari is an avowed atheist – both nevertheless lament religion's fading footprint in the West and predict a parched future for societies that are neglecting their Judeo-Christian roots.

Murray voices a series of ideas already alluded to. In the place of religion has come the ever-inflating language of human rights, a concept Christian in origin. We have left unresolved the question of whether or not our acquired rights are reliant on beliefs that the continent has ceased to hold. But once the roots of the tree are severed, the tree itself begins to die. Harari makes pretty much the same point in more general global terms:

> Even though liberal humanism sanctifies humans, it doesn't deny the existence of God and is in fact founded on monotheist beliefs. The liberal belief in the free and sacred nature of each individual is a direct legacy of the traditional Christian belief in free and eternal individual souls. Without recourse to individual souls and a creator God, it becomes embarrassingly difficult for liberals to explain what's so special about individual sapiens.[19]

Harari then suggests with regret that religion has been replaced by science: 'As we can tell from a purely scientific viewpoint, human life has absolutely no meaning. Humans are the outcome of blind evolutionary processes that operate without goal or purpose.'[20] So we've developed the power of gods, but have very little idea what to do with all that power. This is his closing sentence: 'Is there anything more dangerous than dissatisfied and irresponsible gods who don't know what they want?'[21]

Both authors are thus telling us that if we lose our religious beliefs, specifically the Judeo-Christian beliefs set out in the

Bible that each of us is in the image of God and therefore sacred and possessed of non-negotiable dignity, then the result will be, in Murray's eyes, the end of Europe, and for Harari, the end of homo sapiens.

Having myself noted this similarity, I was pleased to see that Rabbi Jonathan Sacks has also made play of it. He develops the point by noting moments at which earlier thinkers have also issued ringing forecasts of civilisational decline: Ibn Khaldun from an Arab setting in the fourteenth century, for example; or Giambattista Vico in Italy some four hundred years later; and more recently, the American historian Will Durant. Every civilisation, Durant says, eventually goes through a conflict between religion and society or, more specifically, between religion and science. And then it reaches a point when, in his words,

> the intellectual classes abandon the ancient theology, and after some hesitation, the moral code allied with it. Literature and philosophy become anti-clerical. The movement of liberation rises to an exuberant worship of reason and falls to a paralysing disillusionment with every dogma and idea. Conduct deprived of its religious support deteriorates into epicurean chaos and life itself, shorn of consoling faith, becomes a burden alike to conscious poverty and to weary wealth. In the end, a society and its religion tend to fall together like body and soul into a harmonious death.[22]

Durant, too, has no pro-religious agenda. On the contrary, having once tested a vocation to the Catholic priesthood, he later left the Church. Like Murray and Harari, however, he warns that when a society loses its religious base, its civilisation is at risk of perishing. Having recorded all this, Sacks issues a challenge: any public figure who denies the reality of climate change will rightly face accusations of ignorance at best; but what of cultural and civilisational climate change? 'It's real and it's dangerous,' says Sacks:

And we'd better start doing something about it now, because we are rapidly losing the very culture that gave us the foundations of liberty, namely the sanctity of the individual person . . . If we lose that belief, none of the other institutions of the contemporary world is going to save us, not science, not technology, not market economics, and not the liberal democratic state . . . [There is] a pretty simple reason [for this]. Because science can tell us *how*, but not *why*. Technology can give us power, but cannot tell us how to use that power. The market economy gives us choices, but doesn't tell us which choices lead on to human flourishing, and which to self-destruction. And the liberal democratic state gives us freedom, but cannot itself provide the intellectual or moral or spiritual basis of that freedom. So the end result . . . to put it mildly, [is that] we're in trouble.[23]

Sacks's proposal is that we should protect the human environment with as much passion as we are displaying towards protecting the natural world. 'Because if we fail to do so, we will by forgetting our past, lose, destroy our human future. And if that happens, heaven help us and our grandchildren.'[24]

Murray has made a further observation that needs bringing out. His bracing views on Islamism have drawn regular accusations of racism. But far fewer of his critics on the Left would disagree with his *cri de cœur* over the West's civilisational malaise, or what he calls 'existential tiredness'. In other words, conservatives and progressives alike can agree that Europe's cultural fuel gauge is running low. And while agreeing with this, Christians can at least identify means of recharging ourselves.

To start with, belief in creation is plainly a game-changer. The Bible teaches that our world was initially good. Since parts of it are now on fire, it is the job of human beings to dampen the flames. This idea derives from the kabbalistic notion of *Tikkun olam* (repair of the world), reflecting a belief that Jews are responsible not only for their own welfare, but also for that of wider society. And for this reason, among others, the three great monotheistic faiths might give two cheers for contemporary liberalism while insisting that a better manifesto for our time on earth – more satisfying, because more in touch with the truth of our being – would invoke life, liberty and the pursuit of holiness.[25]

My book *The Hardest Problem*[26] quotes a resonant umbrella defence of religion's function given by the philosopher and neuro-scientist Iain McGilchrist:

> And one of the reasons for having a religion rather than just a spiritual sense is constantly to remind us of a broader context, of a moral order, a network of obligations to other humans, to the earth and to the other that lies beyond. Extending beyond our lives, that is, in space and time yet rooted firmly in places, spaces, practices here and now . . . Without [religion], this sense risks being dissipated. Trust depends on shared belief to a large extent. Religion is the manifestation of that trust and the embedding of it into the fabric of daily life. I am not unmindful of the ways in which this can also be harmful, damaging and lead to terrible loss, but it also leads to great creativity as well. Religion embodies awareness of God in the world through deeply resonant myths, narratives and symbols enacted in ritual, conducted in holy places that parallel the cyclical passage of time. We can't make this stuff up for ourselves and I'm not sure the world can afford to lose this . . . wisdom.[27]

Believers who are straightforwardly sympathetic to McGilchrist may say simply that good religion refreshes the parts other belief systems cannot reach. Christians in particular will naturally endorse the principles spelt out by Tom Wright. But there is an abiding challenge represented by Harari's atheism. As we have noted, the secularist who remains sceptical can still retort that while religion may indeed be a rich source of unifying narratives, ultimately the comfort it offers is spurious because God is dead. My exchange of emails with an influential media commentator was instructive in this regard, because McGilchrist's words appeared not to move him at all.

> Dear Rupert — It's a strange situation to be in. To adhere to the rituals of a religion based on pleasing/placating a god you don't believe in (for even if I'm sort of open to theism, the god of Abraham is to me clearly a man-made invention) not because you think someone or something is listening, but because the weight of history, culture and tradition means that only within that invented religion can you find the rituals and community you long for to give life sufficient meaning, warmth and structure: all of this would just leave me trapped in a lie.

My correspondent's words don't quite propel us back to square one, but they should certainly chasten Christians and others. We have noted that the view of religion shared by many opinion-formers remains very unreconstructed. The persistence of this prejudice explains why our ground-clearing remains only half-complete at this stage. We must ask of Christianity the question sometimes asked in jest about French thought: it may be all very well in practice, but does it work in theory? Part of the answer to that question is historical. Christianity rests on empirical foundations. And before confronting this critical question, we must dig deeper still and ask whether belief in God is coherent in the first place.

3
How Credible is the Creed?

Where Have All the Good Atheists Gone?

Suppose that Jack and Jill are debating the subject of nutrition. Jack is a vegan, Jill an omnivore. Jack justifies his choices by insisting that a good diet can be entirely plant-based. Jill answers that there will always be a place for animal husbandry in a mixed agricultural setting. 'Only a vegan lifestyle can avoid direct or indirect involvement in the abusive treatment of livestock,' Jack argues. 'Their welfare should be a big priority,' Jill replies. 'But ethical meat- and fish-eaters can influence the food industry through favouring good practice and avoiding the bad.'

Note that we here have samples of genuine debate. An insight dating at least as far back as Aristotle has it that two parties only start to pass this test if they agree on what it is that they disagree about. This points us to a fundamental problem with the New Atheist assault on religion over the past two decades. The discussion has often barely got off the ground, because the god in whom Richard Dawkins, Sam Harris and others disbelieve is a blown-up creature, not the deity conceived by the classical traditions. Dawkins then mockingly demands 'proof' under laboratory-like conditions that this 'sky-god' exists.*

---

* Harris likewise offers highly one-sided summaries of the religious outlook, as when he informs us that 'the central message of [Judaism, Christianity and Islam] is that each of us is in relationship to a divine authority who will punish anyone who harbors the slightest doubt about His supremacy.'¹ Yes, the 'severity' of God is one element in traditional theism. But a more balanced reading of the relevant texts clearly shows that such severity is more related to the demands of justice and righteousness than to an obsession with suppressing the doubters. This forms one

Developed religious language points to truths that elude scientific treatment, but this should not render it invalid by definition. Take a ready example. Our understanding of others, not as objects to be analysed but as persons to be encountered, is just as real as our knowledge of stars or genes – more so, in fact, because it is more direct and involves a greater spread of our capacities.

---

example among many of what the agnostic thinker Anthony Kenny has described as a use of 'tendentious paraphrase, imputation of bad faith, [and] outright insult' among the anti-God squad.

Strikingly, however, Dawkins and Harris are not on the same page with respect to spirituality. While Dawkins appears to have no use for it, Harris wishes to salvage what he sees as 'important psychological truths' from the 'rubble' of faith. These truths relate to the undoubted reality of spiritual experiences, which 'often constitute the most important and transformative moments in a person's life'.[2] The transformations Harris has in mind are familiar from the claims of many types of Eastern religion, and include a sense of 'selfless wellbeing', 'self-transcendence', 'paying attention to the present moment', a feeling of 'boundless love' (albeit of a fundamentally impersonal kind), a sense of being 'at one with the cosmos', and 'bringing stress to an end'. They stem from a long tradition in which the paramount objective is achieving bliss by detaching oneself from the stressful world of struggle, commitment and dependence. Whether such detachment has the paramount value that Harris appears to assume is of course a vexed issue, but what seems more obviously questionable in the context of Harris's general philosophical position is his claim that the relevant spiritual experiences can be understood purely in 'universal and secular terms'.

A philosopher such as John Cottingham pinpoints the flaw in Harris's argument also noted by other religious believers. 'Harris makes it central to his argument that "nothing in this book needs to be accepted on faith", since all his assertions "can be tested in the laboratory of your own life". But the spurious image of the laboratory masks a vision of ultimate reality that is actually metaphysical, not scientific. Harris's vision is of a reality where there are no true substances and there is ultimately nothing but an impersonal flux of conditions that arise and pass away. Yet once the results of spiritual experience are allowed as empirical confirmation of this kind of vision, then Harris has left himself no justification for dismissing those countless theists whose own spiritual experience has, by contrast, seemed to them to disclose the nature of reality as deeply and ultimately personal.'[3]

Aristotle had already made this kind of insight clear well before the birth of Christianity. Educated people do not expect the word 'certain' to mean the same thing in every context, he argues, adding that it is the mark of a juvenile to think that certainty is fully contained in the notion of mathematical certainty. Mathematics poses no difficulty for a 'juvenile' in this sense. But ethics is difficult, even for a mature person, because certainty isn't so easy to come by. You have to grow into it.

New Atheist standard-bearers and the large company of casual non-believers who support them are therefore doing the equivalent of shouting 'checkmate' during a game of poker. They owe to the objects of their scorn the courtesy of finding out what classical teaching in the Abrahamic faiths does and does not say. Though superficially attractive, polemic of this kind has a dubious lineage. Bertrand Russell, poster boy for atheism in English-speaking circles during the twentieth century, was plainly a figure of high achievement. But *Why I Am Not A Christian* is charitably described as a weak book. In any case, he believed in all sorts of non-natural entities, including 'Russellian Universals', which cannot be demonstrated scientifically. By all means be an atheist, but your case may carry more weight when at least purged of the blatant double standards.

Informed Jews, Christians and Muslims would insist that God is not a thing who competes for space with creatures. You cannot (to posit a crazy thought experiment) add up all the things in the universe, reach a total of n, then conclude that the final total is $n + 1$ because you're also a theist. God belongs to no genus; divinity and humanity are too different to be opposites. By definition, then, no physical analogy will describe our putative creator. We are migrating off the semantic map. But light is among the more helpful. The light in which we see is not one of the objects seen, because we see light only in as much as it is reflected off opaque objects. From a monotheistic standpoint, it is the same with the divine light. The light which is God, writes Denys Turner, we can see only in the creatures that reflect it. 'Therefore . . . when we turn our minds away from the visible objects of creation to God . . . the source of their visibility, it is as if we see nothing. The world shines with the divine light. But the light which causes it to shine is itself like a profound darkness.'[4]

So believers and non-believers alike should remind themselves of the limits of language. On the one hand, theology makes claims about the whole context of the moral universe, so is therefore unlikely at first sight to be content with provisional statements. On the other, religious talk deals with what supremely withstands the urge to finish and close what is being said. Theological rigour therefore partly involves keeping watch over any tendency to claim what has been called the 'total perspective'.

Closely connected to this is an awareness that faith involves the domain of the implicit. And not just faith: much of our apprehension of the world derives from this overlooked dimension. To start with, it is impossible to capture the true essence of *any* object in language, even if it is simple and immobile. In his great work *The Matter With Things*, Iain McGilchrist cites his fellow thinker Bryan Magee's example of the towel left carelessly in a heap on the bathroom floor.[5] Words cannot convey the real look of it. The more words you use, the further away you get from your goal. True as this is of towels, it is truer still of far more important things. They simply cannot be explained without either missing the point, altering their essence, or destroying the very thing sought to be explained. As Magee goes on: 'How does one *say* the *Mona Lisa* or Leonardo's *Last Supper*? The assumption that everything of significance that can be experienced, or known, or communicated is capable of being uttered in words would be too preposterous to merit a moment's entertainment *were it not for the fact that it has underlain so much philosophy in the twentieth century*.'[6] In essence, the explicit is the bright glare of midday; the implicit, the eloquent luminosity of twilight. A half-light can be more illuminating than the full beam – what Wordsworth calls 'the light of common day'. This in turn may be linked to a thesis familiar to readers of *The Matter With Things*, namely that relationships are more important than the things related. These betweennesses are also inherently dynamic. As such, relationships are much more like flames than crystals. They cannot be pinned down or reduced to words. Jonathan Gaisman's account of musical appreciation given in a talk about McGilchrist's work is especially relevant here. The act of listening to music provides not one but two examples, he suggests.

> First, there is the relationship between the notes. Although this is a gross oversimplification of the myriad relationships which arise in a piece of music, take the familiar falling sevenths of Elgar's 'Nimrod'. Each is composed of just two notes: but what an emotional charge they carry. Where is this falling seventh? It is not in the first note. It is not in the second. You cannot see it in the printed score. When does it start, or finish? The only answer to these questions – a half-answer – is provided by the second relationship which listening to music highlights. The musical encounter, such a precious experience that some people organise their lives in pursuit of it, is located in the metaphorical space which arises from the interaction of the purely physical world of sound, and the mental world of intentionality brought to bear by the listening subject.[7]

A mystery, then. But what is mysterious is not for that reason untrue, as quantum mechanics demonstrates. It is only that the mystery invites us to enter into a more profound understanding of where truth might lie. Even in a poem, the essence is not in the words. It is in the spaces between them, like the spaces between the notes of a piece of music. In each case, it is in these gaps that there arises the infinity of associations, conscious and unconscious, constituting true artistic experience.

What applies to areas such as music and poetry is supremely true of spiritual practice. So often when I read the work of figures such as Dawkins and Harris (my book *Outgrowing Dawkins: God for Grown-Ups*[8] is a rebuttal of *Outgrowing God: A Beginner's*

Guide[9]), I feel as though I were in the company of tone-deaf people who dismiss all music as worthless. None of this is to commend some kind of wishful, dreamy approach to the subject. On the contrary, I think the debate would benefit precisely from a more stringent matching of tools to material.

These tools come from anthropology as well as philosophy. An anthropologist might begin by noting that 'religion' as a term is very hard to pin down. A general definition would include rites in the ancient world such as animal and human sacrifice, employed as forms of scapegoating. But dwelling at any length in such territory would be eccentric for our purposes. In a brief overview such as this we are concerned with global faiths that have produced major bodies of critical thought, and with definitions given by the sociology of religion, which sees its subject as involving an apprehension and symbolic representation of sacred or non-ordinary reality. Scholars in this field remind us that human beings do not merely investigate the natural world at a scientific level. We also seek to make sense of our lives via all sorts of evolutionary adaptations – agriculture, dance, literature – that have emerged from animal play, animal empathy, ritual and myth during a long history of tribal societies without much sense of the beyond, through supernatural king-god monarchies, to more recent societies with their religions of value transcending an awareness of the brute givens of existence.

With these patterns in mind, observers have pointed up developments during the first millennium BC. Whether or not one accepts the term 'Axial Age' to encompass this period, it can nevertheless be described as transformational. The ideal was contrasted with the real; visionary horizons of hope were set against the frustrations of the everyday world. The quest for transcendence arose in China, India, Israel and Greece especially.

Ask Jews, Christians, Muslims, Hindus, Sikhs and others today to give a rationale for what they are doing, and – as we have seen – they are likely to reply that their beliefs need viewing in the context of life as a whole. Ritual, narrative, ethics, institutions and personal experience all feed into the mix. Some will supplement this with observations about human nature, and what is implied by a self-examined life. Others will echo words of Simon Conway Morris: 'The unsolved puzzle of why human beings alone among creatures have language, music, cumulative technologies, laughter, morals, teaching and, come to think of it, religions (including atheism) is the elephant in the Darwinian room.'[10] Others again will focus on what they may see implied by these points. We are free, accountable and objects of judgement in our own eyes and the eyes of others. We are motivated not only by desire and appetite, but by a vision of the good. We are not just objects in a world of objects, but also subjects, relating to one another reciprocally. Roger Scruton sums things up as follows: 'Our form bears ... the marks of its peculiar destiny; it is capable of sanctity and liable to desecration; and in everything it is judged by a standard not of this world.'[11] This way of seeing ourselves does not point unavoidably towards a religious interpretation, of course. But it deploys categories that are supplied by religion, 'and to be obtained only with the greatest difficulty without it',[12] he adds.

The New Atheists' neglect of philosophical reasoning strikes me as particularly lamentable given a renaissance in the discipline since the 1980s, forming a significant chapter in the history of ideas. Though the shift cannot be discussed at length here, its main conclusions are worth outlining. The scales of debate on whether a faith such as Christianity deserves more serious attention will tilt a bit if the theistic picture looks more coherent on closer inspection than many had previously thought, and naturalism – the belief that everything is ultimately explicable in the language of natural science – less plausible as a consequence.

Today McGilchrist's explicitly Christian counterparts include figures such as Janet Soskice, Sarah Coakley, John Cottingham and Catherine Pickstock, who have developed complementary expressions of what might be termed 'humane' philosophy – an approach to the subject involving holistic visions encompassing desire, affect, embodiment and other elements until recently dismissed as too subjective by anglophone (but not Continental) practitioners.

Soskice is clear that this approach is not based on fuzzy impulses associated with personal taste. Her point, rather, is that practising a faith may require an appropriate discipline or *askesis* – engagement in a tradition as the means of grasping the polyphony of religious understanding. Cottingham's use of a musical analogy is also pertinent: 'A lifetime of musical discipline may enable the committed musician to discern profundities and beauties of musical form that are . . . quite literally inaccessible to the novice; but this does not mean that they are mere idiosyncrasies of subjective feeling.'[13]

At the same time, some of the most influential champions of belief in God have sprung from the notionally more secular domain of analytic thought. In North America and Britain, leading lights include Alvin Plantinga, Richard Swinburne, Brian Leftow and Nicholas Wolterstorff. For example, a student embarking on a philosophy of religion course today could typically be told that there are six strong arguments for the existence of God: the modal ontological argument, the kalām cosmological argument, the argument from moral truths, the argument from mathematical truths, the argument from fine-tuning, and the argument from consciousness.[14] None of these should be seen as logically coercive, but that hardly renders them redundant. If this form of reasoning can draw one towards the threshold of belief – to the point where one makes a life-changing commitment, moving beyond intellectual assent alone – or if it can build bridges with atheism, demonstrating that religion is not irrational, then it will have served a valid purpose. Believers seeking a more straightforward rationale for their convictions interlacing reason and faith could cite three forms of awareness. First, that we are embodied beings with the capacity to grasp meaning and truth; second, that our status is to be viewed as a gift prompting awe, gratitude and a heightened sense of ethical responsibility;

third, an acknowledgement of this gift as grounded in a reality that freely bestows itself on us.*

Theologically informed observers will also note that divine transcendence is pictured in broadly complementary ways

---

* The argument just traced prompts a provocative but unavoidable question: can we conceive of all the capacities I have listed and associated with the world's created status, *without* belief in God? Atheists who dismiss 'ultimate' meaning may be hard-pushed to account for any meaning in the here and now. An alternative involves seeing all meaning as a human construct. Take an illustration from *The Guardian*. 'If you accept that meaning is something that emerges from sufficiently complex biological machines,' the astrophysicist Brian Cox writes, 'then the only place those machines might exist is here; then it's correct to say that if this planet weren't here, we'd live in a meaningless galaxy. That's different to life. There's a difference between life and intelligent life.'

In suggesting that the only meaning lies in a subjective imposition on the cosmos, he is sawing off the branch on which he, as a scientist who claims to be in pursuit of objective truth, is sitting.[15] A believer standing in the Abrahamic traditions can reply that if you take an all-knowing God out of the picture, then the whole idea of objectivity – and, therefore, intelligibility – becomes problematical. Our finitude means that our grasp of what we term reality is unavoidably partial and fragmentary. For creation to be fully intelligible, there therefore has to be a reality not limited in the ways that we are limited.

The matter could be summed up as follows. Pinning a definition down involves conceptual content of some sort. But conceptual content is not material stuff, nor is it reducible without remainder to material stuff. Whatever else they are, the chains of inference, entailment, logical in/compatibility, and so forth that stitch conceptual content together are not *causal* connections. They are not governed by the laws of nature but by the laws of thought. An analytic philosopher such as Alvin Plantinga thinks it is *a priori* less likely on naturalism than on theism that a world would emerge in which there were beings capable of deriving meaning from it *or imposing meaning on it* (that latter point is important: the theist can grant that we are mistaken in the meaning we do in fact find. But what requires explanation is the capacity to engage the world in terms of meaningfulness, regardless of whether we have ever correctly grasped the meaning of reality).

across the major faiths. The conception I have in mind can be found in various forms of pagan belief deriving from late antiquity such as Neoplatonism; in the three Abrahamic religions; in Vedantic and Bhaktic Hinduism; in Sikhism; in some aspects of both Taoism and Mahayana Buddhist visions of Buddha Nature. They all tend to see God as the one infinite source of all reality: uncreated, eternal, omnipotent, omnipresent, transcending all things and, precisely by dint of not competing for space with creation, immanent to all things as well.

In at least some major strands of Indian religious thought, God is described as infinite being, infinite consciousness and infinite bliss – *sat*, *chit* and *ananda* in Sanskrit – from whom we derive our existence and in whom we are to achieve ultimate fulfilment. St Gregory of Nyssa describes the divine life as an eternal act of knowledge and love, in which the God who is infinite being is also a boundless expression of consciousness, knowing himself as infinitely good and so also an infinite outpouring of love. David Bentley Hart notes that a medieval Sufi thinker such as Ibn Arabi draws attention to the shared root of the terms *wujud* (being), *wijdan* (consciousness) and *wajd* (bliss) to designate God's mystical knowledge.[16] Hart sees that these terms also encapsulate the ways in which several faiths picture the believer's own appropriation of the reality of God:

> [f]or to say that God is being, consciousness, and bliss is also to say that he is the one reality in which all our existence, knowledge and love subsist, from which they come and to which they go, and that therefore he is somehow present in even our simplest experience of the world, and is approachable by way of contemplative and moral refinement of that experience. That is to say, these three words are not only a metaphysical explanation of God, but also a phenomenological explanation of the human encounter with God.[17]

This model need form no challenge at all to the integrity of science, notwithstanding ignorant, authoritarian voices in parts of the Muslim and Christian worlds who oppose the teaching of evolution in schools among other subjects. To show why, some commentators have given the example of a basic act such as heating milk on a stove to illustrate the difference between what is technically known as primary and secondary causation. According to classical monotheistic teaching, the process has been misconceived by believers and non-believers alike in three ways. The first mistake is to suppose that the gas heats the milk and God is not involved at all; the second, that God heats the milk and the gas plays no part; the third, that God makes the gas act on the milk as a puppeteer moves a puppet, meaning that the gas does not exercise a power of its own. The Abrahamic faiths take a more nuanced view. As a canvas supports a painting, so God makes the whole situation to exist: the gas, its power and its action on the milk. God and the gas work at different levels, not in competition. Creation is thus seen as a relationship of radical dependence. God's creation of the world should not be likened to a carpenter making a chest. A better analogy (alongside that of light sketched earlier) would be the relationship between an author and his or her characters.[18]

If we absorb these points, it becomes clearer why the doctrine of creation as classically framed cannot be undermined by Darwin's theories. The priest and Darwinian Aubrey Moore was right to say that 'Darwin appeared, and, under the guise of a foe, did the work of a friend', because he held that God had made a world which makes itself.[19] Moore's insight was that Christians could now free themselves from a deistic conception of God whereby the creator had made a machine-like world, retreated, and then occasionally intervened with a tweak. Moore realised that Darwin had restored agency to the world, while at the same time making that agency an expression of what God is. This was an echo of Aquinas's oft-quoted remark that nature is not like wood being made into a ship, but like wood that *makes itself* into a ship. In this connection some insights voiced by John Cottingham are highly germane:

> Many scientists talk teleologically. It's curious, actually, that many people discussing the modern scientific world view use words like random and accidental. We're just an accidental blip on the face of the cosmos. But that can't be quite right. It does seem that it is quite natural for galaxies to form. It is natural for some stars to explode into supernovas and to produce heavier elements. It is natural for planets to form and most scientists say that, sooner or later, given the right conditions, life will emerge and then, given the Darwinian principles of selection, intelligence is likely to be favoured. So the scientific conclusion from all that seems to be that the universe is, as the British Astronomer Royal Martin Rees puts it, both biophilic and noophilic, that is to say that it will tend in due course to produce life and intelligence. There is a natural tendency there, if you like, so using words like 'accident', 'random' and so on is in a way misleading.[20]

Far more could naturally be said about the subjects discussed so far – including how mistaken Dawkins is about *science*, let alone theology. His assumption that matter consists of meaningless bits of stuff is rooted in outdated assumptions: the consensus in disciplines including physics and physiology has moved on.[21] But a focus on the big picture should probably take in several questions above all, given their salience in general discussion. First, can't a humanist be a perfectly decent person without religion; second, what is to be understood by the claim that God 'acts' in the world; and third, why does a supposedly all-powerful and all-loving deity permit evil and large-scale suffering, especially among the innocent? Having spoken of arguments in favour of God's existence, I fully acknowledge that there is one strong argument *against* theism. It rests on the supposed impossibility of theodicy – that is, providing morally sufficient reasons God has for permitting strife and moral depravity in multiple forms.

God and the World

The opening challenge of this trio is the easiest to answer. Countless people without religious faith plainly live moral lives. The traditional – and correct – view in Christianity is that conscience is the exercise of reasoned judgement. So 'natural law' is just that. St Paul in Romans 2:14 writes of how gentiles can be a law unto themselves for the reasons spelt out above. Yet none of this stops a Jew or Christian – or members of other faith groups, using their own language – from grounding ethics in the structure of reality. Religious believers can say that they are not just exercising a set of individual choices, but somehow making visible the way the world is – and ultimately the way God is. So yes, while you can lead a good life without having religious convictions, as an atheist you will have to work rather hard to explain why your moral compass isn't just arbitrary. Perhaps the secularist could reply that Aristotle's Golden Rule is available to neutral reason on grounds already hinted at. Human beings are animals, with natural needs and capacities. The fulfilment of these needs and capacities amounts to happiness, which partly involves being honest and decent and generally doing as you would be done by. Religious voices across the spectrum might only be half-persuaded by this, however. Since Christians remain the New Atheists' prime targets, it seems right to focus again on church teaching, sometimes framed on the following lines. The 'cardinal' virtues of justice, temperance, prudence and fortitude are indeed rational. But it is religion which can offer the most solid grounding for the 'theological' virtues of faith, hope and charity. The Truth and Reconciliation Commission in post-apartheid South Africa was very much an exercise of the theological virtues. I suspect that Archbishop Desmond Tutu would be among the first to say that while a secular liberal ultimately believes in justice, a Christian, also deeply committed to this virtue, none the less prizes forgiveness above all.

I have outlined my impression that secular visions of the good life often borrow from theology without due acknowledgement.

The results can be confused. A philosopher such as Joel Feinberg, who is broadly speaking a liberal in the tradition of John Stuart Mill, has enormous problems with examples including a voluntary gladiatorial contest. He points out that there are people who will engage in such combat for a sufficiently large sum of money, with an assurance that the millions earned will go to their family if they lose. The spectacle would only be available to paying customers behind high fences. What would be wrong with that on libertarian grounds? For the strict secularist, it is very difficult to say. It is likewise very difficult to spell out what is wrong with bestiality on libertarian grounds. The only way to do so would be by holding that it is incompatible with a strong sense of the dignity of the person. Ever since Kant, people have been trying to give a 'rational' account of such dignity without theological underpinnings. The political thinker Andrea Sangiovanni has tried to do this in his book *Humanity without Dignity*;[22] but many are unconvinced by his arguments. You still require a sense that there is some value there which cannot be fully explicated in purely naturalistic terms. In essence, human rights discourse cannot be disembedded from broader philosophical – and theological – traditions: rights divorced from an innate sense of human dignity can easily descend into a battle over rival entitlements.

In conclusion I suggest that Judeo-Christianity offers the most robust foundation for values such as love, hope, truth and freedom, though this need not in any way preclude an open-handed attitude towards secularists and other faith groups. Some will still see an intellectual land grab in this claim. In my eyes, it rests on the search for a fundamental and inclusive context of meaning. To the goods just listed, I have added the impulse to solidarity, and with it a grasp of symbols. When a fascist paints a swastika on a synagogue, the wrong done goes beyond the cost of cleaning up and repainting. Understanding the symbolic and communicative dimensions of existence takes us beyond the province of cause and effect.

In detecting many marks of grace outside the visible Church, I am conscious of confronting some exclusivist Christians. But natural law as understood in Catholic teaching at its most open-handed and best is not the property of those standing in a charmed religious circle. It is less a pre-existing body of obligations and rights and more a code human beings must write themselves, using their God-given reason. Confronted with debate on matters such as abortion, cloning and euthanasia, for example, conservatives have regularly accused politicians of 'playing God' without realising that playing God rationally is just what the teaching of a figure such as Aquinas demands. In practice, natural law could be reframed as 'natural lawmaking'.

This leaves me critical of certain aspects of Christian thought, starting with strands of Catholic teaching that have held too much sway over the past two centuries especially. Conscious that a huge body of reflection in the world's largest Church defies simple summary (there are inevitably tensions, false starts and blind alleys to be traced), I was gratified to hear an indictment of debased parts of the record in a sermon preached by Fr Alban McCoy of Cambridge University. As Catholic moral theology over time came to be inappropriately equated with canon law and consequently manualised, morality became more and more separated from spirituality, he observed. In consequence, morality came to have less and less to do with holiness and more and more to do with obedience. Though he was too polite to say so, his comments apply as much to sections of the Protestant world:

The outcome of that long process has been, until very recently, a duty-driven moral outlook that many mistake for Christian morality and, understandably, reject as legalism. St Thomas Aquinas, for one, would have certainly disagreed that morality concerns primarily duty, obedience and rule-keeping. For him morality concerns, primarily, not the discharging of duty and fulfilling obligation, but human flourishing and our search for the lasting and true happiness such flourishing constitutes. It's about what we *are*, and only secondarily, what we *do*. The two are not unrelated, of course, but the latter follows from the former. Catholics are now returning – though not without opposition from some – to a much older, more rational, saner and certainly more Christian understanding of morality, evident at an earlier time in the Church's life, when the Sermon on the Mount was the central text for all moral discussion. And it's easy to see why: virtues are attributes of the person, the wellsprings of action. As they come more and more to characterise us, so the need for precepts decreases.

Christians can therefore say loud and clear that morality has less to do with a supermarket model of choice than with the education of desire. A mature person is unlikely to think much about choice in the way it is conventionally understood. Think of Jesus in the Garden of Gethsemane. Could he have fled? Did he really face the same kind of agony that we might face in a similar situation? In the Christian understanding, he could have selected another option. But there was a deeper sense in which he had no choice, because of who he was. A parallel can be seen here with Edith Stein, the Jewish Carmelite murdered at Auschwitz. Arrested by a Nazi officer who greeted her by saying 'Heil Hitler', she replied 'Laudetur Jesus Christus' (Jesus Christ be praised). Here we observe the place beyond consumer freedom reached by the saint. Having become habituated to seeing and responding truthfully, the saintly person's instincts are second nature.

***

What of divine action? I have indicated that from a classical standpoint, the world is itself the act of God. Creation does not just refer to what is believed to have happened a long time ago. It is happening *now*, because contingent existence is not its own cause (or to put it another way, nothing can make itself). On this view, therefore, we should not look around for that space where God might be detected in addition to our own presence and action.

Yet the challenge is that Christians do indeed speak not only of the natural working of finite causes in the universe, but also of supernatural reality. And by supernatural reality believers mean the life of finite agents transformed by, or sharing in, the infinite. Christians believe themselves to be sanctified and adopted as children of the heavenly Father, absorbing and exercising the means of grace. So does that upset the neat idea that what we are is what God does and that's all there is to it? One of the foremost discussions of this subject over the past century comes in Austin Farrer's Bampton Lectures, delivered at Oxford in 1948 and published as *The Glass of Vision*.[23] Farrer points out that we don't simply inhabit an arena of regular finite causes, but one in which the unique phenomena of personal will and personal relation mark the lives of agents such as ourselves. This highest level of finite agency – which is seen as relation to God on the part of creatures – itself allows more to happen in the finite world than if there were no relation with the infinite. And so the challenge for theology is to think through a model of reality in which infinite agency and finite agency are radically distinct – they can't be added together – and yet in which human beings may attain their full dignity and reality in a relationship with the infinite will and reality of God, which will in turn subtly alter mundane reality.

In unpacking this understanding, Farrer holds that God may bring about through finite causes effects which do not arise from the natural power of those causes. Our relatedness to God does not mean that something infinite intrudes into the finite, he says, but that the finite, related to God, produces more than it could alone. Just as we say of complex physical realities that the properties of the whole may be more than the properties of single parts, so our relatedness with God, our wholeness as finite beings in relationship to God, allows more to be possible in the world than would otherwise be the case. So Farrer is claiming that under certain circumstances, finite agency is open to possibilities rooted in infinite agency rather than just its own immanent predictable capacities. Accordingly, what an event or transaction in a sequence of finite causes makes possible is genuinely more than the sum of the finite parts involved, in so far as it is related to the infinite.[24]

Drawing on his Augustinian side, Farrer holds we have some hint of this in the work of our own imagination: that properly supernatural activity in the world is discernible when we recognise, and act in tune with, dimensions, purposes and possibilities that are not just obvious to the natural observer. Something occurs in this 'attunement' to communion with God: this is what Christians mean by revelation. A specific communication from infinite agency to finite mind occurs by means of the way in which finite agencies and substances arrange themselves. The world remains the world; finite causes remain finite causes; God does not tear apart the fabric of the world to insert his word into it. But as the world rearranges itself around the magnetic attraction of the infinite, that rearrangement uncovers something of God's communication.

***

Our third challenge listed above is the stiffest. The problem of evil plainly assails believers as well as sceptics. I myself have felt sufficiently exercised about the subject to devote my book *The Hardest Problem*[25] to it. Outstanding recent contributions to the field include *Wandering in Darkness*,[26] Eleonore Stump's monumental feat of scholarship, and David Bentley Hart's tract-length work *The Doors of the Sea*.[27] Here there is only space to delineate an answer in the broadest terms, starting with the discrete arguments about suffering and moral depravity that the three Abrahamic faiths have tended to advance.

First, it is said, pain cannot be avoided where physical laws have their own integrity. A material world involves inbuilt constraints. Aquinas observes that entities exist by winning the favour of their environments, but there is no chance of harvesting all that benefit at once without any associated rupture. In his view the universe as a whole is better for including some things that cease to survive. Fire must consume air as it burns, pandas must eat bamboo, carnivorous animals must seek their prey. There are ways of improving the situation so as to achieve greater even-handedness, but to have the universe without any of this destruction is impossible. According to this line of interpretation, God indirectly causes natural evils and afflictions as a result of bringing about world order and harmony. Not even divine omnipotence can generate a finite cosmos in which natural evils will not be a concomitant of good. Knowing this, God chose to create, so can be held responsible for natural evils. Earthquakes on Jupiter and other planets without sentient life are neither here nor there. Suppose, though, that you or I were in a position to destroy our own planet instantly and painlessly. Would we do so because of those concomitant evils? Aquinas thinks not. Therefore blaming God is not viable. The true course for us is to accept our environment and assume our own share of the responsibility for it. We could try taking on one of the main tasks for which Genesis suggests Adam and Eve were made, namely to tend and cherish the earth as good stewards.

Evil is also considered unavoidable in a setting where flawed human beings are free to become better or worse. *The Hardest Problem* quotes the answer given by Jonathan Sacks when confronted with the question of where God was at Auschwitz.[28] He said that God had been there 'in the words "You shall not murder." He was there in the words "Do not oppress the stranger", in the words "Your brother's blood is crying to me from the ground." ' Sacks immediately added that the Holocaust was not in and of itself a new challenge to faith. Exactly the same question could have been asked about Cain and Abel, among innumerable other disasters.

Why did God let Cain kill his brother? And the truth is, that is the Jewish equation. We believe that God gave us freedom. It is the most fateful decision he made in the entire universe. Freedom means that if we do well, we are little lower than the angels. But if we do bad, we are lower even than the beasts. That is our world. God teaches what's good and what's evil, what we should

73

do and what we should not do. But God does not intervene to force us to do good, or to prevent us from doing evil.

I went on to record further resonant remarks made by Rabbi Sacks on this subject: here they are reproduced in an endnote.[29]

Church teaching has tended to harness the argument in ways already hinted at. First, by a suggestion that there is some analogy between the divine love that knows self-conscious existence to be a precious gift which can only be bought at a price, and the love of parents who conceive a child knowing perfectly well that they are bringing her or him into a broken world and exposing their daughter or son to risks over which they will have no control. Mothers and fathers 'choose life' because they believe in its possibilities. Second, Christians invoke fundamental articles of belief. A potent answer to the waste and suffering entailed by evolution is the presence of God incarnate experiencing the joys, sorrows, injustices and mortality that we all face. Christians do not merely believe God to be great or transcendent. They hold that he 'transcended' his transcendence by taking off his crown to share our flesh. God was rejected by humankind on the cross, but made of that rejection an example of divine humility. Another biblical theme follows on from this: God's creative process, which began by bringing something out of nothing, will end with the deliverance of everything and everyone out of the nothingness of sin and death into perfection. St Paul plainly had no access to Darwin's discoveries, but was well aware that suffering, death and decay were part of creation, and did not shy away from the idea that God was responsible for that reality. The matter is encapsulated in Romans 8:20ff.

Among the best summaries of a Christian perspective I read during my researches came from Sam Wells, a theologian who as Vicar of St Martin-in-the-Fields in London stands at the forefront of outreach to people in dire need. He writes as follows in his book *Humbler Faith, Bigger God*:[30]

The 'problem of suffering' assumes that God's role is to bring health and flourishing – and if God fails to do that, God is malign or weak. But what if God's role is to be with us always, in person in Jesus, in myriad ways through the Holy Spirit, and forever in heaven? God is not an instrument we discard if it malfunctions. God is the essence of all things who astonishingly chooses to be with us even in desperate hardship – and even, in the crucified Christ, in indescribable agony. That doesn't make suffering go away. But it turns God's engagement with suffering from a reason for rejection into a reason for worship.[31]

These reflections do not imply that I think such a profound conundrum can be answered simply and comprehensively in this life. Anyone who imagines they can do so has failed to grasp the dimensions of the problem. Yet it also seems clear to me that much rejection of theodicy is based on a misconstrual of how a faith like Christianity has traditionally conceived of God and divine engagement with the world. There is something fundamentally reductive, both conceptually and spiritually, about thinking of a deity who tears apart the fabric of creation and intervenes from outside it. Church teaching has laid far more emphasis on the importance of created intermediaries and our place within that whole. Many questions here (and related matters in the philosophy of religion) in the end come down to different models of causality, in that if our understanding of divine and human agency is antagonistic, then fundamentally we're left with a problem. Whereas if creatures are always nested within the divine causality, then we have a different template in which some of these problems may not dissolve, but certainly take on a new kind of structure.

The task for a Christian is to give an account of reality in which awareness of evil on the one hand, and faith in God's omnipotence on the other, cease to be disruptive of the wider story. It is not that questions about suffering and evil evaporate, but rather that it becomes possible for them to reside within a bigger picture. In this picture God is held to be at work repairing creation from within, but going with the grain of what he had made, not through waving a magic wand. From a Christian vantage point, then, the laws of creation are an expression both of the divine love and of the divine understanding that we can only respond freely to that love because of a divine reticence, a refusal to dazzle, coerce or manipulate us. The incarnation is an expression of that reticent yearning for our response. Kierkegaard's famous parable of the king and the lowly maiden expresses this thought very effectively: 'For it is only in love that the unequal can be made equal,' runs the punchline.

Kierkegaard is here echoing Pascal, who thought that God can be expected to appear openly to those who truly search for him, but to remain hidden from those who do not seek. This insight has been recast in our own time by Paul K. Moser, author of *The Evidence for God*.[32] He rejects the demand of militant atheists for 'spectator evidence' of God's existence as though this most mysterious of quests could be resolved in a test tube. His work emphasises a person's motivational heart, including their will, rather than just the mind or the emotions. Whatever its challenges, this path is clearly in tune with the gospel summons to newness of life.

Moser nevertheless insists that faith needs to be 'cognitively commendable', not contradictory or arbitrary. He also draws support from Paul, and especially the 'grace-based' forms of knowledge evident in a passage such as Romans 5:5 – 'And hope does not put us to shame, because God's love has been poured out into our hearts through the Holy Spirit, who has been given to us.' Personal commitment really is unavoidable. Both Paul and his followers become evidence for God's reality. We are now a long way from the 'neutral' terrain characteristic both of theist–atheist debate and of some philosophy of religion courses. Yet the process has been necessary in order to give us the tools for attempting an authentically Christian description of God. No effort to capture the ineffable in words can fully succeed, of course. But the answer given by Rowan Williams to the broadcaster Melvyn Bragg, combining both intellectual and spiritual threads, is among the most succinct one could hope for: 'God is first and foremost that depth around all things and beyond all things into which, when I pray, I try to sink. But God is also the activity that comes to me out of that depth, tells me I'm loved, that opens up a future for me, that offers transformations I can't imagine. Very much a mystery but also very much a presence. Very much a person.'[33] From this it follows that God is not to be thought of primarily as an unmoved mover or first cause (despite being so), but rather as an intimate presence in the life of believers responding to a gift and a richness from beyond their imagining.

The Jesus of History and the Christ of Faith

Faced with the question of how we can know that the gospel narrative is true, Williams has given a potent answer to enquirers undertaking the Alpha Course drawing together some of the points I've tried to outline. It ranks among the best I have encountered from a church leader:

> By listening to what Jesus says, and by watching what he does, people's whole sense of their world changes . . . Reading [the New Testament] is like watching people feeling their way into the new landscape and seeing the light in it. Bit by bit people put together a jigsaw and you end up with that really strange and mind-bending notion that God . . . lives in Jesus in an absolutely unique way . . .
>
> But how do we know it's true? Christians have never been able to come up with a simple answer to that. It's a bit like saying, 'How do you know that your husband or wife is lovable?' . . . There's something about the 'knowing' that is involved with your whole personality changing. But of course Christians have always tried to make some sense of it, and to put it into some kind of intellectual shape. Among the things they've said would be things like:

'Does it never occur to you as rather strange that a random, unintelligent process of evolution should have thrown up beings capable of understanding the process of evolution? Has it never occurred to you as a bit odd that a blind universal system, working in its own regular but undirected ways, should produce the questioning, agonising, imagining, loving people that you are?'

Nobody can prove to you that human beings are not the result of blind chance and undirected process, but from time to time it's worth stopping and asking that question. *Doesn't it strike you as a bit odd?* I sometimes feel I'd like to ask that question of Richard Dawkins, a man who has devoted huge amounts of energy and tremendous intellectual sophistication into proving that there is no structure or meaning to the process which he so elegantly, intelligently and brilliantly outlines.

The other thing Christians say is, 'It's not just about mind, it's about love.' 'Mind' on its own – powerful intelligence – is never creative just by itself. Think of human relationships, think of artists – even scientists – at work. It's not intelligence alone – it's absorption, commitment, love, and the leak of imagination that goes with real love. Only love can make something completely different and rejoice in its difference. God is not just intelligence, but loving intelligence – and you can't pull them apart for a second . . . Our existence as intelligent creatures – loving, risking, questioning – somehow fits with the idea that God is a God of loving intelligence, who loves what's different . . . There is no single, knock-down argument for the truth of all this. If there was, we probably wouldn't need Alpha courses, or indeed anything else. Everybody would just sign up without asking any questions.

There is a leap of faith involved – or what I'd rather call a leap of the imagination – that sudden sense of, 'Yup – it all makes sense, I see how it fits.' And the claim Christians make is that when you see how it fits, everything changes.[34]

And what of the historical element underlying these claims? It isn't oversimplifying a complex picture to say that many scholars are more confident about the Gospels' reliability than several generations ago. One robust summary of Jesus' message might run like this. In common with other rabbis, he expounded Scripture, enjoined his hearers to observe the central elements of Jewish law, and emphasised God's love for the outcast. More remarkable was his absolute renunciation of violence and insistence on self-giving love as the supreme virtue. He proclaimed the arrival of the Kingdom of God, with all that it entailed in terms of the espousal of the poor and weak, the casting out of evil spirits, and the release of those resources of generosity and compassion which are so easily deflected by social convention and spiritual legalism. This mission led to Jesus' death, which he accepted, sensing that his crucifixion and subsequent vindication by God would have redemptive power for the community of believers he had inaugurated.

He believed this because of having made one especially audacious claim from the start of his ministry which we have already flagged up: that the question of how people relate to him and to what he says will govern how they relate to the God he addressed as Father. If Jesus is the one who determines who belongs to the people of God, then Jesus' authority must be connected with the divine purpose. Distinctively Christian theology begins to take shape when two elements are brought together: the actions and the words and sufferings of this particular human being, and the vision of a God whose purpose is unrestricted fellowship with the human beings that he has made.

Christian experience was distilled from the experience of prayer and communal life over generations. As reported in chapter 2, the teaching that emerged in the New Testament and early Church holds that through Jesus' death and resurrection, a new phase in history has been ushered in. Human beings discover their destiny in an orientation towards the source of their being. This is not the orientation of a slave to a master, but the intimate relationship of a son or daughter to a parent.

Why was Jesus crucified and why does it matter? One of the first things worth noting is that his execution was not accidental. He indicates several times in the Gospels that his forthcoming demise cannot be avoided. This was not just because he scandalised the Jewish authorities by presenting his teaching as the fulfilment of the law of Moses, but also because of a more general human trait – our tendency to despise and reject full humanity when we encounter it.

Jesus plainly did not want to die. His anguish in the Garden of Gethsemane is clearly recorded. Yet over and again he is portrayed as wanting to do the will of his Father above all. This is not to suggest that the Father sought Jesus' death either. What loving parents hope for is that their offspring will flower as people. The 'Father's will', of which Jesus was so conscious, consisted in being completely human: this was the path that led to the cross.

Perhaps the toughest question faced by the early Church was how to designate a man who appeared utterly dependent and utterly free – who claimed a divine liberty and who was yet so obedient to God that you couldn't accuse him of trying to stand in the Father's place. The effect of Jesus' career was so extraordinary that it took centuries for the Church to reconceive its understanding of the divine nature. Gradually there arose a conviction that God is not only source, but also loving response, that there is in God the agency of giving that we call Father, and also a derivative responding agency that we call the Son or the Word, and that these agencies are equal.

Belief that Christ was 'of one substance with a Father' did not become normative until the fourth century. The length of time taken to arrive at this definition was caused by a sense that apparently neater theories were inadequate. Some early Christian theologians were happy to think of God in purely transcendent and monistic terms, while designating Jesus as a deputy. This model came to be seen as doubly defective. It didn't do justice to the absolute creative freedom felt to have been at work in Jesus, or to the exhilarating possibilities that Christians believed had been opened up for them by the crucifixion and resurrection. On what has been called the 'unadventurous' model of God and his deputy, the promised outcome was an authorised communication from God that would help us to lead better lives and to pray with a bit more confidence. But a bolder claim was made by other Christians – that our goal is communion with God, not merely communication with him. This is why developed orthodoxy expresses the belief that in God there is room for us, because in God there is not only eternal giving, there is an eternal answering. Christians are called to echo and take in and embody that answer, that loving response.

The doctrine of the incarnation states that there is a full human identity in Christ, which is 'at every moment of its being suffused with the life of the divine answer to the [originating] divine love'. Precisely how this happened is a mystery on which the Church must remain reticent. In the words of one of my teachers, 'I can't say how; I can say what. And the "what" in this instance is a human life that erects no obstacles to the activity of God at any time.'

The Church also holds that an axe was laid to the roots of evil through the passion and resurrection. There is no doctrine of the atonement purporting to explain how this came about, only a variety of theories. Mainstream assessments start by focusing on the cross. What makes the crucifixion of Jesus different from that of other victims is that it is done to someone who claims to speak for God. In Williams's words, 'He promises being with God and his path leads to the cross; so that we are starkly challenged as to whether we can cope with identifying this place of execution as God's place.'[35] That is why it makes sense to speak of the cross as an action as well as a passion. It is the sign and the substance of God's decision to be where his human creation tries hardest to kill itself. And for Williams, the 'price' paid through the crucifixion is not to do with placating God's wrath, but with the way in which 'the bearer of God's life bears the consequence of human self-hatred, the cost of human fear.'[36]

In *The Hardest Problem* I offered seven reasons for accepting the bodily resurrection: they are reproduced below.* But one of my most stimulating correspondents – and now a friend – insisted that there is an eighth and supremely important ground for orthodox belief, namely the willingness of all the inner disciples and apostles to submit to martyrdom for maintaining the truth of what they had seen. The prevalent idea that they had stolen and hidden Jesus' body and then

---

* First, scholars do not dispute that the resurrection was proclaimed in Jerusalem a few days after it allegedly happened. This would have been a puzzling and risky thing to do had the tomb not been empty. The location of the tomb could not have been unknown to the authorities: Roman guards were placed there and Joseph of Arimathea was on the Sanhedrin. Second, it is generally agreed that the disciples were accused of stealing the body (the evidence is thought to be strong, because it's a piece of *testimonium hostium*). But the accusation makes no sense if there was no empty tomb to be explained. Third, if the tomb was not empty, the most straightforward way of arresting the cult would have been to produce and display the body (such public displays were not uncommon). Fourth, the absence of any trace of veneration at the tomb or shrine – or any pilgrimage to it – suggests that the tomb was indeed empty. It was customary in Judaism for the tombs of prophets and other holy men to be venerated. Fifth, the discovery of the tomb by women is historically probable, because of cultural attitudes and legal principles concerning the authority of female testimony which are widely known about. No one concocting literature whose purpose was to persuade people of the truth of the resurrection would have said that women were the prime witnesses. Sixth, the rapid shift among early Christians from observing the sabbath on Saturdays to celebrating the eucharist on Sundays (observed by Pliny in about AD 110 but in evidence much earlier than that) is highly telling. Seventh, it is widely accepted that Paul (albeit indirectly) attests to the empty tomb in 1 Corinthians 15:3–5 given the died–buried–raised pattern, his doctrine of resurrected and transformed bodies, and his belief in the personal return of Christ. Since this chapter arguably contains one of the earliest credal formulas in the New Testament (scholars agree that for grammatical and lexicographical reasons Paul is reciting an established credo), it weighs heavily with many well-informed readers.

concocted a story about his resurrection 'collapses in the face of their willingness to undergo significant trials and suffering and eventually be killed for the truth of what they saw', my friend argues. 'This is also true today. Thousands are willing to die for their experience of the risen Christ. Yes, people are willing to die for political causes, and in war, although I think there is an element of hazard in there – but it is extraordinary that, as far as we know, all of the apostles were executed for their faith while millions of believers since then have undergone the same.'

All of the last few pages could be summed up in a single affirmation: that God has not only made us, but 'spoken' to us in Christ. What is known as the 'scandal of particularity' has been a stumbling block to many. Eternal verities are one thing, say the doubters, but it is absurd to suppose that any set of contingent events carry the unique importance that Christians ascribe to Christ. How can he have done more than heighten our perceptions of the good life? Like others, I have found answers in literature, as well as the Bible – including in Martyn Skinner's remarkable epic *The Return of Arthur*,[37] at the end of which an unbeliever finds himself entranced in a church as he contemplates a plaque of the nativity:

> So Leo gazed, absorbed, a timeless glance;
> And thought of all the trees that nature held
> (Strange instance of a trance within a trance);
> Cedars of Lebanon, green beechwoods delled
> With sapphire; sombre newsprint forests felled
>   At such a rate, each Sunday men were able
>   To read ten acres at the breakfast table;
> Dwarf fairy oaks at Lichen, harled with moss;
> Trunks wide as roads, through which a cart could go;
> A jungle mat a continent across
> Which, piled as logs, would make the Alps look low –
> And yet of all that ever grew or grow

(So ran his thoughts) this carving had been done
Uniquely from a random plank of one.

Was not the contrast much the same in space,
Whose glittering forests were the galaxies?
For if the carver made a special case,
Selecting from innumerable trees
One segment, so from the vast host of these
    Could not the prime Creator, mightier far
    Have carved his story on a single star?

And if he had, ah, if indeed he had,
And come himself to earth, a newborn cry,
Would not the story have been just like that;
And signs accompanied, in earth and sky,
That holy abdication from on high;
    And radiant beings from about the throne
    Of Light, have made the lamplit stable known?

***

Finally, it seems worth answering a more general question about the integrity of the Bible, given the tendency of secular-minded intellectuals to dismiss the most consequential text in history as a relic. In *God Is No Thing* I maintain that, rightly understood, the Bible is an extraordinary and complex human phenomenon, a library of books of every genre, evolved over centuries and held together first in Hebrew Scripture by one nation's quest for identity – its account of what it means to experience God and be in covenant with him – and then in the New Testament by the ministry of an exceptional man believed by his followers to personify the Jewish nation. Fundamentalist interpretations of Scripture are not genuinely traditional: we have already noted that inspiration does not mean dictation from on high.

Genesis starts with two pictures, one of a creation recognised as good, and the other of the source of a deep fracture which spearheads the search for atonement and renewal. It leads to release from bondage, which means both freedom of a people, and deliverance from the self-absorption of sin. It includes the rejection of idols, pictured both as images of the unknowable, and the pursuit of wealth or power that we follow in denial of our real duties towards God and neighbour. The sociologist David Martin has encapsulated the significance of the New Testament as follows:

[It is about God's presence with us] as flesh of our flesh, about the proclamation of an invisible kingdom and a banquet to which we are all invited, as well as about the signs of that kingdom and that banquet, about the absorption of . . . evil in the gift of body and spirit even unto death, the death of the cross, about healing of spiritual and physical wounds, the offer of a sign of peace, and the reconciliation of enmities, about rebirth, death to self and resurrection, and about the taking up of a redeemed humanity to share in the mutual exchanges of love which are the life of God.[38]

It clearly follows that a Christian is not committed to belief in a specific transgression involving a snake in a garden six thousand odd years ago. A literal acceptance of Genesis 1–3 has never formed part of the creed. But what the story reveals about flaws in human nature is abidingly true. A common complaint among critics of Christianity is that God is represented as vengeful in the Old Testament. I do not want to make light of this challenge – only to clarify that there is a reasonable reply to it. Historically, the Church has taught that a full disclosure of God's Trinitarian being did not emerge until the life, passion and resurrection of Christ, and the descent of the Spirit at Pentecost. In other words, the Old Testament is the first stage of an unfolding drama yet to reach its climax. It is therefore no cop-out to say that Hebrew Scripture represents a genuine but partial revelation. Note that one of the first major decisions in the early Church was to abrogate the ritual elements of Jewish law.

Side by side with this should stand a general awareness about textual interpretation. It makes little sense to pluck a single leaf off a tree and pretend that it can represent an entire landscape. If one verse makes God seem cruel, for example, but the thrust of the narrative is that God's mercy exceeds divine justice, then it is the big picture which counts. Jesus himself famously summed up the whole of the Law and the Prophets in terms of radical self-giving love for God, and for neighbour defined in the broadest possible way. Nor is this approach unique to Christians. Rabbinic reflection on the Hebrew Bible displays similar impulses.[39]

Easter in Ordinary

I hope I have demonstrated that Christianity deserves an attentive hearing. If my credentials for attempting the task are passable, I do not think that this is just to do with a broadly Christian upbringing or academic qualifications or the inspiration of fine teachers. Though I studied theology and the philosophy of religion, the experience initially left me less rather than more sure of my beliefs. Years of agnosticism followed. That my worldview only regained a Christian shape after a spell of living and learning tells against any suspicion that I've been confined in a pious bubble. Though I now work in academia (and part-time with asylum seekers), most of my career has been spent in the very secular environs of Fleet Street.

This book is not the journal of a soul, however. I have alluded in passing to my own experience for two reasons. Partly to underline that there was nothing inevitable about my development. Most people I know of a similar background have few if any church connections. Conversion processes can grip those with nominally Christian upbringings like me as much as they affect those with wholly non-Christian backgrounds who embrace the faith de novo. The second reason grows out of the first: believers typically live their way into a new way of thinking rather than thinking their way into a new way of living. Practising a faith chiefly involves doing things that change you.

This imperative famously exercised a pull on the novelist Francis Spufford, which he recalls in his compelling book *Unapologetic*.[40] The clue is in the subtitle: *Why, Despite Everything, Christianity Can Still Make Surprising Emotional Sense*. Recently Spufford's insights have been reminted with equal verve by Elizabeth Oldfield. She enjoyed an ecstatic experience of Pentecostal Christianity during her teens. It felt like falling in love. Joy was later displaced by ennui. Afflicted by growing intellectual doubts, she also fell away from her practice as the grind of life set in. Eventually a further change took root: Oldfield began to entertain doubts about her doubts. Dissatisfied by slick irreligion as well as the slick Christian variety, she began a journey towards the quieter and deeper faith she now holds. It seems to me well worth tracing some of the main contours in her spiritual reflection, *Fully Alive*.[41]

The descriptions of her formation and identity are especially instructive. 'I am British,' Oldfield writes, 'marinated in the irony, scepticism and critique of dominant liberal culture.' She is a feminist with two degrees.

I have worked at the BBC and in Westminster. I have a subscription to the New Yorker (I liked the bag) and know who is on the Booker shortlist, though my actual reading skews increasingly heavily towards golden age detective stories.

In summary: I am supposed to be one of the growing majority of people who have long relegated Christianity to the scrap heap. For my friends who are also desperately seeking ways to settle their souls, it's the last place they'd look. I should have been one of them, dropping the mild cultural Christianity still around in my childhood without regret like most of my generation, retaining only a socially acceptable taste for choral music or Gothic architecture, the festive habit of tipsy Midnight Mass. That isn't what happened. My story went off script.

Like Spufford, Oldfield has a talent for connecting widely touted existential conundrums to Christian answers in unforced ways. We are at a moment in our society where many people feel utterly bereft of sources of collective meaning, places to belong, ways they can settle their soul, she adds. Technology has freed us from drudgery and offers endless ways to increase our comfort and convenience. Product after product promises to help increase our status and performance.

> But still there is a malaise, a sense of impending threat, which many of us feel in our least defended moments and don't know how to speak about. The news scrolls unendingly with stories of war, disease, deepening division, the rise of authoritarian governments and the unimaginable but rapidly approaching prospect of climate collapse. Accelerating advances in AI may turn the world upside down in ways no one can predict. Against this ominous global mood music, we have unlimited choices in framing our identity, but this freedom can sometimes induce vertigo rather than exhilaration. Many of us feel isolated and anxious, or too distracted and overworked to feel much at all.

Her solution to this sickness lies in what she terms wisdom, depth and 'a stability of soul'. She aims for neither a big life nor a small life, 'but a deep life'.

> I want a luminous soul . . . I'm done with cool. That's not actually true. I want to be done with cool. I'm old enough now, surely. It is true that I'm increasingly drawn to wisdom. I am longing for there to be more people I can trust, who reliably act with integrity.

I want more morally serious people, which is not the same as just being no fun, or being good at pointing fingers at other people. My instinct is that morally serious people don't have to perform their virtue. They've learned some things, and suffered some things, and let go of some things. They are resilient, kind and open. They know how to laugh, even on dark days. I want to be like them. My ambition is to be a 'non-anxious presence', to make people feel more peaceful when I'm around. I'm currently too distracted, too scattered for that. I want to be brave and generous and free, and on those I also have a way to go. Sometimes, when I catch myself moaning about some triviality, trudging through a day made grey by my inattention, a voice wells up inside and shouts 'FREEDOM!' Yes, I can be sort of intense.

The result is a vibrant but grounded account of the Christian life purged of technical vocabulary and other varnish. Oldfield's presentation of sin is especially worthy of note: following Spufford, who notes that the term has become evacuated of meaning, she redesignates it as the human propensity to mess things up. There follow chapters on the worst of human vices and the resources Christianity offers for overcoming them.

Her discussion of envy, for example, includes analysis of how 'social science now agrees with theology' about the danger of the self-esteem movement (a trend so pernicious that its devotees will now typically rise at 3.00 or 4.00 a.m. to engage in frantic activity for hours before the day is supposed to begin). A section devoted to wrath unpacks the principle of turning the other cheek in situations ranging from Twitter/X pile-ons to tense conversations in the workplace. Oldfield describes times when she's been attacked online or on the airwaves, and seen 'how quickly the situation can change when I manage to make this unexpected move'. She has invited people calling her a religious bigot over for dinner – and ended up becoming friends with them. Through her podcast, The Sacred, she has listened 'with as much empathy and openness as I can to a range of people whose views I deeply disagree with, and learned a lot in the process'. Unless society learns to listen, she thinks – to hold tension, cross divides and refuse to descend into tribalism – 'our common life is at stake. Theology can help us.'

Her diagnosis of gluttony includes a discussion of her friends' use of psychedelics to obtain oceanic moments of self-transcendence. Aware that her own embrace of Christianity as a teenager involved ecstatic experiences which some may view with suspicion, she is nevertheless clear that such experience is not wholly foreign to her generally more subdued spiritual practice in middle age. 'I go to church and sing with others, cry with others, and often lie on the floor and let myself be flooded by sensation, images and joy. I come away feeling reset.' She notes that Aristotle was a rationalist who none the less appreciated the value of 'unselfing' moments, and pokes gentle fun at sections of British society with allergies to emotion and 'enthusiasm'.

And lastly, her discussion of pride includes a welcome rebuke to those (believers as well as their antagonists) who set too much store by winning arguments. She rightly observes that most people who reject the idea of God do not do so for mainly intellectual reasons, adding that a philosophy of religion seminar can seem like a bad computer simulation compared with a glorious landscape. Desiccated, joyless and beside the point. Her words have stayed with me:

> I believe in God because I feel God's presence. Because I asked a question and felt it answered. When I momentarily stop distracting myself with hurry and dopamine hits and a constant stream of stimulation, when my thoughts slow down, in the beats between the stanzas of life, there is something beyond the silence. In the silence. When I turn my deepest attention it meets an attention that is already turned towards me, patient and faintly amused and always, always kind.

***

This chapter has covered a large acreage. To anyone crying out for more detail, I would respectfully point out that it is not a theological manual; to those puzzled at my taking time to defend the creed in a book about Christian decline, my reply would focus on the need to understand what is being accepted or shunned, rather than a caricature. In this coda my instincts are to return to Rowan Williams, given his talent for weaving disparate strands – historical, spiritual, theological – together, and in the process subverting dogmatism on either side of the pro- and anti-Christian divide. One camp is populated by the credulous: those who consider that their embrace of faith supplies them with privileged spiritual information, along with cudgels to beat others who don't belong to the club. Another is peopled by those who judge that Christian proclamation is a tissue of nonsense with all the stability of cloud-capp'd towers.

The option I commend is the excluded middle. In the early Church, just when people were starting to shape doctrinal formulae, they were also starting to say quite extravagant things about how little we know about God. So it is not a new tension: but a paradox is not the same thing as an outright contradiction. In Williams's words, 'When I recite the creed, I believe I'm telling the truth about God. That what God has shown of himself is best and most truthfully expressed in those words. And at the same time I know that whatever has been said is not adequate, not the whole story.'[42] It's therefore true as far as it goes. 'This doesn't mean I think it's ever going to be exposed as untrue or in need of revising – on the contrary, when Christians describe their Saviour as of one substance with the Father, they mean what they say and are likely to think that their lives depend on it.'

If pressed on what exactly this formula means, he'd reply: 'God knows exactly what it means, but from my side it's the least silly thing I can think of saying – it's the least inadequate way of talking about it. It will take me a huge step forward in advancing towards the truth.'[43] So Christians need not be embarrassed by statements of belief. On the other hand, the worst mistake they can make lies in supposing that creeds somehow sew God up. The process is more like saying that the footprint of a large creature in the forest has been observed.

It's a real mark; it has made a real difference. It's truth-revealing. But you haven't seen the whole animal. We Christians at least have an advantage. We have seen the face of God in Jesus Christ. All our Christian language is an attempt to say that something quite new, quite unexpected and gratuitous has happened. We couldn't have predicted it. It didn't come from us. And we're feeling our way around that great mystery that's been put down in the middle of us.'[44]

4

In Search of the Common Good

So far I have extolled the tools Christianity offers for making the world a better place, while pointing to what could be called missing ingredients in a purely secular take on reality. A positive part of the thesis involves seeing that religious principles can regain relevance after periods of eclipse. For example, the international dimension of Catholicism was devalued by the Reformation and the Enlightenment, but re-emerged after 1945 in the reconstruction of Europe and the founding of what became the EU. A more critical strand in my case highlights liberal enlightenment's status as a form of universalism. Like Christian or Islamic universalism, it is supersessionist and inclined to suppose that it has subsumed whatever good there was in the past. David Martin expresses the point as follows: 'The virtue of universalism always harbours the vice of imperialism, but whereas liberal enlightenment sees that very clearly with regard to religious universalism, it is less clear about its own imperialism.'[1]

For corroboration of my positive argument, take an area such as economics. Over four centuries, the liberal economic tradition (admittedly containing Catholic neo-scholastic as well as Protestant roots) has emancipated the capitalist free market from most of the moral restraints imposed on commerce in medieval Christendom. While too many Christians over the generations have been found either actively promoting or passively acquiescing in the more questionable forms of capitalism, there has always been Christian proclamation and practice of a more demanding economic ethic, ruled by principles and models of love and justice drawn from the Bible. Today we need only look at the strong Christian initiative in campaigns for just international trade and debt relief to poor countries, more conscientious consumption habits in the rich nations, and the development of technologies throughout the world that protect the environment. These priorities have plainly assumed ever-greater importance since the financial crisis of 2008.

Some still query the extent to which supposedly Christian input to political debate really stands outside the range of independent secular formulation. They may cite attitudes to the use of force in support of their view. For non-pacifists (so this line of thought runs), it does not really matter whether a Christian lens is employed, because churchgoers will end up in the same boat as everybody else: assessing likely scenarios within a small range of realistic options. In other words, just war theory may have theological origins, but the arguments are entirely available to 'neutral' reason without reference to doctrine.

It is true that once a given public decision has been identified and described, observers may find it difficult to see how Christians could respond very differently to it from other people. But by that time the interesting part is all over. As an ethicist such as Oliver O'Donovan emphasises, identification and description of decisions is essential work. Why, for instance, did weapons of mass destruction become the sticking point with the second Iraq war of 2003? Because of the UN Convention on WMDs. Why was there a UN Convention? Because of huge revulsion at the Western and Soviet policy of massive deterrence, a revulsion focused to a high degree by the Churches. Why were the Churches interested? Because they had a long-standing if partially buried tradition of asserting the importance of discriminate conduct in warfare. What was the basis of this tradition? The belief that international conflict, though it lies outside the scope of human law, does not lie outside the scope of divine judgement, and that guilt and innocence therefore matter on the battlefield, too.

Can non-Christians not embrace this tradition without believing in God? Yes, many do of course. People often develop their moral convictions in eclectic ways, allowing them to operate with such fragments of Christian or other moral thinking as seem to meet their needs. Just war thinking has been popular recently, precisely because it speaks to pressing contemporary problems. But it was not always popular. Total warfare was at one point the dominant strategic wisdom of the West. So if discrimination in armed conflict is a humane insight of some importance which can be lost, we should ask what the conditions for its recovery in the West were, and the conditions that need to be met if we are to hand it on to future generations with moral coherence. Then the value of the theological train of thought will be a good deal more apparent.

This idea could be pressed a bit further. Not only is it wrong to say that the just war idea is simple rationality: it is not even the simple rationality of the West (let alone of the Islamic world). The tradition has had its high tides and low tides in the history of Western thinking. Having written at length on the subject, O'Donovan summed up his view to me like this:

One can, I believe, search the debates of the Second World War without finding any extensive moral scruple about non-combatant casualties. Even Bishop George Bell of Chichester mounted his great defiance of the wartime spirit of vengeance not primarily on the issue of non-combatant Germans but on the issue of non-Nazi Germans. In the second half of the twentieth century, driven by concerns over the policy of mutually assured destruction [MAD], the category of non-combatant immunity seemed suddenly to recover its relevance. [The ethicist] Paul Ramsey stressed that, while the restraints imposed by the principle of proportionate harm are elastic, the principle of non-combatant immunity from direct attack is absolute. Non-combatants are caught up in a war collaterally, of course, and may suffer gravely; yet to make them the deliberate object of attack is an unqualified sin. It was on this basis that the massive destruction strategies of the 1950s and 1960s were exposed to consistent criticism from Christian sources.

And so [more recently] the climate is different. During the war in Afghanistan in late 2001, we were told, a controversy arose in the USA because commanders in the field were expected to have every potential target cleared by lawyers in the Pentagon for risk of excessive collateral non-combatant damage. A set of moral factors had come into our thinking that weren't there when the Second World War was fought. They can be intelligently or unintelligently applied. But I cannot regret they are there.'[2]

Another robust example is Magna Carta. Eight centuries after it was promulgated 'for the honour of God and the exaltation of Holy Church and the reform of [the] realm', laws deriving from standards set out in this document secure freedom of belief across a vast belt of the world. Christians along with others hailing the theological dimension remind us that the two billion people who live in common-law polities are the document's heirs. Almost every contemporary constitution has drawn inspiration from it. Magna Carta was biblically based. Stephen Langton, the Archbishop of Canterbury who played a leading role in framing the text, was a keen promoter of ecclesiastical independence. But he was no less keen to apply norms first set out in the Torah: that the Israelites were not to be abused or enslaved, and were themselves to do justly. At the heart of such a polity was the administration of justice. 'Appoint judges and officials for each of your tribes . . . and they shall judge the people fairly. Do not pervert justice or show partiality. Do not accept a bribe' (see Deuteronomy 16:18–19). The scriptural echo in clauses 39 and 40 of Magna Carta is patent: 'No free man will be taken or imprisoned or . . . outlawed or exiled or in any way ruined nor shall we go or send against him save by the lawful judgement of his peers and by the law of the land. To no one shall we sell and to no one shall we deny or delay right or justice.'

Magna Carta was reissued in 1216 as the Coronation Charter of a new monarch, Henry III. Speaking at the Church of England's General Synod in July 2014, the theologian Nicholas Sagovsky pinpointed the link with the covenantal theology developed by the biblical King Josiah: 'Just as with the covenant of the Hebrew

Scriptures, which defined Israel as a covenant-people, so Magna Carta became woven into the self-understanding of the English nation. Just as the prophets of Israel recalled the people to fresh observance of the covenant, so the constitutional thinkers and lawyers of the common-law tradition have refreshed and renewed our understanding of Magna Carta over 800 years.'³

My provisional verdict is not just that Christianity has more to contribute to the public square than is often thought. This contribution seems to be essential, rather than just advantageous. One of my intellectual heroes is Justin Martyr, the second-century apologist who saw the divine Logos, or Word of God, as widely seeded in human society, and the Church as the body interpreting the Logos in decisive ways. Justin's strategy in debating with non-believers was open-handed. In effect he said, 'I am drawing out the full implications of beliefs which you are already committed to. As a Christian I see their full significance.'*

***

If asked further about adapting an ancient principle to our own situation, I would cite Article 14 of the German Constitution, with its well-known declaration that property carries responsibilities. Many may suppose that this simply reflects a set of social conventions

---

* This is the light in which I read some very thought-provoking reflections of Jacques Maritain in *The Rights of Man and Natural Law*: 'Finally the conception of society we are describing is *theist* or *Christian*, not in the sense that it would require every member of society to believe in God and to be Christian, but in the sense that it recognizes that in the reality of things, God, principle and end of the human person and prime source of natural law, is by the same token the prime source of political society and authority among men; and in the sense that it recognizes that the currents of liberty and fraternity released by the Gospel, the virtues of justice and friendship sanctioned by it, the practical respect for the human person proclaimed by it, the feeling of responsibility before God required by it, as from him who exercises the authority as from him who is subject to it, are the internal energy which civilization needs to achieve its fulfilment.'⁴

established for practical purposes. There is something inherently valuable in exercising stewardship over one's property. But what are the presuppositions entailed in generating this principle? People often talk about intergenerational responsibilities or environmental responsibilities as 'stewardship', without recognising the Judeo-Christian roots of this metaphor. It does not make sense to be a steward unless there's a lord on whose behalf one is acting.

So Justin Martyr's successors today can deploy a vocabulary enabling people to see that there may be more to their perceptions than they had anticipated. And what might that 'more' consist in? A general overview could draw on some suggestions from Chapter 3. Several major faiths have at their base an understanding of the world as owned and 'selved' by various kinds of agent. At the centre – or one of its centres, if there is intelligent life elsewhere in the universe – stand human beings, who not only occupy existence but are alive to it, taking it in with intelligence and giving it out with loving care. And at its apex stands a creative providence of which human wisdom is to be an instrument.

We have seen that one consequence of such an awareness is a heavy emphasis on human dignity. With regard to the developing world, that is likely to crystallise in opposition to forms of poverty that are offensive to such dignity. In a richer society, Christians and others may see a different menace in the form of idolatry – for example, the worship of GDP or a failure to recognise that markets are good servants and poor masters. Developing this theme, a faith-based approach is likely to value equality, yes – but to prize solidarity even more. The point about responsibilities linked to property ownership rests on assumptions about constitutional government. You might say that it is ultimately about the right ordering of economic and social affairs. Yet as in the case of armed conflict, we cannot tell an uncomplicated story about the ethical foundations of such a picture. It may indeed be possible to explain and justify democracy on pretty rudimentary assumptions about being cautious over who gets power, and related matters such as human fallibility and the need for accountability.

But I do not think it is really possible to explain to people why they should take the quality of their public life seriously without saying something more about the ethical responsibilities of being a citizen in a democracy. A simple egalitarianism will not do.

Those wanting to take Christian insights seriously often stress the importance of economic security across the life-cycle. They also see the family as the foundation of society. It is the capacity to cope with effects of the life-cycle that really marks out a worthwhile social and economic policy. A certain form of dignity can be established without thinking theologically, but whether we can firmly establish the idea of care for people at vulnerable moments without thinking in at least implicitly religious terms is less clear.

The case gains in texture from further exploration of a core term such as the social contract. It is a way of talking about the network of rights and responsibilities that bind us as citizens to one another and which form the basis for government action. Think of it as a charter of rights and responsibilities by which our society is governed. Every so often that charter needs to be refreshed. 'Now is one of those moments', observes the political theorist Albert Weale, writing in the wake of Russia's invasion of Ukraine.[5] When the Berlin Wall was demolished in 1989 and communism was dismantled, many assumed that benign democratic government would spread without hindrance. People even spoke about the 'end of history'. This did not mean the end of politics, but it did imply that fundamental political revolutions would become a thing of the past. Latin American dictatorships were replaced by constitutional democracies. Apartheid ended in South Africa. In the West, economic policymakers – governments, central banks and international institutions – all shared a set of assumptions about how to achieve prosperity involving lean supply chains, competitive tendering for public services, and just-in-time delivery. Governments, it was said, had learnt how to avoid boom and bust. What Weale terms the 'great complacency' set in.

That smugness was ended by the crisis of 2008. But there had been plenty of other dangerous signs before this time. Strong evidence of climate change had begun to accumulate in the 1980s – so much so that even in 1992, the Rio Declaration on the environment urged precautionary action. Though less public attention was given to the issue, global water resources were already being depleted beyond sustainable levels. After Hurricane Katrina devastated New Orleans in 2005, the most powerful country on earth was unable to guarantee physical security to its citizens against an event that was high on American politicians' own list of foreseeable risks. The outbreak of Severe Acute Respiratory Syndrome (SARS) in 2003 in East Asia was a harbinger of Covid-19. Then came the 2008 recession. More recently, the war in Ukraine has formed a chilling reminder of the need for military security and just how internationally interdependent energy and vital food supplies are. 'We took for granted the benefits of a just-in-time world. We had forgotten the need for a world of "just-in-case",' Weale adds.[6]

His prescription for a new social contract putting precaution and public goods at the centre of our priorities is very well judged. Though Weale has no specific religious case to make, his opening suggestion is drawn straight from Catholic Social Teaching (itself often hailed as producing an economics centred on the needs of people rather than of money). In an echo of numerous papal encyclicals, he also thinks that public policies should be based more on the contours of the human life-cycle. It is obvious that we are born vulnerable and utterly dependent. All being well we achieve independence, and in most cases develop responsibilities to our children and/or elder relations. And if we reach old age, we shall ourselves become dependent on others. What is needed are public policies likely to foster resilience over the cycle. Weale also notes that such an imperative is obscured by the seductive but questionable vocabulary of 'levelling up'. This widely discussed term refers to one group of people (the left behind) who are helped by another group (the affluent) to the likely advantage of the former and the financial detriment of the latter. But he sees that things aren't so simple:

The well-off pensioner forced to wait for hours for emergency treatment after a fall, the young professional couple finding that one of them is working solely to pay for childcare, or the business that cannot find trained technical staff: all suffer from the lack of public support that a well-functioning social contract would provide. This lack of support includes adequate provision for health and social care, affordable childcare and high-quality education and training. The lustre of private affluence loses its shine amid public penury. A crucial feature of services such as good healthcare or affordable childcare is that they are both elements in the public goods – those commodities or services that benefit all members of society, often provided for free through public taxation – that all individuals need in order to flourish.[7]

The main lesson is this. Granted that respect for the individual is a mark of civilisation, we should also accept that individual fulfilment will best be realised by a social order serving the public good. Such an order will resist short-termism. The costs of precaution, like all investment, come early and the benefits materialise later. When people are hard-pressed financially, it is tough to persuade them to give up something now on the promise of a benefit in the future. Even more difficult in the pursuit of the precautionary state is a recognition that the benefits are often those of security rather than goods that are experienced in direct forms. Like any form of insurance, the hope is that you do not have to call on the policy. If this is a sobering lesson for individuals, it is an even harder lesson for us collectively. Populist policies overlook planning of this kind through the facile promise that we can have our cake and eat it. Weale acknowledges that even the UK shows a capacity for long-term thinking – through the often unsung work of parliamentary committees, for example, and NGOs and other bodies such as the National Audit Office. In conversation with me, he has not only emphasised the creditable role of the Churches in this context, but also recognised the implicit theology haunting his own thinking overall.

Bad and Good Religion

I trust we are now in a better position to bring more explicitly articulated theology to the discussion. Consider a spiritual leader and thinker such as Jonathan Sacks. Faith, he maintains, is

> part of the ecology of freedom because it supports families, communities, charities, voluntary associations, active citizenship and concern for the common good. It is a key contributor to civil society, which is what holds us together without the coercive power of law. Without it, we will depend entirely on the State, and when that happens, we risk what J. L. Talmon called a totalitarian democracy, which is what revolutionary France eventually became.[8]

Or to put it another way, perhaps metaphysics isn't a candle in the wind after all. After 2008, Sacks reminded his audiences among much else that economic terms such as confidence and credit have religious roots, respectively in the words 'faith' and 'belief' – *fides* and *credo*. He didn't shrink from drawing a bold lesson: 'The whole economy of the West depends on these deeply psychological – you might even say spiritual – states of mind.'[9]

Sacks's contribution has been immense. One of the most vivid snapshots of his ideas comes in the Prologue of his bestselling *The Dignity of Difference*.[10] He sets out his stall with a set of acute observations about the importance of faith in a globalised world, religion's status as a source of harm as well as good, and its potential to supply the antidote to its own poison.

First, he foregrounds the inescapable moral element: politics raises questions that cannot be answered by political calculation alone. And second, that great responsibility now lies with the world's religious communities. 'Against all expectation they have emerged in the twenty-first century as key forces in a global age.' What is more, in conflict zones throughout the world – Northern Ireland, the Balkans, Chechnya, Tajikistan, the Middle East, Sudan, Sri Lanka, India, Kashmir, East Timor – 'they are at the cutting edge of confrontation, reminding us of Jonathan Swift's acid observation that we have "just enough religion to make us hate one another, but not enough to make us love one another".' Bad religion promotes discord; the good variety promotes conflict resolution. 'We are familiar with the former. The second is far too little tried. Yet it is here if anywhere that hope must lie, if we are to create a human solidarity strong enough to bear the strains that lie ahead.'

Sacks goes on to recall the Millennium World Peace Summit of religious leaders held in New York a year before 9/11. Freighted with symbolism, the 9/11 tragedy illustrated some of the perils of globalisation. 'Two icons of global capitalism, the jet and the skyscraper, were turned into instruments of destruction. Office workers going about their daily routine found themselves suddenly implicated in a conflict whose epicentre was thousands of miles away.' And given the exceptional potency of faith ('politicians have power but religions have something stronger: they have influence'), Sacks draws a stark inference: 'If religion is not part of the solution, it will certainly be part of the problem.'

He then explains in more detail why faith is both so important and so combustible. Before the modern era, people inhabited self-contained spaces physically, and therefore intellectually. It was possible to believe that 'our' truth was the only truth. Now we live in the conscious presence of difference. That can be experienced as a profound threat to identity.

One of the great transformations from the twentieth to the twenty-first centuries is that whereas the former was dominated by the politics of ideology, we are now entering an age of the politics of identity. That is why religion has emerged, after a long eclipse, to become so powerful a presence on the world stage, because [it] has become one of the great answers to the question of identity. But that, too, is why we face danger. Identity divides. The very process of creating an 'Us' involves creating a 'Them' – the people not like us. In the very process of creating community within their borders, religions can create conflict across those borders . . . [Faith] is like fire – and like fire, it warms, but it also burns. And we are the guardians of the flame.

Next, Sacks calls for two conversations: one between religious leaders, another between them and politicians and business leaders on the direction globalisation must take. At this point he reveals that he is an anti-liberal, philosophically speaking. He therefore judges Western democracies to be ill-equipped on the whole to confront the challenges he has outlined. 'Britain still has a National Health Service, and most Western countries have some form of welfare provision. But increasingly, governments are reluctant to enact a vision of the common good, because – so libertarian thinkers argue – there is little substance we can give to the idea of the good we share. We differ too greatly.' All recent popes would share this lament.

Beyond the freedom to do what we like and can afford, contemporary politics and economics have little to say about the human condition. They give us inadequate guidance in knowing what to do in the face of the random brutalities of fate. We need to recover an older tradition – essentially a set of religious traditions – that spoke of human solidarity, of justice and compassion – and of the non-negotiable dignity of individual lives.

And in an age of uncertainty, religious creeds remind us that we are not bereft of guidance from the past. The sheer tenacity of the great faiths – 'so much longer-lived than political systems and ideologies' – suggest that they speak to something enduring in the human character. Sacks concludes that it was religion which first taught human beings to look beyond the city-state, the tribe and the nation to humanity as a whole. 'The world faiths are global phenomena whose reach is broader and in some respects deeper than the nation state.'

And how can economic globalisation be assisted by religion? Faith encourages restraint, humility, a sense of limits, and the ability to listen and respond to human distress – 'these are not virtues produced by the market, yet they are attributes we will need if our global civilisation is to survive, and they are an essential part of the religious imagination.' Sacks applauds the sentiment governing the outlook of anti-globalisation protesters. It is right to be very worried about poverty in particular. Unlike many in this camp, he is clear that the free market is 'the best means we have yet discovered for alleviating poverty'. Yet he also grants that the market generates unequal outcomes on an unacceptable scale.* His proposed solution resides in the biblical notion of

---

* The essence of a highly instructive work like John Plender's *Capitalism: Money, Morals and Markets* (2015) is that capitalism, whatever your misgivings about it may be, has brought about a reduction in inequality between nations. Globally, inequality has been reduced, partly because the Asian countries in particular have been drawn into the global trading system, which has given them an enormous economic impulse. And millions have been lifted out of poverty on the basis of accession to the World Trade Organisation set-up, and to global free markets. Plender's reservations are about the internal workings of capitalism in developed countries. Since the Reagan–Thatcher revolution of the 1980s, we have seen a great increase in income inequality. And since the financial crisis of 2007–9, wealth inequality has increased because the central banks poured liquidity into markets on a vast scale. Such action led to inflation in the prices of assets, bonds, equities and property – commentators talk about the 'everything bubble'.

The action of central banks can naturally be defended on the basis that it prevented a depression on the scale of the 1930s. Less welcome was their continuing to pour liquidity into markets and the sustaining of an upward impetus on all asset prices. That has been a bad development, both economically and socially.

Plender's other major reservation echoes that of Sacks. It concerns what might be called capitalism's scoring system, which has often excluded 'external' factors such as environmental costs. It relies for the incentive

tzedakah (righteousness, or a sense of ethical obligation). With its basic idea of the economic requirements of human dignity, it is 'more helpful than the Western polarity of charity and justice'.

Having restated his rejection of liberal relativism ('If respect for human life is only one value among many, what grounds have I for opposing the suicide bomber who believes that by murdering others he is securing his place in paradise?'), Sacks moves on to his final substantive point, which is a rationale for the title of his book. He argues that Western civilisation has known five 'universalist' cultures: ancient Greece, ancient Rome, medieval Christianity and Islam, and the Enlightenment. Three were secular; two religious. They brought 'inestimable' gifts to the world, but also great suffering – 'notably, but not exclusively, to Jews. Like a tidal wave they swept away local customs, ancient traditions and different ways of doing things.' They extinguished weaker forms of life and diminished difference. What Sacks terms the sixth universal order, that of global capitalism, is also a homogenising force. (He might have said the same about the paradox surrounding multiculturalism.) 'It threatens all things local, traditional and particular.'

His pitch – he calls it a revolutionary argument – is that all universalising impulses, whether religious or secular, can be traced to Plato's notion that progress resides in a movement from the local to the universal. Sacks's lesson is that we must resist what he sees as this malign Platonic legacy and recognise that unity can breed diversity. 'The glory of the created world is its astonishing

---

structures that work in an advanced economy on the profit-and-loss account of companies. But that measure does not reflect the damage that companies can do to the environment or to wider society. One of the attractions of the social market as practised in Germany, for example, or the social democratic Scandinavian economic models, is that they try to compensate for that through government initiatives – welfare systems and so forth. Of all the various forms of capitalism, those we see in countries such as Sweden, Norway and Denmark are the most humane and egalitarian. They are more attractive than what is on offer in the US and UK.

multiplicity: the thousands of different languages spoken by mankind, the hundreds of faiths, the proliferation of cultures, the sheer variety of the imaginative expressions of the human spirit, in most of which, if we listen carefully, we will hear the voice of God telling us something we need to know. That is what I mean by the dignity of difference.'

It is perhaps easier for a Jew to voice this argument, since Judaism is not a missionary religion. Many Christians would nevertheless agree with it, and claim a solid theological warrant for doing so, despite the Church's uneven record.

'Interactive Pluralism'

The question of whether and how other communities adapt to a changing world is clearly beyond my remit. But I can reiterate that public Christian voices need to be self-critical as well as measured, and that the right tone of voice is best struck by drawing on religious vocabulary rather than ignoring it. And to boost Sacks's argument still further, we might accentuate an insight serving as a pedal note to this book: that the standard secular narrative whereby the forces of enlightenment gradually threw off religious shackles in the name of freedom and progress is deeply flawed. Treat with due scepticism the story told by a figure like Steven Pinker in his overrated *Enlightenment Now.*[11] Look instead at scholars already mentioned, especially Larry Siedentop, whose grasp of the intellectual history is far more secure. In *Inventing the Individual,*[12] he argues that the roots of liberalism were firmly established in the arguments of philosophers and canon lawyers by the fourteenth and early fifteenth centuries. These included belief in a fundamental equality of status as the proper basis for a legal system; awareness that enforcing moral conduct is a contradiction in terms; a defence of individual liberty through the assertion of fundamental 'natural' rights; and, finally, the conclusion that only a representative form of government is appropriate for a society resting on the assumption of moral equality.

Rowan Williams's gift for recasting stale-sounding debates in fresh ways matches that of Sacks. He has distinguished between good and bad models of secularism, respectively the 'procedural' and the 'programmatic'. Procedural secularism grants no special privileges to any particular religious body, but denies that faith is merely a matter of private conviction.[13] It should at least be allowed to nourish the public conversation. Williams continues to see so-called programmatic secularism in a far less positive light, because it insists on a 'neutral' public arena and hives religion off into a purely private domain. Rather than resolving clashes of outlook, programmatic secularism risks inflaming social conflict by stoking resentment among faith groups. In a series of addresses over the past three decades, Williams has proposed 'interactive pluralism' as a recipe for harmony. This encourages robust dialogue among faith communities and between them and the state. No one has received the whole truth 'as God sees it', so all have something to learn. Such a model contrasts with the subjectivity implied by multiculturalist attitudes. As indicated, a tag such as 'tolerance of diversity' can conceal a multitude of sins.

Williams's account of Lord Acton, the liberal Catholic pioneer, is highly relevant to our discussion. Writing during the 1870s, the future Professor of Modern History at Cambridge made the eye-catching claim that religious liberty or freedom of belief is the foundation of all other liberties, and that political liberty in turn underpins the health of religious communities. The rationale for this lies in Acton's definition of liberty as 'the assurance that every man shall be protected in doing what he believes to be his duty. Against the influence of authority and majorities, custom and opinion, the state is competent to assign duties and draw the line between good and evil only in its immediate sphere.'

The state and religious communities thus owe something to one another. If one is to be free, the other must be free. And the state has a duty to respect conviction and conscience – especially the conscience of a minority – as well as an obligation not to be swallowed up by any religious body or to assimilate itself to one faith group. The state, then, is not a Church. The state guards the possibility of there being 'Churches' (Acton's shorthand for religious groups) and the existence of these communities of conscience stands before the state as a challenge and reminder of what it is and isn't. From this follows a momentous judgement: since the state is the authority that permits you to follow your conscience, it cannot claim the right to dictate what you believe.

It may seem counterintuitive to suggest that religion can only flourish when the state as such isn't religious, but the point is certainly grasped by T. S. Eliot in *The Idea of a Christian Society*.[14] This is the text in which the devoutly Anglican poet famously says that he would prefer to have a competent atheist running a government than an incompetent believer. His point is that the state has its business, but that business has boundaries. Williams's conclusion in a lecture on Acton is forthright, especially in view of his own left-wing allegiances:

When a state believes – and acts on the belief – that there are no loyalties more serious than political loyalties, the state becomes idolatrous and diabolical. Thus the presence within the state of communities of non-negotiable conviction is unexpectedly the best thing that can happen to a state. A state faced with communities which deny its absolute and universal reach is benefiting from that. Once the state recognises that there are, within it, communities that it doesn't, so to speak, franchise – that don't derive . . . their meaning from the state, the state will have reason to hesitate over any attempt to assimilate all communities to itself. The state will have reason to be cautious of any policy that tries to homogenise, totalise and control.[15]

The vision is codified equally well by John Neville Figgis, the early twentieth-century Anglican theologian, who wrote of 'the free Church in the free State'.[16] He held that all you need to make a state a champion of liberty is a community within it insisting on its own liberty over against the state. The state recognising its limits would become more fully itself.

Acton's perspective is far-reaching, given the political horrors of the twentieth century and the melancholy state of the world today. Theocratic states – de Valera's Ireland, Poland under the Law and Justice party, Saudi Arabia, Erdogan's Turkey, Modi's India – are to be deplored for restricting basic freedoms. But the illiberal secular state, by pushing religious conviction into a purely private sphere, ends by instrumentalising its citizens and seeing them as no more than agents of the state's purposes and subjects of its decisions. Authoritarianism of this kind risks forming a secular counterpart to theocracy. In cases such as abortion or assisted suicide, to cite two especially contentious areas, Christian campaigners should advance theologically informed arguments about the sanctity of life, as well as practical arguments endorsed by many secularists. Religious voices will not and should not always get their way in a free society. They need to be held to account on the basis of cogency, viability and other criteria. But if we grant the force of Acton's arguments, it follows that believers cannot be expected to accept an interpretation of their beliefs that reduces them to the status of a buttress for secular morality.

So the Churches should naturally respect democratic norms. On the other hand, the state cannot simply require that conscience or doctrine be jettisoned. If these two principles are acknowledged, what follows is that both Church and state can be influenced by a cross-fertilisation of debate. It may be that on some issues the social consensus pushes the Church to rethinking aspects of its doctrine. This can be a blessing, a major example being the acceptance of same-sex relationships. Yet it could also be that Christian expressions of conscientious dissent obliges the state to think again about the coherence of some of its own arguments. Debate over sexuality, and on gender self-identification for trans children, are instructive examples. The mainstream Churches have regularly been well behind the curve in accepting gay equality.

Catholic teaching, in particular, is sometimes likened to a broken computer program. There is therefore a solid case for revisiting traditional teaching. Conversely, governments in several European countries have introduced highly permissive legislation on gender reassignment for minors which are contentious in themselves, and do not enjoy a critical mass of popular support. Mainly spurred by pressure groups rather than grassroots opinion, the changes (including allowing male prisoners in women's prisons and male competitors in women's sport) draw understandable criticism from gender-critical feminists, thereby discrediting assumptions that intolerance only resides in the religious camp.[17] Christians have something to contribute after all in commending the wisdom of caution.

The Actonian model I have commended allows for genuine exchange and debate about complex matters of public policy. Williams sums things up epigrammatically by suggesting that the best citizen is the person who is not only a citizen, whose loyalty to the political unit is qualified, enriched and fleshed out by other kinds of morally significant loyalties. And this second area of concern has to do with how bridges are built between the discourses of human dignity as theologically understood, and human rights as legally framed. If human rights discourse becomes just a matter of individual entitlement, then something is missing. A discourse of rights without a discourse of dignity risks becoming, if not trivial, at least a recipe for endless contention and growing individualist rivalry. We need that myth, to use the word neutrally, of what human beings actually are in relation to 'the Eternal', to talk about the image of God in human beings, and about that completely non-negotiable, unchangeable core of human identity, which (to use Christian terms) is constituted by our relation to our maker and redeemer.

In this light it perhaps becomes easier to see how public conversation can be enriched in perhaps surprising ways when a self-critical theological awareness is kept in mind. Another apt example involves current anxieties about free speech. When language about human dignity becomes hollowed out, we can become more protective of vulnerabilities at the same time as growing less confident of one another's strengths. Accordingly, the impulse to protect people from certain kinds of speech, while laudable in itself, can carry with it a fundamental lack of trust in the human adult's ability to digest, respond and argue. I am not at all against curbs on hate speech – incitement to violence and violent attitudes. My worry is that if we simply allow this to run over the whole area of our public discussions, we shall be undermining the very possibility of argument. There is sense in the view that a good democracy is an argumentative one. If free speech is so interpreted as to limit the possibilities of robust interaction, then the public square is left the poorer.

***

A separate cluster of insights barely hinted at so far must also be registered. Christian representatives should feel able to voice judgements that many politicians are not allowed to express, given the tacit assumption that voters should always be deferred to. Churchill was no doubt correct to comment that democracy is the worst form of government apart from all the alternatives. While agreeing, Christians can also air two unpalatable truths in particular. First, that the West's problems are at least as much a result of affluence as of want and an inability to accept deferred gratification; second, that our electoral choices reflect wishful thinking.

Boris Johnson and Donald Trump have been widely derided for offering pie in the sky or 'cakeism', in Johnson's case. But it was voters who swallowed populist messages in the first place – not only in the UK and US of course, but in Spain, France, Germany, Hungary, Turkey, Brazil and other countries. The hunger for having our cake and eating it starts with us. One survey after another shows that the British among others strongly support cheap energy but also oppose onshore wind, fracking and anything else that might provide it. Voters back cheaper housing but oppose the loosening of planning restrictions needed to implement that goal. And people support higher spending on healthcare, but not the higher taxes also required.

A journalist such as Matthew Syed writes as follows: 'It has become commonplace to blame problems in democracies on polarisation, and it is true that on certain issues, such as Brexit and trans rights, electorates are bitterly divided. But what we haven't quite recognised is that the deepest form of polarisation is within ourselves.'[18] This isn't altogether true. Christians and other faith groups *do* recognise it. Christianity diagnoses the scale of human self-delusion with greater precision than any other worldview. Syed (no less that Matthew Parris and Polly Toynbee) has a notable blind spot about religion. But in some ways that makes his account of an inner malady all the more striking. He argues that in polls, 'it wasn't as if one group was in favour of better healthcare while another worried about what it might mean with regard to taxes. It was the self-same people who wanted both better healthcare and lower taxes, without noticing the contradiction between the two.'[19] Given what the Church has to say about individual and corporate sin, it is in a strong position to offer a searching diagnosis of what's wrong with us. Instead of indulging the temptation to pin all woes on politicians, the mainstream media, tech platforms, or any number of other sources, we would be well advised to take a hard look into our own souls. That is just what believers are enjoined to do every time they go to church.

Rock of Ages

In glossing the notion that religion embraces the whole of life, Christian thinkers have sometimes spoken of six dimensions to belief and practice: doctrine, ritual, myth, ethics, institutions and personal experience. Doctrine is necessary as a means of relating tradition to developing understandings of the world. This implies that the Christian way should involve a mixture of creativity and receptiveness. The community should aim at making professions of faith that are broad and inclusive, yet at the same time clearly derive from what has been received from the past. Ritual is the main way of giving voice to faith in a religious setting; myth in the technical sense is the core underlying ritual. The great biblical narratives – culminating with Easter and Pentecost – will shape the outlook of the believer at both conscious and unconscious levels. Ethics naturally entails certain forms of behaviour, from decent conduct to at least an awareness of the radical self-giving love that has prompted greater feats of spiritual athleticism among the saints and countless others. Christians should have two priorities in particular already signposted in this chapter. Both are essential if not always easy to balance: solidarity and social cohesion on the one hand, and a willingness to engage in a radical critique of society on the other.

If this sounds like hot air, look (to take but one example) at the evidence collated in a work such as Luke Bretherton's *Resurrecting Democracy: Faith, Citizenship and the Politics of a Common Life*.[20] It is based on a four-year study of the groups London Citizens and Citizens UK, examining ways in which community organising constitutes a form of democratic politics, bringing together people of different faiths and none to answer pressing social needs. Or – casting the net more widely – consider what a volume such as *Peacebuilding*[21] reveals about the Christian contribution to conflict resolution in scores of societies from Colombia to South Africa to the Philippines.

That many remain unconvinced by these claims is partly connected to what I have designated secular liberalism's self-appointed role of referee rather than contestant in the public square. I have described it as acutely sensitive to the perceived imperialism of other worldviews, but coy about its own imperialism. And I have just observed that Magna Carta was grounded in biblical ideas. Needless to say, the law in most Western societies does not consider national life to be anchored in any particular religious text. In 2004, for example, many politicians and civil servants resisted calls for a reference to God and the continent's Christian roots in the preamble to the EU Constitution. One clerical observer after another has pointed out that celebrations to mark the Magna Carta anniversary in 2015 rarely if ever mentioned divine law; we are therefore confronted with a tension between the enormous cultural footprint of Christianity on the one hand, and its negation in a secular multicultural society such as Britain on the other. For evidence of a related situation in France, one could cite the writings of Pascal Bruckner or Alain Finkielkraut or Michel Houellebecq. They voice a sense that self-criticism in Europe has shaded into self-hatred. The nostalgia for past standards felt by conservatives is matched by a determination to wipe the slate clean on the part of their opponents.

Preaching during his enthronement sermon at York Minster in 1983, John Habgood qualified his liberal impulses with a set of observations that are no less applicable in the twenty-first century. Far from seeking to impose his views on others, he was more concerned to warn of how the denial of deeper commitments and aspirations could leave a relativistic blank state. 'I am constantly surprised by what people *do* believe,' he noted,

> half-remembered bible stories, odd bits of science fiction, snippets of proverbial wisdom passed on through grandmothers or glossy magazines. There is evidence, too, of a huge and largely unrecognised reservoir of religious experience in all sorts of people who would be horrified to class themselves as religious. There seems to be a widespread diffuse awareness of some sort of religious reality, which can attach itself to whatever materials happen to be around.[22]

A society was liable to lose its bearings in the absence of focused awareness, 'a public frame, a shared faith, which can sharpen vague feelings into prayer and commitment and action', Habgood added, before immediately noting that many would think an archbishop presumptuous for saying so. Negotiating between the

Scylla of a free-for-all and the Charybdis of authoritarianism has rightly been called a lifetime's work. But I share a sense that there need be no final contradiction between a public framework of faith and a critical awareness of its limitations.

Given all these factors, a viable conclusion might run as follows. Religious bodies are not incapable of error; their representatives can make statements going far beyond the basic natural perception of the mystery of existence. Such statements can lead to mistakes, conflict and other evils, including the idolisation of community identities. In certain respects, the history of religion maps onto the entire social history of humanity. The problem is especially felt in significant sections of the Muslim, Hindu and Buddhist worlds today; Christian societies were deeply marked by such stains as recently as the 1930s and 1940s but are now on the whole much more tolerant: true to a combination of their direct roots, and to secular Enlightenment – soil itself partly watered by Judeo-Christianity. Two conspicuous exceptions are the Russian Orthodox Church, the leaders of which are under the thumb of Vladimir Putin, and the American fundamentalists who oppose science and legitimate political diversity.

The second part of this verdict could be that the Churches are most conspicuously forces for good when they display love of neighbour – especially where definitions of neighbour are stretched to include the stranger – through magnanimity towards other belief systems, as well as feeding the hungry and clothing the naked. To restate one of the main messages I have transmitted: secularists tend to take their creed too much for granted, forgetting its theological underpinnings. As I have argued, reason can transport us to the domain of prudence; it is the spiritual dimension which can advance us further, towards goals including grace and forgiveness.

I ended my book *Does Religion Do More Harm Than Good?*[23] with some general reflections that I now endorse even more keenly. For pastors and other spiritual leaders, the need is for public expressions of faith which are broad enough to be inclusive, fostering the ability to live and move within a given spiritual heritage and not be narrowed by it, but also firm enough to be rooted in what has been received from the past, and to cast necessary judgement on the spirit of the age where appropriate. Though the vision is not easy to implement in every particular, it can nevertheless be spelt out with reasonable clarity in headline terms. Conviction and dogmatism are not the same. There is a difference between having seen some truth and claiming to speak in the name of all truth; between knowing what one believes and refusing to respect the beliefs and experiences of others. People of faith should speak with a humble authority combining real knowledge with an awareness of the limitations of that knowledge. Their authority is not that of the wise woman or man and the scholar, important though wisdom and scholarship are, but that of lovers who express their delight in what they love, even though they have scarcely begun to glimpse its full extent.

***

I do not regret concentrating on principles in Part I of this book, even if the foregoing pages may appear strongly theoretical to some. Later chapters will draw much more on practical matters. Meanwhile, church decline can only be seen as a matter of regret in the first place if Christ's followers are acknowledged to have a message worth hearing. My aim has been to describe the message accessibly but without too many short cuts. Stopping after a rehearsal of notionally robust ideas may not be sufficient either, though. It could easily look complacent in the context of claims that Christianity's institutional arm is in trouble. Sturdy materials in the form of a solid bedrock of teaching are a necessary but not sufficient condition for assessing a religious body.

To round off, it seems more relevant to cite a figure like Williams speaking not about ideas, but of his experience at the sharp end of ministry in conversation with the journalist Jon Snow. Their interview is available online and worth digesting in full.[24] Despite being the son of a bishop himself, Snow represents a secular everyman who sits very lightly with regard to questions about belief in God. By his own admission, he only attends church occasionally for a mixture of musical appreciation and a sense of fellowship. But though his initial questions are hostile, bit by bit Williams's reasoned answers serve to cast matters in a different light. The following extract strikes me as revealing, especially as what the then Archbishop says about Wales also does duty for much of Western Europe.

JS: How would you characterise the state of faith in Britain today?

RW: Institutionally, not very strong. Emotionally, still quite a bit stronger than some people think. I don't like the dichotomy between spirituality and religion that some people use: I think that's far too easy an opposition. But I continue to be fascinated by two or three things which suggest that we're not secularised in the way some people would suggest. One is the bare fact of how the Church – my Church, anyway, but others too – work in deprived and challenged communities. Still there is the assumption, which can load a huge burden onto parish clergy, that the Church is there for their well-being twenty-four hours a day [to make] the community's wheels turn. Whether that means an endless stream of people wanting passport forms signed, whether it means the pressure on the parish priest to be chair of governors of the local school, whether it means the parish priest convening a group to discuss bids for grants for community development: all of these I've seen in spades over the years. That's one side of it.

The other, I think, is this issue which I've touched on more than once over the last few years. The sense that part of that 'being there for': is it still a context where people expect to find a space in which significant experiences, significant emotions, can be registered? And the example I've quoted several times is from my days in South Wales [as Bishop of Monmouth, 1992–2002], when we'd had a particularly horrible murder of a schoolgirl in one of our parishes, and the local curate was talking to some of the schoolgirls at the bus stop, obviously in great distress. And she said, 'What if we opened the church for a couple of hours on Friday night? Maybe you could just come in and light a candle and sit in the quiet for a while.' And that Friday night, eighty to a hundred teenagers from the local school flocked into the church. There had to be somewhere for things to be put, to be recognised. It's a bit Philip Larkin [in his poem 'Church Going']. Now that's part of the condition of faith in this country. It doesn't add up to a wonderful success story for any of the Churches. It doesn't have very much doctrinal content in itself, yet it remains one of the ways in which the communities of faith have a foot in the door of the culture. And I don't think it's trivial.

JS: No, I think it's incredibly important and you've certainly chimed with something which I feel very strongly, [namely] that for me . . . faith in the human spirit is a very big driver. Now I go to church perhaps once every month and why do I go? I go because I like the coming together of the community. The aspiration to do better, the joining together in music and in the same environment every time, the going through of various rotes, the detail of which I couldn't necessarily deconstruct and say 'I believe in that.' But at the end of it, there is a faith that what you have done is to come together, and you emerge at the end . . . collectively and say, 'We're going to do better.' But you want God in it.

RW: Well, to put it bluntly, it's not a question of what I want! If God is there, God is in it. That's an end of it.

JS: But I'm not talking about him.

RW: And I am!

JS: Which is what I think those girls were doing lighting candles. They were coming together. They were sharing a space. There was a feeling of comfort within where they were: it wasn't essential to believe that God was in it.

RW: Nobody was asking the questions as they came in. But I believe very strongly that that instinct in people like those teenage girls is God-oriented. I don't ask them what exactly they believe. I think that's an insult. They're coming into somewhere which holds open the possibility of humanity being more than you thought it was. To me that has everything to do with God, and I couldn't imagine it without God. You can. Well, good luck. But that's not where I'm starting from. And I think one of the really significant things about the practice of faith is exactly as you say, it is an affirmation that humanity is capable of something extraordinary. And that human dignity, the absolute irreducible dignity of the person, all those things: that is crucial here. For me, that is simply a natural outgrowth of what I believe about God. And I'm not quite sure where else it comes from. Other people have other answers. That's where I start.

Something crucial, yet also fragile and in danger of being lost. Here, I hope, we have a foundation from which to understand and justify much of the discussion ahead.

Part II
Earthen Vessels

5

Christians Don't Count Either

In 2021 the writer and comedian David Baddiel published *Jews Don't Count*,[1] a widely praised tract laying bare the prejudice summed up in its subtitle: *How Identity Politics Fails One Particular Identity*. His opening example gives a flavour of Baddiel's argument overall. It concerns Charlie Kaufman's novel *Antkind* (2020), which received a hostile notice in *The Observer* from Holly Williams.[2] Among her complaints was that the story's narrator operates from a 'white-male-cis-het' perspective. As Baddiel notes, '[a]nyone occupying this square of characteristics is considered, by those who assume that all social structures are underpinned by power, privileged.'[3] Straight white men who inhabit their gender without ambivalence thus have four head starts in life. But although the narrator of *Antkind* is called B. Rosenberger Rosenburg, wears a tie emblazoned with the legend '100% Kosher', and endures extensive antisemitic abuse, the review failed to mention his Jewishness at all. Partiality of this kind and the attitudes underlying it are widespread.

Baddiel has lifelong left-wing loyalties. When someone of his standing questions fashionable hierarchies of victimhood, it is worth taking note. I would only qualify this by adding that the structure he challenges is more rickety than he thinks. Christians often don't count either. An even more accurate subtitle for his book might have been 'How Identity Politics Fails One Particular Identity Among Others'. This claim will no doubt appear counter-intuitive to some. Why bracket Judaism, by some way the smallest global faith, with Christianity – not only the largest, but itself the source of so much antisemitism and other oppression in the past? Because for all their earlier mistakes and abiding faults, Christians endure around four-fifths of all oppression on grounds of spiritual allegiance. If Judaism is proportionately the most persecuted global religion, Christianity is by far the most persecuted numerically. It just isn't on trend to say so. Beyond media ignorance stand innumerable cases of deep strife arising from criminality.

A belated awareness of this problem has surfaced in some quarters, including when Jeremy Hunt was Foreign Secretary in Theresa May's administration. Warning in 2018 that Christianity is on the verge of extinction in its Middle Eastern birthplace, and that Britain's current efforts were not matching up to the scale of the problem, Hunt announced the setting up of an independent commission led by the then Bishop of Truro, Philip Mounstephen. Published in the following year, the commission's report rests on a wealth of serious research – including that Christians are being targeted in 144 countries. It offers a highly troubling conclusion:

> Evidence shows not only the geographic spread of anti-Christian persecution, but also its increasing severity. In some regions, the level and nature of persecution is arguably coming close to meeting the international definition of genocide, according to that adopted by the UN. The eradication of Christians and other minorities on pain of 'the sword' or other violent means was revealed to be the specific and stated objective of extremist groups in Syria, Iraq, Egypt, north-east Nigeria and the Philippines. An intent to erase all evidence of the Christian presence was made plain by the removal of crosses, the destruction of church buildings and other church symbols. The killing and abduction of clergy represented a direct attack on the Church's structure and leadership. Where these and other incidents meet the tests of genocide, state parties to the UN Convention on the Prevention and Punishment of the Crime of Genocide have a duty not only to bring perpetrators to justice but also to prevent attempts at genocide.[4]

A glance at the historical background tells us much. Before the partition of Sudan in 2011, the regime in Khartoum was responsible for the deaths of around two million Christian and other non-Muslim civilians over a thirty-year period. Before East Timor gained independence from Indonesia, 100,000 Catholic non-combatants were killed by agents of the Suharto government during the 1970s, 1980s and 1990s. Also in 2011, the Grand Mufti of Saudi Arabia, Sheikh Abdul Aziz bin Abdullah, announced that 'it is necessary to destroy all the churches' on the Arabian Peninsula. In Egypt, at least 600,000 Copts – a figure equivalent to the population of Manchester – have emigrated since the 1980s in the face of systematic discrimination on the one hand, and the regular destruction of churches and church-owned property on the other.

Now take in an even longer time frame. Hitler notoriously thought that the Holocaust could be carried out without obstruction, because no one recalled the Armenian genocide that unfolded between 1894 and 1924. He was half right. At least two million Christians perished during and after the disintegration of the Ottoman Empire: the catastrophe is charted in meticulous detail by Benny Morris and Dror Ze'evi in their book *The Thirty-Year Genocide*.[5] During this period onslaughts were launched against Assyrian and Greek populations, as well as the Armenians. To describe these events as neglected is a colossal understatement.

It was concern shading into frustration about an unacknowledged elephant in the room which led me to write my book *Christianophobia*[6] between 2010 and 2012. The news hasn't just been under-reported but also wrongly framed, for reasons already alluded to. A priest friend offered a few more when we corresponded on the subject. Here is a extract from his list:

1. The persecution is so widespread that it offers no single and geographically close locus on which to focus. As a teacher before ordination, [my friend] regularly took parties of students to KL Sachsenhausen to give them a deeper awareness of Nazi persecution of Jews, Roma, gay people and political opponents. Where would teachers take their pupils to raise

their awareness of the Armenian genocide or of atrocities in Nigeria?

2. Knowledge of world Christianity among what passes for our intellectual and cultural elite is very limited. Some of Baddiel's peers on the comedy circuit are happy to lampoon Christianity because they perceive it as part of the establishment (which one numerically dwindling branch of it is) and as overwhelmingly white.

3. That limitation is also shaped by a sense that the global Church is in part the product of imperialism and therefore at best a historic embarrassment and something over which it is hoped that Western secular values will eventually triumph.

Though a loyal listener to BBC radio, I have never heard the Corporation describe the 276 Chibok girls kidnapped in Nigeria in 2012 as *Christian* girls. Most Muslim girls would not have been allowed to attend school in the first place. When Mariam Ibrahim, the Sudanese Christian and presumed convert was forced to give birth while shackled in her prison cell in 2013, much of the mainstream British media cast the story as an instance of gross misogyny. The reporters and commentators concerned were apparently unaware that a male 'apostate' would have received even harsher punishment under sharia law than a woman. (Ms Ibrahim had in any case been a Christian all her life. Raised by her Christian mother, she had been abandoned by her Muslim father as a baby.)

I looked at the situation in almost twenty countries, mainly in the Middle East, Africa and Asia. An allied impulse for the project had been growing in my mind for years. One Islamist suicide bomber after another cited the deaths of Muslims in Iraq and Afghanistan as a warrant for terrorism in the West. The video made by Mohammad Siddique Khan, ringleader of the 7/7 attack in London, forms an example of this tendency. I wasn't just struck by the moral horror of claiming an excuse for indiscriminate murder on a bus or train. That sense was widely shared. But something vital was missing. Muslims enjoy freedom of worship in Britain and most other Western societies, yet there is scarcely a single country across a vast belt of the world between Morocco and Pakistan in which Christians and others can worship without harassment.

An important caveat should be entered. *Christianophobia* is emphatically not based on polemics about a supposed clash of civilisations – still less on an uncritical attitude towards my fellow Christians. The Church's past record of violent intolerance (a record that persists in Russia, the Balkans and other parts of the Eastern Orthodox world) is obviously shameful as well. China was a victim of Western chauvinism during the nineteenth century and is still smarting from what it sees as a major humiliation. Equally plainly, a number of grievances felt by Muslims are reasonable. For example, I believe (in line with the clearly broadcast views of most church leaders around the world) that the Iraq invasion of 2003 was a serious mistake, and have a keen sense of the West's role in promoting the sense of injustice felt by many Arabs in particular. More broadly, it seems equally clear to me that Christian mission in nineteenth-century Africa was often politicised, and geared to undermine the spread of Muslim influence; that Western (above all Anglo-French) adventurism in the Middle East during the twentieth century played into the hands of Arab nationalists and watered the seeds of Islamic revivalism; and that al-Qaeda drew strength from the West's indulgence of dictators in the region before the Arab Spring. Furthermore, a good deal of 'Christianophobia' – in China, North Korea and other communist societies; in India; in mainly Buddhist domains such as Sri Lanka and Burma – has nothing to do with militant Islam. While supplying context to my argument, however, these points do not invalidate it.

The hounding of Christians in the Middle East seems to me all the more heart-rending given that the roots of their communities are almost as old as the New Testament itself. Westerners are often shamefully ignorant when it comes to the Middle East's patchwork of faiths: many even assume that Christianity is an import to the region rather than an export from it. For two millennia, the Church's profile across the region was an integral part of successive civilisations: in one senior cleric's words, 'a dominant presence in the Byzantine era, a culturally very active partner in the early Muslim centuries, a patient and long-suffering element, like the historic Jewish communities of the Maghreb and the Middle East, in the complex mosaic of ethnic jurisdictions within the Ottoman Empire and, more recently, a political catalyst and nursery of radical thinking in the dawn of Arab nationalism.' Several sources later told me how some London schools had unwittingly borne out these points by their inept treatment of refugee children from Syria. Arab pupils had been pulled out of assembly by over-zealous staff who assumed that they must all be Muslims, when a significant proportion were in fact Orthodox Christians.

Any bid to reframe perceptions of this subject must fill out the picture further still. Beyond the Christianity of Byzantium, beyond the Euphrates and into Persia, Central Asia, China and India, thousands of congregations arose during the first millennium. The faith spread early into modern-day Iraq from southeast Turkey and established itself during the second century in the city of Seleucia-Ctesiphon, on the banks of the Tigris near what would become Baghdad. Here, as a leading scholar of Middle Eastern Christianity such as Anthony O'Mahony has noted, the Assyrian Church – also known as the Church of the East – became the most successful missionary launchpad in the world, all without ever becoming a state religion.[7]

Why is this seam of history so unfamiliar to Western eyes? A full explanation would entail a chapter in itself. It partly centres on the fallout of theological disputes about how to understand Christ's human and divine natures that came to a head during the fifth century. Separated from the rest of the Christian world after the Council of Ephesus in AD 431, the Church of the East was thereafter known by the inaccurate label 'Nestorian', at least until the modern era. The Oriental Orthodox Churches went their own way after the even more momentous Council of Chalcedon, held near Constantinople in 451.[8]

Doctrinal differences were naturally magnified by geopolitical factors, among them that a large proportion of Assyrian Christians lived outside the Eastern Roman Empire. Much later, the frisson of discovering another Christian culture at once familiar, alien and exotic was expressed by an early twentieth-century traveller such as Adrian Fortescue. 'The stranger who passes the Turkish–Persian frontier near Lake Urmi, the stranger who goes to delve among the ruins of Ninevah, will perhaps wonder to find in these parts buildings which are plainly Christian churches,' he wrote.[9] What the visitor had stumbled across was the 'last tragic remnant of a Church whose history is as glorious as any in Christendom'.[10]

Though professing a confident strand of Catholicism, Fortescue has the grace to acknowledge the Assyrians' extraordinary missionary endeavours. These led not just eastwards, but also to westward expansion – especially after the rise of Islam, because caliphs in regions such as Egypt and Syro-Palestine were indifferent to doctrinal disagreements between Christians and allied attempts to outlaw 'Nestorianism'. But it was the Assyrians' missionary ventures into Asia, including countless places where the gospel had never yet been preached, which most impressed Fortescue. He salutes them as follows:

Those forgotten Nestorian missionaries, they were not Catholics but they were Christians. Braving long journeys, braving heathen tyrants and horrible danger, they brought the name of Christ north to Lake Baikal [in Siberia], south to Ceylon, and east right into the heart of China. They must have baptized thousands, and they taught the wild men of Tartary [the Great Steppe, stretching from the Caspian Sea to the Pacific] to worship one God, to serve Christ . . . to love his mother . . . Let that be remembered to their honour.[11]

The point is summed up in a different way by Philip Jenkins in *The Lost History of Christianity*.[12] In terms of 'the number and splendor of its churches and monasteries, its vast scholarship and dazzling spirituality, Iraq was through the late Middle Ages at least as much a cultural and spiritual heartland of Christianity as [were] France or Germany, or indeed Ireland'.[13] Jenkins's subtitle is again revealing: *The Thousand-Year Golden Age of the Church in the Middle East, Africa, and Asia – and How it Died*. The author deals with longer-term civilisational currents, but judges the impact of the death of Genghis Khan in 1227 to have been decisive. His Christian deputy, Kit Bugha, was defeated by a Mamluk army from Egypt in 1260. This tide of Mongol conquest – and with it a tradition of religious tolerance – now came to an end. Churches and church-run institutions were razed in Mesopotamia and Egypt by radical adherents of Ibn Taymiyyah (1263–1328), sometimes seen as a spiritual ancestor of today's Wahhabis. The Christian population then plummeted.

Though involving extensive travel, my project began locally with a visit to the Coptic church in West London. I met one of the congregation's long-standing members, Dr Ibrahim Habib. Originally from Minya, near Asyut in Upper Egypt, where about a third of the population is Christian, he has enjoyed a distinguished career in England for several decades. But his blithe manner contrasted with the dark tale he went on to recount about his first medical school:

> Christians were either passed or failed; not a single one was placed in the 'Good', 'Very Good' or 'Excellent' categories. This meant that none of us Christians would achieve a high-flying career. The modern phase of anti-Christian violence in Egypt really began in 1972, with the establishment of the Gama Islamiya, a militant group. They started attacking Christian students on the university campus at Asyut, barging into our rooms and tearing down pictures of the Virgin Mary and other religious materials. A fight ensued. I and other Christians were expelled from

university accommodation, but the Muslims who caused trouble were allowed to remain.

The upsurge in militancy [since the Second World War] can be blamed to a great extent on President Sadat. After the assassination attempt on Nasser in 1954, many fundamentalists were rounded up and sent to prison. Sadat, faced with heavy challenges from the Left, indulged the Islamists and let many in from Saudi Arabia. He also called Egypt a Muslim country, even though 15 to 20 per cent of the population were then Christian. That figure has now fallen to 12 per cent, because of all the emigration.

In the lead-up to my own graduation from Asyut in 1976, several Christian students were thrown from the balconies of buildings and injured. Others were killed. A local priest in Asyut, Fr Gabriel Abed al-Motgaly, was murdered. I felt that my decision to leave Egypt was vindicated, because a major flare-up took place in 1981. A piece of land belonging to a Christian in the Al-Zawiya al-Hamra suburb of Cairo was seized by Muslims who wanted to build a mosque. At least eighty people were killed in the violence, some people were burnt alive in their homes, and the police just looked on, according to eyewitness accounts.

There were many similar attacks on Christians in Upper Egypt as well, and no prosecutions, apart from in one case. A monk was murdered in front of the gates of his monastery at Al Muharraq. Two men were arrested, and eventually received prison sentences of three years.

The situation deteriorated steadily during the 1980s and 1990s. Hundreds of Christians died in many attacks during this period. A few Christians I knew were given good jobs for propaganda purposes, and because they were very loyal to the Mubarak regime. But my own prospects would have faded if I'd stayed.[14]

Egypt's future is pivotal to interfaith harmony in the Middle East, owing to its substantial Christian population. Most of these are Copts – part of the Oriental Orthodox family which includes the Syrian, Armenian and Ethiopian traditions. The country was a more tolerant place a hundred years ago than today. Muslims of both sexes were widely involved in culture and education. The Salafist Wahhabi ideology deriving from Saudi Arabia became more deeply embedded from the 1970s onwards. Alaa al-Aswany, journalist and author of acclaimed fiction such as *The Yacoubian Building*, has ascribed the rise of Salafism in Egypt to a chain of causes. With the quadrupling of oil prices in 1973, Salafists suddenly acquired the finance to export their ideas around the world. Millions of Egyptians sought employment in the Gulf States, where they came under the influence of Wahhabi ideology. In time, Wahhabi sympathisers infiltrated Egypt's security forces as well: unlike the Muslim Brotherhood, the country's largest organisation, Wahhabis did not menace the state directly. They are nevertheless widely seen as heralds of theocracy. As well as opposing music, theatre and general education, or insisting that women wear the burqa – jettisoned by earlier generations many decades ago – the Wahhabis deny that Christians can be full citizens. Rather, they see the Copts as *dhimmies* (protected non-Muslims) occupying a subordinate role. As al-Aswany puts it:

In Wahhabis' eyes, Copts are . . . infidels and polytheists prone to hating Islam and conspiring against it . . . Anyone who follows the portrayal of Copts on dozens of satellite channels and Salafist websites is bound to be saddened. These forums, followed by millions of Egyptians daily, openly declare their hatred of Copts . . . Often they call on Muslims to boycott them. There are countless examples, but I will cite here what I read on the well-known Salafist website 'Guardians of the Faith', which devoted a whole article to the subject, 'Why Muslims Are Superior to Copts'. 'Being a Muslim girl whose role models are the wives of the Prophet, who were required to wear the hijab, is better than being a Christian girl, whose role models are whores,' it says. 'Being a Muslim who fights to defend his honor and his faith is better than being a Christian who steals, rapes, and kills children,' it adds. 'Being a Muslim whose role models are

Muhammad and his companions is better than being a Christian whose role models are Paul the Liar [*sic*] and the whoremongering prophets.' As this enmity towards Copts spreads, is it not natural, even inevitable, that it should end in attacks on them?[15]

While contemporary Egypt has a poor record on religious toleration, Nigeria's is far worse. This is partly because the country resembles a bundle of limbs rather than a body politic as such. Its population of over 220 million consists of almost five hundred ethnic groups. Very unusually, there are roughly equal numbers of Christians and Muslims. By agreement between the British and the long-established local emirates, Christian mission in the north was heavily curtailed during colonial times. A small church presence was tolerated for the sake of non-indigenous migrant workers from the south, but evangelism among Muslims was largely banned. These factors help to explain the country's volatility (though large areas of the west and south are relatively calm), as well as its tight interlacing of politics and religion. All the most toxic strands in the post-colonial experience are here too: military dictatorship for most of the period since independence in 1960, oil wealth giving rise to gigantic inequalities, terrorism in the Niger delta, a general absence of civil society, and widespread female genital mutilation.

More benign or competent rulers would not have had an easy ride. The chief divisions – between the mainly Muslim Hausa in the north, and the predominantly Christian Ebo in the east – mask numerous other conflicts, including between the Hausa and substantially Christian Berom in the central Plateau state. The Yoruba, who occupy much of the south-west, are a mixed group with a Christian majority. Muslim influence rose during the dictatorship of General Sani Abacha between 1993 and 1998 – so much so that the south threatened formal secession. This was averted when the north accepted the presidency of Olusegun Obasanjo – a Christian and former military ruler during the late 1970s – who won the election of 1999.

As a trade-off, northern states introduced sharia law. A dozen had done so by 2006, in defiance of Nigeria's secular constitution. Sharia had long been used to resolve family disputes among Muslims. Christians were now threatened by an attempt to extend Islamic codes of conduct into their own communities. In some northern states, Christian girls have been obliged to wear the hijab; in the north-central state of Kano, a large body of enforcers frequently break into Christian households in search of alcohol. It is estimated that the expansion of sharia has led to the deaths of well over 60,000 people,[16] most of them Christians or adherents of traditional religions. As in Pakistan and Egypt, punishment for ex-Muslim converts to Christianity is severe. *Religious Freedom in the World,*[17] a vital resource edited by the highly respected human rights monitor Paul Marshall, reports that there are many documented cases in which child abduction has been combined with forced marriage and conversion to Islam in the sharia states. Bauchi, which lies to the east of Kano, is a case in point:

> The State Shar'ia Committee has itself been implicated in these abductions in Bauchi state. Christian women are especially vulnerable in shar'ia states since, according to the Christian Association of Nigeria (CAN), 'a woman [who is] not married, irrespective of her religious background, is seen by Muslim enforcers of the Shari'ah as a prostitute'. In 2003, all girls of Bauchi state above the age of 16 were given 90 days to marry or face arrest on charges of prostitution. Eight women were subsequently arrested, fined, and given 10 lashes for being unmarried.[18]

Nigeria is still the place where Christians are most likely to face violent deaths. In the North and Middle Belt of the country, at least 3,700 church members were killed in 2018 – almost double the number seen during the previous twelve months. Entire villages of Christian residents faced a torrent of armed attacks, forcing them to flee. Deaths were highest in Plateau State (1,885), where the murders of Christians at the hands of Muslim Fulani herdsmen were described as 'genocide' by the Nigerian House of Representatives.

Evidence collected for the most recent edition of Aid to the Church in Need's biennial report *Persecuted and Forgotten?*[19] suggests that the spread of violent jihadism in Africa remains a prime threat to Christians. Groups like Boko Haram in Nigeria and Islamic State West Africa Province (ISWAP) are still trying to establish caliphates in the Sahel region, each with its own *wali* (governor) and governing structure. Islamic State in the Greater Sahara (ISGS) has banned music and parties. Social events such as weddings are also heavily regulated. In June 2021, ISGS fighters executed five Christian civilians seized at a roadblock between Gao, Mali and Niamey, Niger. In Mozambique, Al-Shabaab stepped up its terror campaign, killing Christians, attacking Christian villages and burning down churches. The group is affiliated to ISIS, which claimed responsibility for the March 2021 attack on Palma in north-east Mozambique.

Jihadism funded from the Middle East forms one reason why Nigeria teeters on the brink of becoming a failed state. Kidnappings, the murder of clergy and deadly attacks on churches remain common. According to ACN analysis, more than 7,600 Christians were killed between January 2021 and June 2022. Controversy arose in November 2021 when the United States government removed Nigeria from its list of 'Countries of Particular Concern' in regard to religious freedom. Deploring this decision, the Revd Samson Ayokunle, president of the Christian Association of Nigeria, hit back, making it clear that a militant extremist agenda to 'wipe away Christianity' had not gone away. Extremists also exploited pandemic-related restrictions to attack Christian settlements. A letter from UK parliamentarians and charities warned the British government that militant members of the Fulani herder community had been 'taking advantage of Covid-19 lockdowns to intensify attacks on villages' in Nigeria's Middle Belt. Two major cases of anti-Christian persecution in

Nigeria made international news. First was the stoning to death and setting alight of Deborah Samuel, a twenty-five-year-old Christian in May 2022 after she shared purportedly 'blasphemous' messages on WhatsApp. Second was the deadly attack on St Francis Xavier's Church in Owo, Ondo State, during Mass on Pentecost Sunday of that year, killing at least forty. Armed men fired indiscriminately at members of the congregation, killing children as well as adults.

An especially distressing overview of Nigeria was given by the Ven. Mark Mukan, Director of Mission in the Anglican diocese of Jos, on a visit to Britain in June 2023. Speaking at a gathering in Eastbourne organised by the charity Release International, he described a campaign of murder and arson, with churches, hospitals and farmland 'burned to ashes' in north-eastern areas of the country. One denomination above all – the Church of the Brethren – had been more or less wiped out, Archdeacon Mukan said. 'Many are traumatised, frightened, and living in shock. Those who survived have run for safe haven in cities or in Cameroon.'[20] The Nigerian NGO Intersociety also reported that 1,080 Christians suffered violent deaths during the first quarter of 2023 alone. During the previous year, 5,100 were killed in attacks by Boko Haram, Islamic State West Africa, and Fulani militants.[21] The wider picture has been summed up even more soberingly by David Landrum of Open Doors, another prominent NGO:

> Emboldened by the victory of the Taliban in Afghanistan, the persecution of Christians is now expanding beyond Nigeria, and beyond the Islamist strongholds of Somalia, Sudan, Eritrea, Libya, and Algeria. Today, we see the terror replicated in places such as the Democratic Republic of Congo, Mali, Burkina Faso, Niger, Cameroon, Central African Republic, and Mozambique.[22]

A double standard betokened by neglect of these horrors is underlined by the Algerian novelist Boualem Sansal. 'The stubborn silence of European leaders on the question of religions,

Islam in particular, astonishes and disappoints', he has written.[23] (Still living in the country of his birth, Mr Sansal has shown exceptional courage in declaring publicly that Islamist extremism is shaking Algeria's moral foundations.) 'Their attitude is simply irresponsible ... It's like living at the foot of an angry volcano and not understanding that it is preparing to erupt.'[24]

Turkey represents a different set of scourges. While Christians have certainly been murdered from time to time in recent decades, the chief menace is discrimination against religious minorities and the creeping authoritarianism of Recep Tayyip Erdogan. That this has happened in a country once regarded as a beacon of the Muslim world counts as a tragedy.

Modern Turkey is the remnant of the Ottoman Empire. Many Ottoman achievements were admirable. When heretics were still being executed across Europe, the seventeenth-century Huguenot M. de la Motraye maintained that there was 'no country on earth where the exercise of all religions is more free and less subject to being troubled, than in Turkey'. The *millet* system operated by the Ottomans involved conferring limited rights and status on minority communities, but non-Muslims were generally second-class citizens all the same. 'The existence of Christians was always seen by the authorities as a matter of Ottoman forbearance,' as a Turkish Christian who wanted to speak anonymously later told me:

We are not talking about a widely acknowledged sense that Christians enjoyed inherent rights. The anti-Ottoman rebellion by subject peoples – above all the Greeks in the 1820s and the Bulgarians half a century later – left a deep scar on Ottoman consciousness. It embedded two things above all. A suspicion of non-Turks, and a belief that if you're Turkish, this automatically means that you're a Muslim. Religion and ethnic identity became closely joined.

This comment offers a key to grasping the treatment of Christians in Turkey today – especially of converts with a Muslim background. Hardline readings of the Qur'an are interlaced with a nationalistic mindset which holds conversion to Christianity or Judaism to be synonymous with treason. The government controls all religious activity, heavily monitoring the majority Sunni population and actively discriminating against others. The distribution of non-Muslim literature is an arrestable offence. At least a fifth of Turks are Alevis, a Muslim group considered heretical by the Sunni community for their embrace of certain Shia-inspired practices: they have suffered systematic discrimination for decades. No mention is made of Alevi beliefs in Turkey's compulsory religious studies curriculum: Alevis are officially described as a cultural rather than a religious group. Successive governments have ordered the construction of Sunni mosques even in towns and villages where all or virtually all the inhabitants are Alevis. No Alevi has ever been appointed to the Directorate of Religious Affairs.

Conversion from Islam to Christianity can be very costly indeed. Until the turn of the millennium a Christian convert needed to open a legal case against the state, with witnesses, to declare his or her change of belief. After this had been confirmed by a judge, the convert had to make a public declaration in a national newspaper. Although the procedure has now been relaxed, the newly professed Christian is still required to make a public declaration.

A good illustration of Turkey's internal chauvinism and external indifference to it comes from the plight of Hagia Sophia, formerly seat of the patriarchs of Constantinople. Dating from the early sixth century, this spectacular building had a claim to be the world's greatest church for the better part of a millennium before it was turned into a mosque by Ottoman invaders in 1453. Atatürk's stroke of genius when the Ottoman Empire collapsed after the First World War was to make Hagia Sophia a neutral space as a museum. Though deplorable, Erdogan's decision to redesignate the building as a mosque in 2020 met with barely a ripple of protest.

***

I have emphasised that the hounding of Christians naturally extends well beyond Muslim-majority countries, especially in China and India. It is almost a truism that memories of the Churches' near-demise during the Cultural Revolution must now be supplemented by a grasp of this process in reverse: a spiritual renaissance since Mao's death sometimes called the greatest religious revival in history. There are now well over twenty million Chinese Christians. The swinging pendulum points in turn to clashing official perceptions of Christianity and its representatives as both cherished and unwelcome influences.

The impact of the West for both good and ill has been momentous in what is due to become the world's most powerful state within two decades. After the Tiananmen Square massacre in 1989, the Chinese government introduced its Patriotic Education Campaign to reinculcate in school pupils ideas about the crimes of Western imperialist 'devils'. Though hardly objective, the producers of this material had plenty of content to excavate. In 1832, officers of the East India Company had marched into the Shanghai regional administrator's office, demanding that the terms of trade between China and Europe be freed up. Britain provoked the First Opium War, terrorising Shanghai's civilian population in the process. Similar atrocities followed in the Second Opium War of 1856–60, and during the crushing of the Boxer Rebellion by a large international alliance four decades later. Less widely recognised are either the staggering capacity of the Chinese for harming one another – about twenty million people perished during the Taiping Rebellion of 1850–64, for example – or the benign effects of the Christian presence in China. Matteo Ricci and other Jesuit pioneers revolutionised the Chinese understanding of mathematics, astronomy and geography in the late sixteenth and early seventeenth centuries. British missionaries in the so-called treaty ports immunised the inhabitants on a wide scale during the Victorian era, just as British engineers laid China's first telegraph lines and railways.

These and other pieces of evidence are collated by Vincent Goossaert and David A. Palmer in their study *The Religious Question in Modern China*.[25] Of special relevance are the examples of Sun Yat-sen (1866–1925), the revolutionary founder of the first Chinese Republic, and his successor, Chiang Kai-shek (1887–1975), both of whom were Christian converts who held their faith to be compatible with science and a unifying political force.

Some elements in China's early twentieth-century transformation were clearly cultural. Astrological techniques for measuring time were replaced by the Gregorian calendar in 1912. Many traditional practices were abolished. But Goossaert and Palmer are clear that in the eyes of figures such as Sun and Chiang, 'the decline and decay of China were due to idolatry, while the strength, prosperity, and . . . civilization of America were due to the Christian religion. Christianity, for them, could bring dignity and equality to China.' Church life blossomed steadily during this period.

The communists' chief aim after 1949 was to neuter spiritual faith rather than abolish it entirely. They began by doing away with Confucianism, temple cults and other practices judged to be relics of a feudal mindset. Foreign missionaries were told to leave. The main bodies of believers – Buddhists, Taoists, Muslims and Christians – were categorised under the so-called 'Three-Self' basis (self-governing, self-financing, self-propagating). Then as now, Protestantism and Catholicism were counted as separate religions. As well as the Protestant–Catholic divide, a further subdivision would later develop between registered (that is, official) Churches and unregistered (underground) Churches which refused to accept participation within the Three-Self formularies.

The scale of the tragedy that engulfed China under Mao is now widely grasped: Jasper Becker (author of *Hungry Ghosts*) and Frank Dikötter (in *Mao's Famine*) estimate that 45 million people died between 1958 and 1962 alone. The Dalai Lama fled to India in 1959 after the Chinese government reneged on an agreement allowing religious autonomy in Tibet. Religion was proclaimed to be a matter of class struggle during the Cultural Revolution: Christian clergy were purged; re-education officers were sent to villages across the country to wipe out practices deemed 'capitalistic' (an umbrella term that included religious rituals); then came the 'Smash the Four Olds' campaign – the quartet in question being old customs, culture, habits and ideas.

The political clampdowns of Xi Jinping's rule since 2012 also apply to religion. Members of the Chinese Communist Party and the armed forces are required to be atheists. The government has effectively banned under-18s from receiving religious education or taking part in worship (via the national law that prevents people or groups from 'interfering' with school curriculums). In 2019, the CCP launched a five-year plan to 'sinicise' Christianity. This called for 'incorporating Chinese elements into church services, hymns and songs, clerical attire, and the architectural style of churches', while proposing to 'retranslate the Bible or rewrite biblical commentaries'. Two years later, it emerged that the story of Jesus' encounter with the woman caught in adultery (John 8) had been rewritten in an official ethics textbook. After waiting for her accusers to depart, Christ is represented as stoning the woman himself, saying, 'I too am a sinner. But if the law could only be executed by men without blemish, the law would be dead.'[26]

A stream of diktats from Beijing purport to control all religious practice. Henrietta Blyth, who heads Open Doors UK and Ireland, comments: 'In China our figures indicate persecution is the worst it's been in more than a decade – alarmingly, some church leaders are saying it's the worst since the Cultural Revolution ended in 1976.'[27] Yet church growth remains strong. China is still predicted to become the world's largest Christian country before 2050. For this reason, perhaps – and crucially, because Christians are so often heralds of more open societies – public worship not controlled by the state remains perilous. Take one Protestant body among many, the Church of Almighty God. In 2018, at least 10,938 CAG members were arrested across thirty of the thirty-four province-level administrative divisions in China; 6,653 were detained. More than five hundred were tortured or subjected to forced indoctrination; 354 were given prison sentences. This snapshot is fully representative of the situation in other years.

Within the past decade the Open Doors NGO has placed India in its World Watch List top ten for the first time, as Hindu extremists attack Christians and church buildings with impunity. Nationalism is also fomenting intolerance of religious minorities in Bhutan, Burma and Nepal. 'Suddenly,' Blyth observes,

> to be Indian or Nepali is [seen] to be exclusively Hindu, and to be Burmese or Bhutanese one must be Buddhist, so those from minority faiths are considered outcasts . . . It's shocking that India – the country that taught the world the way of non-violence – now sits alongside . . . Iran on our World Watch List. For many Christians in India, daily life is now full of fear – totally different from just four or five years ago.[28]

Communal violence nevertheless has deeper roots in the subcontinent. Often spurred by hate speech flowing from far-right Hindu nationalist sources, it fuels hostility to minorities. Matters are abetted by officials in the ruling Bharatiya Janata Party (BJP), who persistently fail to investigate attacks – still less bring the culprits to justice – and allow the spread of fake news through social media. Documentation from another leading NGO, Christian Solidarity Worldwide, reveals that the survivors of communal violence in Gujarat in 2002, Kandhamal in 2008 and Muzaffarnagar in 2013 have not received justice. Large-scale 'homecoming' (namely reconversion) ceremonies across India are staged by offshoots of the Sangh Parivar movement, who claim to be custodians of Hindutva, the prevailing ethno-religious creed. Their programme is grounded in an insistence that Hindu allegiance is part and parcel of being Indian. Converts to Islam and Christianity are viewed as suspect by definition.

Paradoxically, there are signs that in parts of the Middle East Christians are now in a worse situation than during the ISIS occupation. More recent evidence shows the threat to the survival of some of the world's oldest Christian communities has significantly deepened. The decline is most marked in Syria, where the Christian community fell from 1.5 million (10 per cent of the population) in 2011 to perhaps 300,000 a decade later. In Iraq, where the rate of exodus is much slower, the Christian population fell from around 300,000 before the ISIS invasion of 2014 to as few as 150,000 by early 2022. Research by ACN shows that in parts of Iraq where Christians had formed a strong minority, such as Baghdad, the community has become a shadow of itself. Of the seven Middle Eastern countries reviewed, however, Iraq was the only one to see at least some signs of improvement. 'A comprehensive post ISIS stabilisation programme involving the rebuilding of Christian towns and villages, homes, schools, churches, and other public facilities was crowned by the long-awaited papal visit of March 2021.'[29] Yet *Persecuted and Forgotten?* adds that 'in Iraq, as in so many other Middle East countries, the Christian community feels the danger posed by the underlying menace of jihadist groups. Continuing Islamist violence, for example, in northern Syria, showed that even denunciation of extremism by senior Islamic leaders was apparently making little impact on the ground.'[30] More than five years on from the military defeat of ISIS, 'the threat of a full-scale resurgence has by no means disappeared,' the report adds. 'A revival of jihadism has the potential to deliver a knockout blow for Christianity in its ancient heartland.'[31] In brief, the impulse to emigrate is intensified in a setting where Christians are treated as second-class citizens across the board.

The menace extends to parts of Israel/Palestine. Nearly three-quarters of a century on from the creation of the state of Israel, Christians in the West Bank have declined from 18 per cent of the population to less than 1 per cent. Islamist militancy is once more a major trigger. Groups such as Hamas are driving Christian migration from the West Bank. Although the overall number of Christians in Israel grew by 1.4 per cent in 2021, continuing attacks by fringe groups prompted church leaders to speak of 'a systematic attempt to drive the Christian community out of Jerusalem and other parts of the Holy Land'.[32]

ACN's conclusion can be readily guessed at. Indicators strongly suggest that over the period under review, the persecution of Christians continued to worsen in core countries of concern. In Nigeria and elsewhere, this violence clearly passed the threshold of genocide. Although governments are starting to recognise the importance of freedom of religion or belief, *Persecuted and Forgotten?* shows there is a long way to go to ensure the liberty of Christians and other minorities around the world is protected. A comment later made to me by John Pontifex, Director of Communications at ACN, is salutary:

In my experience, while there are some within government and the civil service who recognise the importance of religious freedom as a foundational human right and who are passionate about it, there are too many who do no more than pay lip service to the principle. This is particularly the case when it comes to the question of persecution of Christians, which is either seen as exaggerated or just not important. The reality of this was brought home to me especially in response within some quarters of government to the Bishop of Truro's Review. We soon found there were signs of resistance to both carrying out the review and then implementing it, even though it was government policy. There seemed to be a determination to skirt round the topic of Christian persecution, which was the specific focus of the review. I remember one conversation in particular where I suggested that increased religious literacy would be of service to all of us, not least those in government. The response I had to this was dismissive. The individual told me they found it 'patronising' when people criticised government commitment to religious literacy.

When we have raised specific cases of persecution either affecting particular individuals or groups or more generally, we have been guaranteed strong expressions of concern and even outrage, but all too often the one thing that has been lacking is action.

Seeking Justice and Charity

What if any lessons can be drawn from all this disparate material? *Does Religion Do More Harm than Good?*[33] underlines the need to untangle strands – cultural, ethnic, linguistic, geographical – in conflicts that can be falsely ascribed to faith differences. There is a widespread idea that faith is a greater cause of conflict than other factors such as access to resources or status, or questions of honour, or ethnic or political solidarity, or the use of superior power to exploit or eliminate rivals. The truth is that these elements are permanent features of intergroup relationships. They have continued to provoke strife under secular regimes into the present. As already suggested, the idea that religion is especially to blame derives from an Enlightenment narrative whereby the state, itself a major source of conflict, offloads blame onto the Churches and other communities of conviction in particular.

Despite its pretensions to objectivity, this worldview (often paired, we have noted, with the idea that a secularised providence has led to a liberal, god-free present) rests on a pile of lazy assumptions. Since religions are held to be irrational sources of violent behaviour, this means that when a particular body of believers is targeted sympathy gets withheld on the basis that the victims would inflict comparable aggression on others were they able to do so. In the case of the Churches, misjudgements are compounded by the association over the past two centuries of Christianity with Western imperialism, as though the link between institutions and wielders of power were not a much more general and tangled phenomenon. Exponents of this premise tend to forget that all imperialisms, secular or religious, are linked to ideologies of domination. A further ingredient in the mix is drawn from tensions that developed in the early twentieth century between Christian missionaries on the one hand, and, on the other, anthropologists promoting the ideology of 'authenticity' – often in alliance with the interests of post-colonial elites. This meant that Christians in countries like Pakistan could be written off as part of the detritus of empire. As it happens, academic anthropology widened its horizons long ago – a shift reflected in a work as *Missions and Empire*[34] in the Oxford History of the British Empire series.

Some are thus readier to acknowledge the substantial part played by indigenous people in Christian expansion. In Africa, Asia and Latin America, many local Christians have long been critical agents in missionary work, given the small number of expatriate missionaries in relation to the size of these continents and their populations. The nurses, medical assistants and compounders in mission hospitals, the teachers in the mission schools and colleges, the evangelists and 'Bible women' who go into villages and homes across vast areas of the world – these people are not only physical intermediaries with vastly varied local societies, but also 'translators', in a deeper sense, as they help interpret Christianity in local languages and cultures.

Anti-Christian feeling can regularly be based more on envy than on fear. Indian Christians in Kerala, for example, are often richer than their Hindu neighbours, and resented for the same reasons that prompted historic prejudice against Jews in Europe. In other parts of India, Christians are loathed by Hindu extremists for opposing the caste system. Sometimes Christians are resented as well as admired for their enormously influential work in education. In Taiwan, only 3 or 4 per cent of the population is Christian (nationalist Chinese persecuted the Churches as much as their communist counterparts), but the Taiwanese educational system was largely founded by Canadian and Scottish Presbyterians. Taiwan itself is not noticeably hostile to Christians. The climate is less benign, though, in other countries where the Christian educational legacy remains strong. I have already suggested that Chinese Christians are feared with reason, because they are heralds of a more open society. That the Churches face large-scale persecution in China and elsewhere says much about their remarkable strength, as well as their vulnerability – a point well made by the journalists John Micklethwait and Adrian Wooldridge in their book *God Is Back*.[35]

A further factor can be almost as challenging for churchgoers in comfortable societies as for secularists. The victims of anti-Christian persecution frequently have more in common than the perpetrators. And among these shared characteristics is a reluctance – by turns admirable, understandable and heart-breaking – to tell out news of their respective Calvaries. Some brave souls, in obedience to the Sermon on the Mount and St Paul's appeal in Romans 12:12–14 ('Be joyful in hope, patient in affliction . . . Bless those who persecute you'), accept their suffering as a source of unity with Christ. But this does not mean that news of their plight should be suppressed. Nor, of course, does it exonerate the perpetrators.

Consider the words of Sr Gloria Cecilia Narváez, a Franciscan, speaking to ACN in January 2020 several months after her release from captivity in Mali. 'My God, it is hard to be chained and to receive blows. But I live this moment as you presented to me. And in spite of everything I would not want any of [my captors] to be harmed.' Imprisoned by Islamist militants for four-and-a-half years, she had faced sustained physical and psychological torture. Sr Gloria made clear that her Christian faith was the source of the animus against her. She described how her captors became enraged when she prayed. On one occasion, when a jihadist leader found her at prayer, he struck her, saying, 'Let's see if that God gets you out of here.' 'He spoke to me using very strong ugly words,' she continued. 'My soul shuddered at what this person was saying, while the other guards laughed out loud at the insults.'[36]

* * *

Being clear that religion is over-blamed for conflict is hardly to suggest that it should not be blamed at all. Pascal's famous warning – that men never do evil so completely and cheerfully as when they act from religious conviction – retains a blistering relevance. Yet different traditions plainly cannot be lumped together in an undifferentiated mass. The repertoires of the major faiths are in some respects very different.

Statistics cast a sidelight on this point. Of the forty-one countries judged religiously free in a survey[37] conducted some years ago by the Freedom House think tank – that is, scoring 1, 2 or 3 on a scale of 1 to 7 – thirty-five are traditionally Christian. Only two traditionally Christian countries out of forty-five, Belarus and Cuba, were deemed to be 'not free' – that is, scoring a 6 or a 7. The other countries rated highly included three traditionally Buddhist domains: Japan, Mongolia and Thailand. Buddhist societies scoring poorly were those with communist governments: China, Tibet, Laos, North Korea and Vietnam. Among the small number of Hindu-majority countries, Nepal scored poorly on both political and religious freedom, while India was rated highly in the former category, but badly in the latter.

Since the survey makes clear that the greatest curbs on religious freedoms take place in Muslim-majority countries, I used the Epilogue of *Christianophobia* to confront a subject shadowing much of my discussion. Is there a problem with Islam as such, or is the trouble more a matter of geopolitical contingencies? The importance of this question was crystallised by Pope Francis's meeting with Sheikh Ahmed al-Tayeb in Dubai in 2019. Both leaders signed a widely reported 'historic pledge of fraternity'. Many praised the Pope's bridge-building efforts as prophetic.

Some of those with misgivings about the encounter complain that the Sheikh – Grand Imam of Al-Azhar, and thus probably the world's most influential Sunni Muslim – preaches a much more hardline message to his flock.

Bringing focus to a broad picture is an arduous task. One approach seeking to avoid the twin pitfalls of incendiary language and politically correct bromides might run as follows. Like Islam, Christianity is on one level saturated in the language of victory. But the Christian vision is of triumph *over* the world, while Islam enjoins victory *in* it. Eye-for-an-eye morality (though itself an advance on disproportionate retaliation) is repudiated even more comprehensively in Christianity than in either Judaism or Islam. Neither the Hebrew Bible nor the Qur'an goes quite as far as enjoining believers to turn the other cheek, though the Scriptures of all three faiths include the immensely important story of Joseph/Yussuf, seen as a paragon of self-giving love. The Qur'an contains injunctions rising above the *lex talionis* – for example, 'Withold your hand' (from self-defence against persecution), 4:77. Yet the difference between Jesus and Muhammad is stark in some respects. Jesus entered Jerusalem unarmed, riding a donkey before going on to convert the city and its Temple into his own spiritual body. Muhammad took Mecca at the head of an army, arguably calling on his followers to effect global conquest.

I am not denying the worldliness of many Christians. The language of Islam, especially in the Sufi tradition, can be world-renouncing, while that of Constantinian Christianity has sometimes resembled Islam's realism about political power, especially when Christendom was at its zenith during the Middle Ages. Furthermore, the Churches have often looked both ways, at times endorsing the self-subversive vision of the gospels, while regularly settling for alliances with secular power. Mary became patron of cities and countries while the cross was being recast as a sword. But the appropriation was far from total. Monarchs and popes washed the feet of the poor in Holy Week; Christian vocabulary is used to dethrone the powers that be, ecclesiastical as well as temporal, in Dante's *Divine Comedy* among many other texts.

Perhaps the fundamental difference is that Christianity's political ambitions do not, *in theory*, allow for violence, while Islam's do. For example, although both faiths have their saintly ascetics, Sufi masters have throughout history taken up the sword in religio-political defence of Islam; and though Christianity has had its prince-bishops, they were scarcely renowned for their holiness. Saintly monks who were also warriors have not been unknown, especially during the Crusades. But they have been fewer in number. A better way of framing the contrast could be to say that, politically, Christianity is a civil society that became a state, and Islam is a state that became a civil society. Remember the variables, however. The Churches have changed much over the past century, jettisoning their former high-handedness along the way. Like communism, Nazism was a godless creed. But the collusion of Christians in the Holocaust is and should remain a source of deep shame. Muslim thought, too, is constantly evolving; what we think of as Islam has in any case been shaped by the adverse legacy of colonialism.

So just as Christianity has developed in positive ways – notably by rediscovering parts of Jesus' teaching obscured by the accretions of Christendom – there are reasonable grounds for judging that Islam will do so as well. Civilisations do not clash: they are more or less civilised, as a character remarks in Lucy Beckett's timely novel *The Year of Thamar's Book*.[38] I have stated forthrightly in this chapter that the Churches – Orthodox, Protestant and Catholic – face grievous levels of discrimination and oppression in the 2020s, much of it unreported or downplayed. I am also keenly aware that since Christianity and Islam are the world's two most formidable belief systems – and both are growing strongly in global terms – the future will partly hinge on progress in interfaith co-operation. It thus seems right to end on an irenic note by reprising the conclusion of *Christianophobia*: that common features uniting the two faiths are at least as significant as the differences. When they are true to their guiding principles, both traditions insist on the sanctity of the person as a seeker of God: from this should duly follow a recognition of religious freedom as the first of human rights.

Whether this awareness will spread is not for me to predict. For the Christian, it is hope – not more malleable impulses towards either optimism or pessimism – which really counts. Hope, in St Augustine's resonant words, 'has two beautiful daughters: their names are anger and courage. Anger that things are the way they are. Courage to make them the way they ought to be.'

6

A Field Hospital for Sinners

With a membership almost equalling the population of China, the Catholic Church is by far the world's largest public body. That it is a profound force for good, and also flawed, ought to be more widely accepted across the spectrum of belief. Yet what strikes many as obvious is insufficiently recognised either on the secular side or by some of the Church's most ardent devotees.

Varied terrains can throw up challenges for the would-be traveller. Different kinds of equipment (in our case conceptual as well as sociological) may be needed. Though much of the trip must take in peaks represented by the papacy, I would begin and end it a long way from Rome in the secluded valleys of pew, parish and personal witness. Some people less well acquainted with Catholicism may be surprised to learn that the Church is the largest single supplier of healthcare and education on earth, the strongest glue of civil society in Africa, a bulwark of opposition to the caste system in India, and a leading player in global campaigns for sustainable living. It also provides almost the only charitable presence in blackspots forgotten by the rest of the world. When Russian bombers flattened the city of Grozny and other parts of Chechnya in 2000, for instance, the Catholic charity Caritas was initially one of the only NGOs to help survivors. Almost all local people faced total destitution. A similar point could be made about the Democratic Republic of Congo, probably scene of the greatest (though still chronically under-reported) bloodbath of the twenty-first century.

Such marks of health and holiness contrast sharply with the sometimes poor standard of the Church's leadership. The anomaly is crystallised by the position of Catholic women. If access to education forms one of the most important elements in a girl's advancement, then the Church gets a major part of the equation wholly right. It also makes a serious mistake in continuing to teach that all artificial contraception is sinful. When Pope Benedict XVI spelt out what he held to be a corollary of this teaching – that the provision of condoms makes the spread of HIV more likely[1] – then wrong-headedness shaded into severe irresponsibility.

The mixed picture is well summed up by Ian Linden in his magisterial study *Global Catholicism*.[2] He begins with a Chinese proverb: when a tree falls it makes a big noise; when a forest grows nobody hears anything. Media interest in ecclesiastical affairs focuses on the falling trees marked by sex scandals, 'unholy rows' and popes who demonstrate their fallibility. While Linden does not shirk these topics, the main task he sets himself is to chart how a Eurocentric body, which to a large extent spread on the coat-tails of empire, has evolved over the past few generations into an astonishingly diverse and far-flung structure.

Change has unfolded on a vast scale. Long noted for its fortress-like mentality, the Church began a rapprochement with the contemporary world during the Second Vatican Council (1962–5), recovering long-buried strands of its own tradition in the process. Linden's dialectical *tour d'horizon* shows how apparently contradictory notions can reflect significant portions of the truth. Do liberal democracy and science itself owe far more to theology and a Christian cast of mind than many realise? We have already seen that the answer is yes. But was nineteenth-century secularism a necessary corrective to ecclesiastical and other forms of unaccountable authority? Certainly. Did Vatican intransigence grow because of the aggressively anti-Catholic policies seen in Bismarck's Kulturkampf and under France's Third Republic? Yes. Was Pope Pius XII right to judge that Hitler's anti-Stalinist credentials constituted a virtue that outweighed his vices? No, but that judgement is easier to make in hindsight.

Similar factors apply to debate between Christians. A Protestant view of the Catholic set-up is likely to concentrate on the damaging effects of papal authoritarianism. Catholics may reply with some justice that a major thrust of Vatican policy in recent centuries has consisted in much-needed bids to protect the Church from secular interference. The example of Russia and other countries of Orthodox heritage, where religion has too often been locked in the suffocating embrace of nationalism, goes a good way to vindicating Rome's stance. (In any case, the absolute power enjoyed by popes over the past 150 years was only made possible by the railways. Before the spread of modern communications, ideas about the universal reach of papal authority were more a matter of theory than practice.) Two contrasting comments of Cardinal Newman in his *Grammar of Assent* are helpful in this context. The first is damning: 'It is not good for the Pope to live twenty years. It is anomaly and bears no good fruit; he becomes a god, has no one to contradict him, does not know facts, and does cruel things without meaning it.' This view was voiced during the reign of Pius IX – the longest in papal history, and one of the most damaging. Why, then, did Newman leave the Church of England in the first place? Part of the answer is signalled in his second remark, this time much more supportive: 'Without the support of a strong papacy the Christian hierarchy would have long ago degenerated into a feudal semi-clerical . . . caste, endowed with hereditary benefices and more and more a slave to civil authority.'

Like other good commentators, Linden subverts easy answers to the big questions he poses. His discussion is consistently fair-minded. Typically, a reasoned, pro-Vatican thesis will lead within a few pages to an equally compelling antithesis – in this case that a leader such as Benedict XVI and his twentieth-century predecessors were unduly fearful of delegating power. And whether Rome likes it or not, Africans and Asians are not just converts to or opponents of Catholicism. They have long been critical agents of evangelisation, given the small number of expatriate missionaries in relation to the size of these continents.

All this is charted in *Global Catholicism*. It demonstrates strong familiarity with church life across much of the world, especially Latin America. Linden was formerly director of the Catholic Institute for International Relations. He has a fund of knowledge to put the concerns of Europeans and North Americans in perspective. As he remarks tartly at one point, the bioethics that matter in the developing world are not stem-cell research but whether governments will find enough money in their health budgets for mothers to survive childbirth and their offspring to reach the age of five. Preoccupations are thus more mundane: clinics too far away with no drugs, corrupt police and officials, land reform, drought, dirty water, crop failure.

Yet commentators, campaigners and others are hardly wrong to focus on deficits in the balance sheet. I have myself written a critical Life of Benedict XVI,[3] while trying my best to set out the case for the defence. Though I agree that due awareness is needed of how Catholic life unfolds in innumerable mundane contexts, the Church remains highly centralised. With due caveats, then, we can learn much of what is both robust and unseaworthy about the Barque of Peter through brief portraits of its most recent helmsmen. What follows is not a potted history. My aim, rather, is to look at prominent elements in the record accounting for both decline and rebirth. I also recognise the justice of liberal and conservative arguments alike. After Vatican II, for example, a large-scale exodus from the Church was certainly spurred by the retention of compulsory celibacy for priests and the reavowal of earlier bans on contraception. But some form of flight was inevitable given the sexual revolution, the rise of individualism, and the spread of a worldview summed up as 'there's nothing more to reality than my private self and the physical world out there' – namely all the changes outlined in the first part of this book. Catholicism offers the richest available rationale for taking tradition more seriously.

Three Popes in Profile

John Paul II (1920–2005; in office from 1978) was a great man with great faults. Gripped by an unquenchable sense of his own destiny, he knew from childhood some lines of Juliusz Słowacki, the nineteenth-century Romantic poet who predicted the coming of a Slav pope unlike Pius IX: 'This one will not Italian-like – take flight / At canon's roar or sabre thrust / But brave as God himself stand and give fight / Counting the world as dust.' Among other achievements he played an outstanding role in the defeat of Soviet totalitarianism (Poland's Vatican-backed trade union Solidarity formed the first in a row of dominoes in the lead-up to epochal change in 1989) and did much to support the spread of democracy in the Global South. He immediately forgave his would-be assassin, Mehmet Ali Ağca, in 1981: the attempt on his life was to cause him sustained physical suffering. John Paul's personal nobility of character plainly constituted an impetus for his canonisation in 2014.

Nevertheless, he also displayed a double standard in championing democracy and human rights for the secular sphere while failing to practise what he preached internally. There are good grounds for judging that he betrayed the spirit of Vatican II by persecuting theologians and subjecting the Church at a local level to tight central controls. In an apparent rejection of papal absolutism, the Council documents had assigned to laypeople a share in 'the prophetic office of Christ', though little was heard about that under either John Paul or Benedict. The Council also emphasised the principle of collegiality – that church government is a matter for all bishops, 'with and under' the Pope, as successors to the apostles. But in 1998, for example, national episcopal conferences were told that they could not make statements on theological matters without both two-thirds majorities and explicit authorisation from Rome. This measure formed part of a pattern. The future Pope Benedict's Congregation for the Doctrine of the Faith (CDF) acted as judge and jury in investigating claims of heresy among figures ranging from the Dutch Dominican Edward Schillebeeckx (1981) to the Sri Lankan Tissa Balasuriya (1997), thereby falling far short of the minimum legal standards operating in most secular democracies. Not only was the ban on the ordination of women reaffirmed; even discussion of the subject was strictly forbidden.

This ruling reflected a climate of paranoia and obduracy. About a hundred thousand priests and twice as many nuns returned to secular life between the 1960s and the turn of the millennium – a development for which Paul VI, John Paul's predecessor but one, can also be held responsible. The number of ordinations in Western Europe has fallen exponentially. Critics see the hand of the Vatican civil service, or Curia, in all manner of regressive moves including attempts to stamp out inclusive language in worship, and an insistence by the authorities in Rome that Latin texts be rendered with strict literalism in vernacular languages. During the 1990s, members of the International Commission on English in the Liturgy expressed outrage at being told how to do their jobs by officials whose grasp of languages other than Italian and Spanish was slim.[4]

John Paul's refusal to moderate teaching on sexual ethics is held to have played a calamitous role in the spread of AIDS across developing countries. Evidence of child abuse among the clergy was meanwhile often ignored. A veteran analyst such as John Cornwell believes that compulsory celibacy has been a source of immense damage in this connection. In his book *Breaking Faith*[5] he quotes the estimate of Richard Sipe, a psychiatrist and former cleric, that as many as 7 per cent of priests in Western countries have been involved in sex with minors. Although John Paul condemned such conduct in general, he took no action against Cardinal Hans Hermann Gröer (Archbishop of Vienna, 1986–95), who was accused of indecent assault by several of his ex-students in 1995.[6] Most Austrian bishops, including Gröer's successor, considered him guilty. But he retained the favour of the Vatican, presumably through being an unbending doctrinal traditionalist.

He was even invited to meet John Paul for a joint celebration of their eightieth birthdays in 2000.

The huge payments made to the victims of sexual abuse by clergy has gravely affected church finances, especially during the first decade of the new millennium. The bill in the United States alone exceeded $2 billion. A scandal which has severely undermined the credibility of the Church in the US and Ireland, while causing considerable embarrassment elsewhere, has thus served to underscore the lack of transparency in the Church's handling of regular donations from laypeople.

Findings set out in *Render Unto Rome*,[7] Jason Berry's exploration of the financial impact of this crisis, are grim. The author's main focus is on America. In Boston, the former Archbishop, Cardinal Bernard Law, and a clutch of auxiliary bishops failed to act against child molesters while reaching court settlements muzzling the victims. The predatory priests were given psychiatric treatment before being moved on to other posts, where they had access to more potential victims. When details at last emerged in 2002 thanks to the *Boston Globe* (a saga dramatised in the film *Spotlight*), Pope John Paul felt obliged to apologise. But he exonerated the bishops, declaring that 'a generalised lack of knowledge, and also at times the advice of the clinical experts, led bishops to make [the wrong] decisions'. This was mealy-mouthed. The Pope also turned down a request by US bishops for permission to defrock severe sex offenders. On resigning as Archbishop, the disgraced Cardinal Law ought to have faded from view. Instead he was appointed to a plum post in Rome.

Then came a poorly conceived plan to sell off assets and close parishes under Law's successor, Sean O'Malley, and the new Archbishop's right-hand man, Richard Lennon. A vigil movement sprang up. Outraged parishioners occupied churches, many of them financially viable, that were scheduled for closure. In Boston, O'Malley was reluctant to bring in the police to eject them. His counterparts in other parts of the country had fewer scruples. When Lennon subsequently became Bishop of

Cleveland, Ohio, a diocese plagued by financial scandal under his predecessor, he needed a police escort when saying final Masses at closing churches. Meanwhile the Boston vigilantes took their case to Rome, where it sank in a mound of paperwork.

This lack of accountability is easily explained. Catholic bishops have until recently enjoyed great discretionary power, especially in relation to money. The funds provided to them by parishes were not subject to audit. Disclosure requirements of the diocesan finances were minimal. As John Plender put it shortly before Pope Francis's election, '[t]he attitude of the Catholic hierarchy to the laity is summed up in the old adage: pray, pay, obey. As for the bishops' accountability to the Holy See, it is rudimentary, consisting of an unaudited five-year statement of financial condition.'[8] In 2010, the Vatican Bank attracted the attention of the Italian authorities over alleged breaches of money-laundering rules. Pope Francis would later entrust oversight of the clearing-up process to Cardinal George Pell – himself later accused, and subsequently acquitted, of sexual abuse.

Another highly disturbing aspect of *Render Unto Rome* centres on what have been termed rewards for failure. Three years after the American Church's introduction of a youth charter, Cardinal Francis George (Archbishop of Chicago, 1997–2014) put an accused paedophile back in ministry despite warnings from his advisory board. The priest reoffended and went to jail, and the archdiocese had to stump up for the victims. Cardinal George was then elected President of the United States Conference of Catholic Bishops.

Plender has spent most of his career on the *Financial Times*. His positive assessment of Berry's researches deserves to be set out in full:

In any commercial organisation, a key to ensuring ethical behaviour is 'tone at the top'. The same is surely true of any religious organisation. And the question has to be asked: how could men of such strength of character as [Benedict and John Paul] have been so deficient in leadership and morally flabby in their handling of the sexual abuse scandal? As Prefect of the Congregation for the Doctrine of the Faith, the future Benedict XVI was initially slow in responding to the crisis. While brutal in his handling of some errant Catholic theologians, he found it hard to punish cardinals and bishops, as exemplified by his refusal to accept the resignations offered by two Irish bishops for their complicity in harbouring predators. As for John Paul, Berry refers with some justice to his 'surreal dissociation' from the crisis and to his apparent indifference to traumatized abuse victims. There may be no wholly satisfactory answer to this fundamental question, but the corrupting effect of power without accountability in a flawed governance structure must be an important part of it, especially when, as in the old Soviet Union, death is the only form of succession planning for the man at the top.[9]

Though not endowed with the charisma of either John Paul or Francis, Benedict shaped policy in decisive ways during his twenty-three years at the CDF, and then as Pope from 2005 to 2013. On his election he was widely portrayed as the hardline architect of a return to more centralised forms of church government seen during the 1980s and 1990s. Critics charged him with high-handedness; even many observers without an axe to grind saw the former Cardinal as a contemporary Grand Inquisitor. While no stranger to harsh judgements, though, he was also often very charming. Given that the iron fist and velvet glove were both undeniable elements in his repertoire, his record overall is hard to sum up simply.

There is further complexity to untangle besides. Benedict was a poacher-turned-gamekeeper. As Fr Joseph Ratzinger, an independent-minded young priest, he had often complained about the sterile intellectual atmosphere in the Catholic Church of the 1950s, even putting his name to a statement complaining that the hierarchy had 'reins that are far too tight, too many laws, many of which have helped to leave the century of unbelief in the lurch, instead of helping it to redemption'.[10] He served as a *peritus*, or theological expert, at Vatican II. This enabled him to help draft some of the most effective interventions made by a leading reformer, Cardinal Josef Frings. *Gaudium et Spes (Joy and Hope)*, one of the Council's most important documents, mines a long-dormant seam of Christian humanism: 'The joys and hopes, the griefs and anxieties of the men and women of this age, especially those who are poor or in any way afflicted, these too are the joys and hopes, the griefs and anxieties of the followers of Christ. Indeed, nothing genuinely human fails to raise an echo in their hearts.'

Why, then, does Benedict remain a prime exhibit in the liberal chamber of horrors? The short answer is that although there are many continuities in his thought across the decades, he still changed his spots to a remarkable extent mid-career. He concluded during the later 1960s that the Church had opened up to the world just as the world was heading in a very different direction. Outside Catholic ranks, *les événements* and other outbreaks of student unrest in 1968 were apparently demonstrating that Marxism now posed a pressing threat to Western civilisation; while inside the Church disagreement over official teaching on faith and morals was proving hugely divisive. As an academic theologian at Tübingen University, Ratzinger felt the spirit of the age very keenly. He concluded that the faithful must now pull together, shun the luxury of freethinking, and never forget that authentic Christianity is supposed to entail costly witness against what John's Gospel terms the standards of 'this world'. With the eclipse of Marxism, he later came to view postmodern relativism as the most insidious contemporary threat to Christian values.

His outlook on church affairs, and on human nature generally, grew ever more sombre during the 1970s – a change consistently reflected in his work. Ratzinger's books – especially the bestselling *Introduction to Christianity*[11] – were greatly admired by Paul VI, who nominated the professor to become Archbishop of

Munich in 1977. Even greater honours were to follow when the recently elected John Paul translated Ratzinger from Bavaria to Rome. Having been placed in a quasi-judicial role at the CDF, he ought to have kept his sometimes highly partisan opinions under wraps. Critics of his tenure as the Vatican's doctrinal watchdog often base their case on reservations about his combined status as referee and player.

That he sometimes displayed excessive zeal is evidenced by the stream of fiercely worded documents flowing from the Cardinal's pen during the period. Among the most contentious of these was *The Ratzinger Report* (1984),[12] originating as an extended interview with the journalist Vittorio Messori. Giving an almost unremittingly downbeat verdict on church life during the previous two decades, the book implies that a genie was let out of the bottle after Vatican II:

> A new Catholic unity had been hoped for. Instead, a dissent has divided us which, in the words of [Pope Paul VI], has gone from self-criticism to self-destruction . . . I have the impression that the misfortunes that the Church has encountered in the last twenty years are to be ascribed less to the 'true' Council than . . . to the fact that latently present polemical and centrifugal forces have [generated] a cultural crisis in the West, where the affluent middle class . . . with its liberal-radical ideology of individualistic, rationalistic, hedonistic character, is placing Christian values fundamentally in question.[13]

Liberal Catholics were repeatedly accused of selling the pass. The preface to *Introduction to Christianity* illustrates Ratzinger's point with a parable called 'Honest Jack'. A man carrying a burdensome lump of gold exchanged it successively for a horse, a cow, a goose and a whetstone, 'which he finally threw into the water without losing much; on the contrary, what he now gained in exchange, so he thought, was the precious gift of complete freedom'. For Ratzinger, this tale was a warning to theologians drawing ever closer to secular norms. Add together beliefs about the truth of Christianity and the concealment of this truth by sin, and it is not hard to see the inference traditionalists may draw: that discipleship is more about duties than rights, and a global Church must be subject to strong central controls.

Some of these concerns were quite fair. More liberal bodies such as the German Lutherans have suffered steep decline for generations. Other theses aired by the then Cardinal were not only over-pitched but offensive. He effectively insulted other Christians in documents such as *Ad Tuendam Fidem* (1998) and *Dominus Iesus* (2000) – released with John Paul's blessing, but written by Ratzinger – which assert that non-Christians and even non-Catholics are in grave spiritual peril. A hardline Vatican condemnation of homosexual partnerships issued in 2001 mentioned neither the love gay partners bear for one another, nor the Church's love for them. The mystery has been well encapsulated by Henry Wansbrough, the New Testament scholar and monk of Ampleforth who worked with Ratzinger on the Pontifical Biblical Commission: 'I don't know how someone so polite, so perceptive, so open, so intelligent, could also have put his name to so many severe pronouncements.'[14]

Ratzinger's many admirers include the Australian theologian Tracey Rowlands, who has published two intellectual portraits of her subject.[15] She contrasts what she sees as his prophetic, counter-cultural stance with the supine attitudes of his comfortable Western flock:

The emergence of a wealthy Catholic middle class in the US and the countries of the British Commonwealth, desperate for acceptance by Protestant elites and wanting to accommodate its faith to the culture of modernity, including the adoption of a decidedly modern attitude to sexuality, created numerous intellectual and pastoral challenges which were simply beyond the capacities of many of the clergy to address.

Again, this seems reasonable up to a point. Believers do often lack the spine to swim against the tide. We have noted the classical Christian insight that genuine liberty derives from the education of desire. On this view just action should not be based on the freedom to do what you want, but on the right to do what you ought. The thoughtful believer will thus always be counter-cultural in some ways. Ratzinger's convictions were hardened by long-standing worries about a cocktail of ills such as family breakdown, over-consumption and violence, seen as marks of 'neo-paganism'. The vocabulary may be different from that of secular political parties, but the sentiment is of course familiar. Whatever the weaknesses of its execution, David Cameron's Big Society idea owes a clear debt to Catholic Social Teaching.[16] What is more, as a Christian moralist the future Pope could diagnose deeper layers of explanation – above all a sickness of spirit – that are usually assumed to lie beyond the competence of mere politicians.

Ratzinger's distaste for liberalism obviously ran deep. Traditionalists of a philosophical bent (including Alasdair MacIntyre) also rebut liberalism in root-and-branch terms. Their pitch is that the ethic of self-sacrificial love on which Christianity is based implies a certain kind of community drawn not from liberal principles of contract and non-interference, but from shared senses of meaning. Liberals, of course, feel vindicated by the same data. The counter-argument hinges on the undeniable reality of pluralism, and a connected belief that shallower social bonds are both more realistic and more desirable than the elusive goal of 'thick' unity. Those who see the force of conservative and liberal arguments alike may point out that the Church has regularly sought to bind the consciences of the faithful in areas where its teaching has been erroneous. Many of the features making modern life tolerant – and, indeed, tolerable – derive from secular thought. In important respects Western society now casts the net of compassion more broadly than did the Catholic Church under John Paul and Benedict. One could cite, for example, a more grown-up attitude towards divorcees, members of sexual minorities and other former pariahs. Nor is criticism of the Bishop of Rome necessarily a mark of disrespect. On the contrary, many Catholics argue that since he has unrivalled influence, and is the pre-eminent advocate of values without which the world will perish, it is vital to pitch the message credibly.

Linden published his book in 2010. He ends it as follows:

> Rome, the flawed but wise teacher for an age that justifies torture and makes war a first resort, remains the indispensable unifying centre of Catholicism . . . Whether this antinomy, lived out daily as a dilemma by committed Catholics around the world, is a creative tension or a crushing burden will determine the future of global Catholicism. One thing is sure, the distribution of Catholics world wide means that the days of the old Eurocentric Church directed by Europeans are numbered. The future conversation about Catholicism in the twenty-first century will be conducted increasingly by Latin Americans, Africans and Asians.[17]

These words were prophetic. The Catholic arena rapidly started to feel very different under Pope Francis. Commentators have singled out one change above all: an acceptance that the Church no longer embodies political power. He sees it as a field hospital for sinners, not as a fortress. The fresh face elected to Peter's chair in 2013 ushered in a move back towards a pre-Constantinian phase of history, in which the Christian voice was one among many. Francis is not unhappy with the shift. Partly inspired by Jesus' message in Luke 12, he sees grace in the witness of a smaller but more committed flock and feels little nostalgia for Christendom. The message has been repeatedly hammered home – most forcefully, perhaps, during his 2015 address to the Roman Curia. In his eyes the Church is as present in a small Middle Eastern parish staffed by a priest and two religious Sisters, say, as in a richly endowed German setting. Francis's appointments to the College of Cardinals mark one obvious sign of this change. He recently conferred a red hat on a forty-seven-year-old Italian missionary serving a small body of believers in Mongolia.

Benedict also foresaw a leaner Church. But a difference between the two chief pastors lies in what they think the attitude of the flock should be. A foe of what he sees as cosy traditionalism, Francis is sceptical of powerful institutions with levers galore at their disposal. The Catholic Church in Europe has therefore largely stopped trying to control political debate. As recently as the turn of the millennium, John Paul II could stand at his study window on St Peter's Square and deplore a gay pride march taking place elsewhere in Rome. With a senior aide such as Cardinal Camillo Ruini, he successfully lobbied Italian governments on medical and social policy. When Italy legalised same-sex unions in 2016, by contrast, the Church did not put up a fight. 'Who am I to judge?', Francis had famously replied when asked about gay love. He later touched on the heart of the matter in making clear that it is not the Church's business to try to strike down democratically passed laws without popular consent. The principle applies as much to same-sex unions as to divorce: most European democracies decided many decades ago that the state is entitled to relax a strict Christian line on the indissolubility of marriage. Much the same could be said of contraception, where European bishops have essentially given up on the public defence of poor arguments; and abortion, where the Catholic case is much stronger.

This is not to imply that Francis has stayed out of politics, or that he considers it right to do so. He has been especially robust on the environment and migration. *Fratelli Tutti* (2020), his third encyclical, is highly critical of trickle-down economics. Based more on persuasion and an appeal to hearts and consciences, the approach can also display eye-catching savvy. When the right-wing populist Matteo Salvini called for a census of gypsies, Francis met a Traveller family at Rome's cathedral, St John Lateran. And when Salvini had voiced further anti-immigrant rallying cries, Francis appeared in a popemobile surrounded by displaced people from

Africa. These eye-catching moves have attracted far more coverage in the secular media than Benedict ever secured.

That a big name in the realms of economics and public policy such as Jeffrey Sachs takes Francis so seriously is also revealing. Though not a churchman, Sachs has engaged regularly with the Pontifical Academy of Science and praised the Pope as a highly positive influence in international affairs. *Laudato Si'*, Francis's encyclical on the environment, forms an especially significant contribution to debate on the common good.

The strongest opposition to this abrupt policy change is internal. Francis's relaxation of the hard line taken by his predecessors in areas such as Communion for remarried divorcees has drawn heavy fire from conservative cardinals and others. His bid to create a more consultative Church through the Synod on Synodality, held in stages in 2023 and 2024, has likewise set nerves jangling. What to supporters appears like a welcome break with the past is seen by opponents as a surrender to secular mores. Both sides have serious backers, not least owing to a certain cloudiness surrounding the Synod's design. Liberals in Germany gained the impression that existing teaching on questions like clerical celibacy and women's ordination were up for debate. Disappointment was the inevitable result. A summary of the Synod's agenda appears in Appendix I.

Francis's vision of synodality emphasises listening, dialogue and a sense of shared mission between laity and hierarchy. He wants a new way of being the Church for the third millennium. The programme is well summed up by Jenny Sinclair, founder of the group Together for the Common Good.[18] 'The Synod . . . is not about saving the Church. It is about saving the world . . . [The Pope] emphasises that the Synod involves "discernment of the times in which we are living, in solidarity with the struggles and aspirations of all humanity", in order to deliver the Church's mission in a de-sacralised world . . . ' The gathering 'isn't a parliament or an opinion poll', she continues; more a call to a leaner, more focused and outward-facing form of Catholic life:

To develop relational power, we need to become a relational Church. That requires reframing our conception of 'church' as more than a . . . place of worship. It is to conceive of church as a community of faithful people committed to a place, outward-facing to the world, living in loving friendship with others in the neighbourhood, and with a commitment to building local rela-tionships – personal and institutional. The need for these rela-tionships is especially great in places that have been abandoned; politically, economically and spiritually.[19]

The disappointment is not just felt by reformers. A British priest with long experience of Germany's highly influential Catholic community complains that the Synod process has evolved into a liberal echo chamber, notwithstanding its good intentions:

Yes, we're hearing calls for a greater role for women, which I'm all in favour of. But the chief participants – middle-class people in their fifties, sixties and seventies – ought to be more willing to hear different kinds of voice too. Other women who don't want women priests, for example. Or young men who are critical of sexual liberalism and of a contraceptive culture which has led to demographic collapse. Or others who ask, 'Now that we've got lots of old people and not enough young people, what do we do?' These are some of the questions we're not prepared to hear.

This observer's diagnosis of what he terms the 'intense ration-alism' of many German Catholics matched the views of one of my German sources (a recently ordained priest) to a remarkable extent. 'It's partly a reaction to Nazism,' he explained.

The ruling paradigm of recent decades among liberals in my country could be summed up as 'No to mystery and fog. Not only does mystery make Christianity intellectually disreputable, but it opens the door to dictatorship and fundamentalism.' I cari-cature the mindset a bit, but the attitude seems to be, 'Anything which can't be proven by reason or by reference to Heidegger must be suspect. It's reinstating dictatorship by the back door and it's befuddling. It's controlling people.' But in the process of expressing such views, I think these liberals – many of whom are bossier than they realise – have downplayed any sense of the sacred and the spiritual.

All this can in turn be said to have exercised a secularising influence on theology, including an unrelenting urge for Christian proclamation to be 'democratic'. In practice that has meant a sidelining of the principle that the Church is the vessel of a revelation: traditionalism becomes tainted by the suspicion that it is 'right wing'. Things have been taken to bizarre extremes in some of Germany's theological faculties. Critics of the status quo allege that anyone professing a debt to central pillars of the Western tradition such as Augustine and Aquinas – as opposed to expounding their work for historical reasons – can be viewed with suspicion, or even as beyond the pale. A distinguished German theologian who moved to Austria in protest against this intellectual climate sums up the matter tartly. 'What you are now supposed to do – following a big name in contemporary Catholic theology such as Magnus Striet at Freiburg – is make God fit in with modern sensibilities.'

Striet and his acolytes are in turn the offspring of another prominent Catholic thinker, Thomas Pröpper (1941–2015), who himself took his cues from sources including Schleiermacher, the father of modern Protestant theology. This movement's overriding concern lay with making Christianity palatable to contemporary tastes. Such subjectivism is far more questionable than most of its practitioners appear to realise. Theology's relationship to secular currents of thought should involve criticism (or at least caution), as well as creative dialogue. The dynamic has resurfaced in one situation after another throughout church history. During the second and third centuries, Christians both harnessed and reframed the prevailing Neoplatonism in the service of mission.

Writing about a millennium later, St Thomas Aquinas saw potential for pressing the recently rediscovered philosophy of Aristotle into the service of Christian thought. For his admirers, he thereby succeeded in strengthening Christianity's intellectual foundations. For his critics at the Reformation, however, he was overinvested in philosophy at the expense of 'unsullied' biblical proclamation. The pendulum representing attitudes to secular culture has swung back and forth. Spool forward to the 1920s, for instance, and we see Schleiermacher's paradigm falling into disrepute as Karl Barth smashed the cosy liberal consensus that so influenced German Protestantism before the First World War.

Striet's reverence for twenty-first-century secular liberalism is especially problematic in the eyes of his critics. As well as denouncing pre-Enlightenment thought and hailing 'freedom' as the apex virtue, he has gone so far as to claim that he understands Christ better than Christ himself did. A high proportion of those appointed to the major chairs of Catholic theology in Germany over the past few decades share this outlook: it partly accounts for the revisionist attitudes prevalent in the Church more generally. One point seems incontrovertible: liberalism hasn't filled pews, or even staunched the wounds of decline. Recent figures show that a record 523,000 Catholics died or chose to leave the German Church in 2022, compared with 359,000 the year before (already a record). The decline has been most pronounced in traditionally Catholic Bavaria and North Rhine-Westphalia. Ordinations also continue to plummet: only forty-five men were priested across Germany's twenty-seven dioceses during this period. Also in 2022, Germany's twenty registered Evangelical (i.e. Protestant) Churches recorded a drop of 575,000 members, or 2.9 per cent of their membership. With 20.9 and 19.1 million members respectively, the Catholic and Evangelical Churches now represent under half of Germany's eighty-four-million-strong population for the first time.[20]

Here, perhaps, we can see a further reason for Benedict's conservatism, and for 'rebellion against rebellion' in general:

a mood of dissent among those who think that Christian witness should be like the salt of the earth, not icing on an essentially humanist cake. There is plainly nothing wrong in principle with an urge to keep pace with the times. Religious language can indeed look far-fetched from the outside. It may need refreshing from time to time. While aware of the good intentions underlying liberal theology, however, traditionalists are not wrong to warn of the pitfalls associated with slimming doctrine down. As a response to divine revelation, Christian thought is in no position to manipulate its object. The Church is not just a fellowship of like-minded people, but a gift created by God's act.

An English priest with strong links to Germany also complains of a climate of intense rationalism there. When he was invited to celebrate Mass in a university chaplaincy in North Rhine-Westphalia, the lay chaplain – whom he describes as 'an impressive young woman' – announced that on the following Sunday, as a protest against the non-ordination of women, there would be a liturgy led by female ministers rather than Mass. This struck the visitor as disproportionate. 'They were prepared to deprive the whole congregation of the Body of Christ, the greatest thing we have on earth, in support of their campaigning.' In such a climate, he concludes, there is a danger that prayer is reduced to mindfulness, the Church becomes an NGO, and religion is reduced to ethics and social activism. 'The result is actually a very cold essentially liberal Protestant religion.'

Significantly, my English interviewee was also keen to call out the damaging effects of Vatican high-handedness. He illustrated the point by explaining how the theologian Bernhard Häring (1912–98), who risked his life to perform clandestine priestly functions while serving as a conscript stretcher-bearer during the Second World War, was later unfairly disciplined by the Congregation for the Doctrine of the Faith. Häring said that if faced with a choice between interrogation at the hands of the Nazis and questioning by the Vatican, the former was preferable because the Nazis marshalled their facts and accused people understood the case against them. 'That comment was of course deeply shocking. We cannot go around adopting the moral high ground condemning social injustice if we inflict injustice on our own people. But it isn't only conservatives who can be unjust. With a heavy heart I have to say that even Pope Francis's treatment of traditionalists is unjust – and indeed, unsynodal.'

This propels us into disputes about liturgy, a minefield in which many groups – centrist, as well as liberal and conservative – have grounds for feeling aggrieved. Benedict always lamented the demise of Latin as the language of worship in favour of vernacular languages. In his 2007 document *Summorum Pontificum*, he authorised a revival of the Tridentine Mass or Old Rite for congregations who preferred it. Concerned that the change was unwittingly giving rise to a Church within a Church, Francis introduced much tighter restrictions on the celebration of the Old Rite with another apostolic letter, *Traditionis Custodes*, issued in 2021. The thrust of his argument was that the *Summorum Pontificum* experiment had caused division and thus failed to bear fruit.

Traditionis Custodes stipulates that there are to be no more Old Rite Masses in parish churches except with express permission from the Vatican. Many have therefore been stopped very abruptly. A diocese may allow the Old Rite, but not in parish churches; some bishops have abolished them altogether. Not all. Some have been very accommodating. The Archbishop of Westminster, Cardinal Vincent Nichols, said in effect that the division Francis describes in *Traditionis Custodes* is not affecting his patch in London. 'Nichols has been very supportive with the Old Rite,' one of his clergy comments, 'because he sees that a lot of them are very loyal Catholics. They have large families, their children are practising, and so forth. In other words, the Old Rite has continued in Westminster relatively unscathed.'

Another priest I interviewed with a special interest in liturgy was keen to denounce what he sees as disobedience and spite towards the Pope among conservative factions. Yet this did not stop him from also arguing that liturgical conservatives have been hard done by.

> Yes, there is a problem with the traditionalist movement. Francis has put his finger on something real, but I can tell you from the Latin Mass congregation at my church, they're not disruptors. And if they were, I wouldn't have wanted a Latin Mass here. It's not part of a huge anti-Vatican II polemic or some kind of political weaponisation of the Old Rite.
>
> The tide of venom against Francis has been incontrovertible. There is a certain sort of theologically and politically extreme right-wing traditionalist who has abused the generosity of the Vatican and particularly of Benedict's *Summorum Pontificum*. They've had Old Rite Masses in parishes and then they've started trying to recruit people and tell them that the Tridentine rite is the real Mass – and generally they're disrespectful. People like that do exist. I've seen them. But they're a minority.
>
> What I don't think Francis understands – and I think it's a tragic mistake because it risks pulling down the whole synodal process – is that what the Old Mass people want now is not the same as the Old Mass before Vatican II. I've canvassed traditionalists extensively and talked to so many people who aren't against Vatican II or newer liturgies in principle. But they love the gesture, the experience of reverence, silence, a sense of timelessness, and other dimensions which they don't find in vernacular rites.

Asked how things could have been tackled things differently, this priest replies that he would have sent out a task force from the Vatican to look at the troublesome parishes and find out what was going on:

> If I were as charming as Francis undoubtedly is, I would have used my charm to say, Right, I want to have a Zoom call with a traditionalist parish in the United States, or wherever. All you

tell the parish priest is that somebody from the Vatican wants a chat with you by Zoom when you're having coffee and dough-nuts after Mass. And he wants to hear why you like the Old Rite. And he wants to report back. And lo and behold, they'd all tune in on the screen, and there would be the Pope himself. And he could say something like the following: 'I admit to you that this isn't really my thing, but I want to know why it's *yours*.' I wish he'd done that: he's definitely got enough personal charm to do it. I know that he's getting older and ill and so forth, but he could still have done it.

Imposing all these restrictions will just drive people to the Lefebvrists [ultra-conservatives whose standing in relation to the Holy See remains unresolved]. We need to take the heat out of this situation and examine a deeper problem of liturgical anthropology here. Sometimes I think that as priests and theolo-gians we decide how we want people to behave in church, but we don't actually look at how they *do* behave. How, in other words, people relate to the holy – and how they behave when there isn't an adequate sense of the holy. So in that respect, I think [Francis] has failed on this.

It is worth emphasising that these words come from an influential figure who considers Pope Francis to have done a fine job overall. 'There's so much that he's done well,' he continues.

Laudato Si' and *Fratelli Tutti* are terrific. *Amoris Laetitia* [deal-ing among other topics with Communion for remarried divor-cees] could have been better framed in terms of canon law, but I think it's a great document of mercy. He's acknowledging that sometimes it's morally impossible for somebody to go through the annulment process. Essentially, he's sanctioning what used to be called the internal forum [i.e. an informed conscience]. And in doing that, he's taken the worry, the doubt and the guilt out of it for plenty of hard-working parish priests. But I am also hear-ing from canon lawyers that it's a mess legally. And it doesn't adequately guard against a bishop saying that the divorced and remarried can have Communion across the board. Francis didn't intend to usher in a free-for-all, but could perhaps have thought matters through more carefully with experts.

Structures and Safeguarding

In seeking to make sense of all the material above, I suggest once more widening the focus away from the Vatican through snapshots of Catholic life in Germany and Austria, and then in England, all in their different ways representative of the wider picture in Western Europe. With respect to Germany, the main lesson I draw (like my interviewee above) is of a Catholic community losing its way through the spread of secularism. One person after another confirmed and put flesh on points already outlined. In England, a historically more marginalised body much shaped by the Irish diaspora resembles its German counterpart in certain respects, despite very different financial arrangements (Christians in Germany pay a voluntary church tax administered by the government and duly disbursed to the relevant hierarchies). Being smaller, poorer and less inclined to activism, however, the Church in England and Wales – as in Scotland – is more marked by a pragmatic impulse to press on in low-key ways.

Benedict's worry about the sensitive relationship between form and content in Christian proclamation was further illuminated for me by a convert from atheism to Catholicism raised near Leipzig. Now training for the priesthood in Austria (where he also teaches in a university), he expressed views strikingly reminiscent of those I have already reported:

German Lutheranism is in severe decline. Its critics see it more as a secular NGO than a credible platform for gospel teaching. But Christianity is of course much more than ethics tinged with emotion. As far back as the 90s, Ratzinger would point out to liberal Catholics that the reforms they were seeking – on married clergy, women's ordination and greater democracy – had already been introduced decades previously by Protestants. But far from growing, the Lutherans in particular have declined even more rapidly.

Several Vienna-based clerics I visited shared this analysis. A regularly repeated observation is that when people – especially the young – embrace Christianity in postmodern societies, they often become either Catholics or Evangelical Protestants, precisely because of the combination of rigour and vigour associated with these traditions. Moreover, given the levels of infighting now taking place among German Catholics especially, Catholic converts tend to opt for low-church, evangelical expressions of Catholicism. 'You'd be surprised by the number of young Austrian Catholics who admire Holy Trinity, Brompton [the Anglican evangelical parish in West London which pioneered the Alpha Course for enquirers], and its clergy, especially Nicky Gumbel,' one Viennese priest told me. 'In Austria, the Loreto Community [for Catholic Charismatics] is very popular, as are other new movements such as the Emmanuels. The Loreto Community can pack 8,000 young people into Salzburg Cathedral for some of their gatherings.'

Another German priest resident in Austria broadly agreed with this picture. As a fortysomething, he seemed to me especially well placed to understand earlier and later generations alike. 'Older, left-wing Catholics usually have a firm faith background,' he told me.

In consequence they have a tendency to reduce all concerns to social matters focused on bettering the world. That is a major part of Christianity of course. Jesus' words are clear. But the reduction of the faith to political and social concerns in the 1970s paved the way for an inarticulacy on the Church's part when it encounters people who are asking deeper questions about meaning. This is the problem with many people who share Pope Francis's outlook, a good number of whom I respect personally. If you want to understand the right-wing turn in the Church associated with Benedict that doesn't caricature conservatives, I think the best way to understand it is to see the movement as a reaction against a kind of ecclesiastical and theological reductionism.

The priest in question – and the many for whom he speaks in his urban parish – do not buy into a straightforwardly right-wing counter-narrative either.

> In the US especially, there are groups I'd be critical of: those who combine strong liturgical conservatism with an uncritical loyalty to neoliberal economics and a dim view of multiculturalism. As a post-liberal, however, I do notice that priests who preach theologically solid sermons about redemption and grace tend to be conservative-leaning, while those who say less about God and more about social issues tend to be on the Left. For me the most important thing in life is the search for God. That's why I'm anti-reductionist and somewhat more conservative. Someone often accused by the Left of being right-wing is Cardinal Christoph Schönborn [the long-serving Archbishop of Vienna]. In fact he's a centrist whose sermons are resolutely focused on the core tenets of the faith. So I tend to gravitate towards people for whom this metaphysical connection is the most important thing.

This priest's outlook might be summed up as follows. There is a big difference between millennials and the Baby Boom generation who, when they were young, still experienced a solid form of Catholicism. They came to kick against it precisely because they grew up thinking of it as so rock-like. The focus of these older believers tends to be is on the reform of structures. What millennials have often experienced, by contrast, is an institution that seems much more fragile. Over the past twenty years especially,

Catholicism has come to look less confident against the back-drop of society as a whole. It is that instability which probably accounts for their urge to build things up, and maybe also their defensiveness.

The Vienna seminary, where I spent part of my time in Austria, is by far the largest in the German-speaking world. There are about forty men in training. Most German semi-naries have under ten students. One Catholic contact after another in Germany voiced a fear that the faith is dying out in their country. In their view there is no longer a thriving parish network devoted to the propagation of the faith. 'Even in the rural areas, the old system is collapsing', according to another cleric. Tellingly, he, too, preferred to speak off the record.

I have suggested that the dynamics of Catholic life in Germany can be seen elsewhere on the continent, albeit in more muted forms. Having revisited Spain every year for decades, I can confirm that there are many older Catholics in the Iberian Peninsula, as well in Britain and Ireland, with outlooks akin to those of their German counterparts. I also know conservative young believers from a range of countries, including France, Italy, Poland and Hungary, some of whom belong to traditional-ist movements such as the Neo-Catechumenate. There is a thriv-ing Loreto community in Twickenham, West London, priding itself on a 'tradismatic' spirituality. Postmodern Catholicism has been transposed into many other keys besides. A Catholic church in central London is likely to offer Mass in several languages. Working for many years in the News Building, head-quarters of News UK, I spoke to immigrant catering staff every day who were mostly either Catholics, ex-Catholic recruits to Pentecostal or Charismatic Christianity, or Muslims. There is plenty of variety well outside the capital as well. In the West Sussex town of Haywards Heath, for example (the popula-tion of which is 92 per cent white), a Syro-Malabar or Keralan liturgy is regularly available to hundreds of parishioners, most of whom are under thirty-five and fervent in the practice of their faith. A statistic like this could be multiplied across the board. The Ukrainian Catholic parish in West London has a vibrant and youthful congregation; elsewhere in England there are Syro-Malabar liturgies being celebrated every week as far north as Preston.

***

In many other places from Portugal to Poland (including Germany of course), church life chugs on faithfully, undemonstratively and without theological arm-wrestling. Having spoken to a group of laypeople in parishes around England, I spotted enough family resemblances outside London and other major conurbations to produce a composite sketch. One leitmotif was the role of deacons and laypeople. 'We have more people training for the diaconate,' one interviewee in a county town told me. 'That is really good. And it takes place in the community rather than the seminary. Women form a part of the training team.' She also reported that growing numbers of people are being prepared for pastoral ministry. In due course they will be running parishes. 'There's no room for complacency,' this source added, speaking off the record. 'The shortage of priests is acute. Most of our priests are fairly elderly.' On the other hand, though:

> an increasing proportion of those in training to become deacons are from very diverse backgrounds. Some are Polish, some are Goans, some are Africans. We have a very good bishop who has encouraged more open patterns of formation.
>
> I associate fragility in the Church more with questions of infrastructure and organisation. In [our diocese] we're going to be moving from a parish to a deanery model, where you might have a couple of priests in a deanery who will serve a number of parishes. And already a number of parish priests might have several parishes that they look after. One of my priest friends looks after four parishes with the help of only two other priests,

both of whom are retired. It would be hard for him to keep going without a very energetic lay pastoral assistant.

My source worships at a large church. She describes herself as 'not uncritical' of the set-up. 'We don't have a pastoral council, for instance. Every parish in the country is obliged to have a finance committee. Our bishop recommends that each parish in his diocese should have a pastoral council too, but they're not compulsory'. Several laypeople I spoke to felt that Synod on Synodality in Rome should encourage a change in canon law.

Parishes were invited to forward their vision of the Church to Rome before the Synod's first sessions in the autumn of 2023 (the final sessions are due in late 2024). Another of my contacts belonging to a large congregation in a provincial city felt the preparatory process had been good overall. 'We've had a number of facilitators who've set up online consultative groups, as well as face-to-face gatherings arranged at convenient times for the elderly. The person running adult education and formation in our diocese supported us strongly. Participation was robust.' Less successful had been the process of taking things forward. 'A group of us in our congregation are supposed to be transmitting the vision of laypeople to the powers that be and making things happen. But it hasn't taken off well.' The terms of reference were said to be unclear; one person involved in the process told me that it lacked energy and vision. Yet this source was also upbeat about the scale of activity 'beyond internal church matters'. Much work with local students takes place, as well as with the homeless and elderly. When Pope Francis proclaimed the Year of Mercy in 2015–16, a member of my interviewee's church started a group which anyone feeling isolated or in financial hardship or weathering any other kind of trauma was welcome to join. It meets every week and regularly draws fifty or sixty people.

Another of my contacts had memories of Catholic life in his West Country town extending back to the 1980s. There were naturally more priests then – and more youth groups. But lay participation was far more limited. Two months before our conversation in the summer of 2023, he took part in a lay-led parish retreat. 'That would never have happened in the past. The same applies to catechesis, which is now largely performed by women.' The other big positive change is that people are no longer ostracised for their sexuality. 'Today the pastoral minis-try we receive is based on the priority of compassion, mercy and inclusion rather than dogma. That doesn't mean we think that anything goes, or that we regard canon law as expendable. But [the emphasis is on] listening rather than finger-wagging.' A resource used for pastoral theology in the diocese concerned is Bill Huebsch's *Promise and Hope*.[21] The author, a prominent American gay Catholic, is himself married.

What my first interviewee above terms 'our more significant shortcomings' relate to two discrete areas. One, she says, 'is our failure to talk about God in ways that makes sense to sceptical, scientifically literate, younger people. There's a shortage of good popular apologetics of the kind produced by figures like C. S. Lewis a few generations ago.'

Tragically, the second still relates to safeguarding. The Cumberlege Commission report (2007) was meant to herald a new era. In response to its recommendations, the bishops accepted that within a year they would draft an amendment to canon law making it compulsory for any institution in England and Wales calling itself Catholic to sign up to the safeguarding standards of the Church. But by the time the Independent Inquiry into Child Sexual Abuse [IICSA] was set up in 2014, the bishops had only just produced a text on the subject to send to Rome. Widely described as scrappy by its critics, the document involved only limited consultation. Safeguarding experts were excluded. The testimony of Cardinal Nichols to IICSA has been described as 'shameful' to me by an array of lay Catholics. Among other lapses it gave no explanation as to why it had taken the bishops all those years to come up with a piece of paper to submit to the

Vatican.* What is more, Rome itself had still not formally replied a decade later.

Where the Light Gets In

All this and more needs to be reported. A scandal has been unfolding in the diocese of Hexham and Newcastle as I write. The Bishop, Robert Byrne, had to resign in late 2022 after revelations of serious safeguarding failures. Among other examples of

---

* The position sketched above was confirmed to me by other laypeople involved with safeguarding, including Baroness Hollins. Their shared view is that while matters are taken far more seriously on Pope Francis's watch, problems remain with the design of institutional responses – and in particular with clericalism.

Matters were summed up in Sheila Hollins's Craigmyle Lecture in 2022, held under Catholic Union auspices. Formerly President of the Royal College of Psychiatrists, she has worked closely with victims of sexual abuse for many years. Lady Hollins was among the first to be recruited to the Holy See's Pontifical Commission for the Protection of Minors in 2014. Describing her decision to step down from the Commission, she was especially critical of its being placed under the aegis of the Vatican's doctrinal department. 'It's anomalous to put a safeguarding commission into the department that deals with allegations against priests, given that its brief is to prevent abuse and to address the care and healing of victims/survivors. The dicastery [department] for the family and laity seems much more in tune with the overall goals of the commission.' Also in 2022 emerged evidence that most of the world's 114 national bishops' conferences had yet to establish proper systems that would enable alleged victims to report cases of abuse by priests and church employees.

A shaky hand on the tiller in Rome contrasts with often excellent work done on the ground, however. In London, the Southwark archdiocese has a highly praised programme, From Grief to Grace, first pioneered in the United States. It is run by two priests, both themselves survivors of abuse. Psychologists, therapists and other experts are also involved. Another venture led by survivors is Survivor Training – Beyond Words. Based in Yorkshire, this church-backed organisation concentrates on safeguarding in educational settings across the board.

misconduct, he had tried to secure a job for a fellow priest despite knowing that the man concerned had been convicted of possessing indecent images of children. Needless to say, abusers should face legal sanction and the vulnerable should be protected. Without in any way playing down the seriousness of clerical paedophilia though (rather the reverse), an array of figures urge that sexual misconduct should be viewed in a wider context. There are also many abusive teachers and doctors; evidence is gradually emerging of extensive levels of child abuse in sport. That some people betray their callings does not stop parents seeking medical help for their children, or sending them unchaperoned to football practice. It is also worth recalling the grim fact that historically most paedophiles have been fathers preying on their own daughters.

Notwithstanding the crimes of a minority, the value of doctors and teachers is still generally taken for granted. Why does it matter that the Catholic Church – as well as observing the unsurpassably important priority of protecting children – should itself have a robust public presence? The question haunts me, given that hostility to Christianity in general and Catholicism in particular is still one of the few acceptable prejudices widespread in the UK. A sense that Catholics are required to believe six impossible things before breakfast doesn't just derive from Protestant or atheist propaganda. It is even there in fictional works by and featuring Catholics such as *Brideshead Revisited*. Better templates are available. Catholic novelists including Graham Greene, Shusako Endo, David Lodge and figures already mentioned such as Lucy Beckett give far more textured accounts of Christian practice than Evelyn Waugh ever contrived.

Yet caricatures persist. After his success with *Jews Don't Count*, for example, David Baddiel published a disappointing companion volume, *The God Desire*.[22] In reviewing the book, I argued that its premise is fundamentally flawed.[23] The truth of atheism is assumed from the start, meaning that no argument is ever engaged over what ought to be contested territory. For all Baddiel's stylistic verve his stance betrays a mixture of flippancy and ignorance. A telling moment comes when he recounts a conversation with his comedy partner Frank Skinner, who returned to the practice of his Catholic faith some years ago. Skinner is represented as sticking to church teaching through a terror of burning in hell. At no point does Baddiel consider why someone so bright should have paid serious attention to Christianity in the first place.

An attitude based more on a lack of curiosity than any sinister motives still strikes me as widespread in Britain, even though things have naturally changed a good deal in half a century. A member of my parents' generation such as the journalist Hugo Young once told me that he and his classmates at their Catholic school in the 1950s were warned that their faith would impose a glass ceiling on their careers. Fortunately, the forecast was mistaken: by the 1970s *The Times* had a Catholic Editor; twenty years after that a Catholic had been appointed Director-General of the BBC. But this hardly stopped old biases from emerging on occasion. I experienced them regularly at my Anglican school during the 1980s. A later case – one among many I could cite – has stayed with me owing to the media splash it caused. In 1999, Glenn Hoddle, then manager of the England football team, was obliged to resign after telling an interviewee that a belief in karma made him think that disabled people are being punished for sins in a former life. Christians and non-believers alike excoriated Hoddle's view. Shortly afterwards a *Guardian* editorial opined that people of faith entertain all sorts of 'other' outlandish ideas with no pushback: Catholic belief in transubstantiation was cited in support of this claim.

The example reflected an old irony: scoffers and naive believers often form two sides of the same coin. I have already indicated that I am an atheist with respect to the deity Richard Dawkins does not believe in. So why as a Catholic am I prepared to accept teaching on transubstantiation? Because God's creation, taken totally, is larger than the material creation. In the new world brought about by Jesus' life, death and resurrection, the final significance of bread and wine in the Mass is greater than their significance in nature. For Aquinas, what is meant by the 'substance' of something is its ultimate meaning to God. So there is a sense in which the 'substance' of Christ's flesh and blood has replaced the 'substance' of the bread and wine at the Eucharist. Transubstantiation is not 'replacement'. In the words of a scholar such as Timothy McDermott,

> Christ's body and blood have not taken the place of the bread and wine, if by that you mean that the bread and wine have been transformed into Christ's flesh and blood. This Aquinas denies. The bread and wine are indeed *signs* of the real presence of Christ's body; what has been 'replaced' is the real significance in God's eyes of those signs.[24]

On this understanding the Eucharist is the kiss of a God present to the touch, and (as McDermott also put it to me privately) as a moment of love and friendship in action, strengthening the mystical body of the church community.

If you ask self-aware Catholics to provide a general rationale for their beliefs, the answers will come on several levels. First and fundamentally stands the confidence that Christianity is a coherent belief system for the reasons set out in Chapter 3. A gift has been given in the incarnation of God the Word and the establishing of the fellowship animated by the Holy Spirit for communion with God the Father. This gift is to be celebrated and shared. And it is precisely these convictions which can allow Christians to see traces of the divine presence across human culture.

Second, that the Church of Rome, for all its manifest wounds, transmits an especially rich and solid form of the faith. A Catholic vision in its broadest sense (a vision shared by the Eastern Orthodox, and many Anglicans and others) is likely to involve some form of Christian Platonism. Catholic theology asks the baptised to see themselves not as single individuals, because their lives are bound up with one another and with higher realities of God's creation all the time. To perceive that higher level, believers must be reorientated by worship. Those who lack such a discipline are liable, as we have seen, to be left with a thinner diet of political campaigning. Far from being an optional extra, then, the Eucharist is the 'source and summit' of Christian worship.

Third, Catholics in particular may suggest that, even though the Church has lost much credibility through the child abuse scandal and a pig-headed reluctance to accept LGBT equality, there is none the less much to be said for its grasp of the big picture. Certainly, there are ditches that some old-school moralists ought not to contemplate dying in. (I have sharp memories of a highly ill-advised bid by Cardinal John O'Connor, a former Archbishop of New York, to stop screenings of *Priest* (1995), the drama featuring a young gay curate in Liverpool.) A revisionist but theologically solid pro-gay case can be simply stated. The Bible condemns corrupt forms of same-sex desire, but does not reckon with stable, monogamous partnerships. What I think Scripture condemns (because the biblical authors had no understanding of the concept of homosexuality – a word of nineteenth-century coinage) is straight people behaving perversely. St Paul inherited that point of view but was also critiquing a Greco-Roman culture in which it was acceptable for men both to indulge in what we would now term paedophilia and to enter into heterosexual relationships for the purposes of acquiring status, property and offspring. Needless to say, such practices were morally reprehensible. Teaching can therefore be revised in accordance with Scripture's underlying message about the link between sex and commitment rather than in defiance of it.[25] The Church (at least as represented by senior clerics) has been slow to take these points on board. *Fiducia Supplicans* (2023), a Vatican Declaration conditionally allowing priests for the first time to bless same-sex couples, has received short shrift from conservatives. The tragedy is that all this eclipses the prophetic side of Catholic teaching. Calmer preachers than O'Connor who decry the sexualisation of children or promiscuity or family breakdown are right to do so.

Fourth and finally, a host of Catholics are animated by a faith innocent of theological or political strife. I sense this most keenly of all in my daily WhatsApp exchanges with a devout and immensely big-hearted woman living on a shoestring in the disaster zone that is contemporary Caracas. Since this book centres mostly on Europe, though, let me give the penultimate word to Christoph Warrack, a London-based social entrepreneur. His strength partly lies in pointing to the difference it all makes on the ground.

He received a Catholic upbringing in the north of England before ceasing to practise his faith for several years in his early twenties, having first explored Eastern religion during a prolonged stay in India. A period of personal turmoil ensued, after which he moved to the capital and found an oasis at Corpus Christi, Brixton, a vibrant church then run by Jesuits. There he encountered a body of people – older women especially – radiating 'the authentic glamour of the Kingdom of God, very much in contrast to the synthetic glamour I was also finding in the secular world'.

His working day was in the film industry at an office in Soho. As a parishioner he had already become motivated to volunteer in care homes, visit people in prison, and assist the needy with drug and alcohol problems. Then Warrack saw a way of integrating his Christian witness more closely with his work: the ritzy offices of several big film companies were cheek-by-jowl with Soho's walking wounded. Didn't vagrants need cultural nourishment as well as food and shelter? Open Cinema was born.[26] Founded in 2009, the venture provides film clubs for the homeless across Britain. It has also spread to Ireland, Finland and California, and inspired similar projects more widely still. Being part of a mixed congregation in Brixton changed his life, Warrack says:

> it made me someone who wanted to serve those completely outside the system and helped me understand the hell of being outside and the heaven of being inside – in everything that's meant by those words 'inside' and 'outside'. And so Open Cinema

was the culmination of my attempt to combine the things I was becoming accomplished at as a professional in the film industry, with the things that I was absolutely passionate and committed to doing something about, namely exclusion, poverty, deprivation, injustice.

Further initiatives followed. In 2018 came Airbase,[27] focused on community skills development. Its aim is to connect anyone with an expertise with anyone with a need for that expertise through harnessing unused or undeveloped spaces. 'The focus is on real-world engagement,' he explains. 'It's not about digital learning. A big part of the motivation lies in making use of buildings whose potential is not fully exploited. That's where the magic happens.'

After living in Brixton Warrack had moved to the West End of London and dropped anchor at St Patrick's, Soho Square, served by a remarkable priest, Fr Alexander Sherbrooke. That church's outreach to the homeless has developed steadily over the past fifteen years or so: I have occasionally joined troops of volunteers serving evening meals to large groups of people. 'Alexander has no interest in preferment,' Warrack adds. 'Some assumed he'd fail at St Patrick's, especially because he has a privileged background. In the event he'll probably be there for life.'

Reflecting further on his journey of faith, Warrack rejects the widespread association between Catholicism and guilt as 'far too hackneyed and clichéd':

I carry much more sense of regret than of guilt, because I feel loved and accepted and held and forgiven by God. Among other things, the awareness assists with achieving what's been called the 'flow' state, when someone is at the upper end of their capacities. When you're neither under-performing nor overperforming, that's when your abilities can be harnessed in their optimal state. And in the case of spiritual practice, I believe that this is when grace can pour out.

The lustre remains undimmed: along with a group he terms his 'brothers in arms', Warrack has set up several further initiatives. B Foundry[28] is a climate finance consultancy. 'You could call it connecting climate ventures with finance,' he says.

> Then there is Gather,[29] a platform for enhancing community collaboration in the face of climate change. It's piloting with the London Borough of Lambeth now. And Moving Beyond[30] convenes senior corporate leadership on climate collaboration across finance, retail, the tech sector, government and civil society, as well as bringing together people from the worlds of activism, scientific research and the creative industries.

The project Warrack now works most with is called Woodland Savers.[31] It helps communities across the UK to crowdfund the purchase of their own woodlands. 'We help them raise money, then match that with institutional finance.' When land has been purchased, the group partners with charities like the Woodland Trust and Forestry Commission to ensure that the areas concerned are properly managed. 'Having immersed myself in [Pope Francis's encyclical] *Laudato Si'*, but also in the science of what's happening, I feel very exercised indeed about the climate emergency. The future of the human race will be very bleak indeed if the ocean food chain collapses. Given climate change, there is a terrifying possibility that this will happen.'

I end by asking about his most transformative spiritual experience. Warrack's reply lays heavy emphasis on a retreat at St Beuno's, the Jesuit centre in North Wales, undertaken soon after he moved to Brixton. Far from suggesting that his faith is just ornamentation, his memories demonstrate that it has formed the governing impetus of a highly creditable career:

> I've never forgotten the visualisation that I was invited by my guide to make on the scene in the Gospels where there's a wealthy, ostentatious man making donations at the Temple and

an old lady giving a few pennies [see Mark 12:41–4]. I became fully immersed in the scene. The spirituality at St Beuno's was so profound, so rigorous, so dependable, so timeworn, that even a clueless, floundering character of twenty-three like me could be reoriented to a place that was not just grounding but inspiring, energising and renewing . . . I could just look across at the disciples observing this scene. Look at their reactions, listen to the Lord talking to them. In brief, it showed me a goodness forming the tip of a very important iceberg.

***

In conclusion, I would reiterate the obvious truth that people without faith in God can be great sources of good as well as believers. But religion in general and Christianity in particular supply an especially intense focus for such work: the Pew Foundation estimates that faith-based endeavour in the United States contributes about $1.2 trillion a year to the economy. And the faith concerned in a historically Christian society springs from the Gospel. Closer to home, I have come across some remarkable testimony from the journalist Martin Newland, who with his wife has fostered dozens of children with a broad range of needs since their own offspring flew the nest. He reflects on his experience as follows:

> Many of those we have cared for have many siblings, often produced by a single mother and host of absent fathers. One boy had seven brothers. Another fourteen-year-old girl who visited had fourteen siblings. Thus a vast tapestry of care provision is created at soaring public cost, delivered by a host of public servants, from police to social workers. The father of one child we cared for moved on to get another woman pregnant a few months later, the baby being placed almost immediately under supervision.
>
> There are not enough social workers or foster carers to cope with this. Too many children, some of them moved between

different carers and care homes ten, twenty or thirty times, are released into society at eighteen – bitter, incapable of trust, with little education and destined to repeat the whole pattern.[32]

What Newland is perhaps too modest to declare is that he and his wife are devout Catholics strongly motivated by their faith. In trying to put my finger on the extra ingredient Warrack, the Newlands and countless other people of faith offer, I would invoke a penetrating distinction drawn by the Anglican theologian Sam Wells between working *for*, working *with*, and *being* with. Working *for* requires one to cultivate and enhance one's skills and shape one's compassion to be alert for opportunities to use those skills to make other people's lives better. 'It doesn't necessarily involve conversation, understanding, or mutuality,' Wells notes. It is action without relationship. Working *with*, like working for, is focused on active steps to overcome problems. 'But unlike the previous assumption of acting on another person's behalf, it seeks in every way to make the project a collaborative exercise, not just with the person encountered, but with a wider range of people experiencing the same or a similar plight.'

Being with – highly evident in the patterns of life I have just described – is different from working for and working with, because it focuses on the relationship itself:

> [B]eing with differs . . . from working with, because it requires a focus on enjoying the person and growing through what they truly are (being), rather than assuming the encounter is an opportunity to exercise one's agency in bringing about change. Being with thus requires a transformation of heart and mind from conventional forms of encounter. It's not [just] about solving problems. It's about enjoying relationship for its own sake.[33]

With these ideas in mind, I end with some testimony of a religious Sister ministering at a provincial parish in England far from centres of power. Her remarks carry all the more conviction because of her low profile: nothing she told me is ever likely to reach the newspapers. Perhaps that in itself is proof of its importance.

Statistically we'll become smaller, but I also see a lot of growth. I see saints all around me. When I look at the people who give catechesis to the kids at our church, for example, doctrine, spirituality, psychological realism and human care are all integrated very impressively. I see incredibly generous Catholics who actually also repent before their atheist friends, by being determined to be more human. So I do have hope. I don't know what God is doing. I think there will be collapses, but I also see deep marks of renewal.

7

Beyond Establishment

Stephen Sykes, Bishop of Ely from 1990 to 1999, once gave a crisp account of why he feels both attracted and repelled by Anglicanism.[1] On the positive side were four big strengths: a 'quiet and confident Catholicism', an openness to a range of spiritual traditions, the exercise of authority with consent, and an honouring of the ministry shared by all baptised people. The negatives included 'the triviality and superficiality into which our eclectic openness can fall', 'the proneness of Anglicanism to fashionable causes', and 'the all-consuming ruthlessness of the campaigners, for whom politics is all'.

The Church of England, along with the worldwide scatter of Anglicanism that grew from it, famously makes a virtue of accommodating a spectrum of views within its ranks. Such unity as it has enjoyed traditionally came from orderly liturgies of shared origin. At its best it can still embody respect for many-sidedness. But what happens when liturgical variety becomes a symptom of clashes over what are held to be central matters of belief? Coherence of message now perhaps forms the Church's chief challenge alongside falling attendance and the care of thousands of historic buildings in a climate where indifference to Christianity would be spreading relentlessly, even in the face of more confident proclamation based on seamless teaching.

The theological divisions in play have deep roots. *Love's Redeeming Work*[2] – a major anthology also serving as an apologia for the C of E's spiritual heritage – acknowledges on its opening page that various ecclesiastical parties have always considered themselves true heirs of the traditions established after Henry VIII's break with Rome. Evangelicals, for instance, have often stressed that the English Reformation was fuelled by an insistence on the supremacy of Scripture in all matters of faith and morals. Many of their successors have thus seen the purification of the Church as unfinished business in every generation. Others have long stressed continuities between Tudor and Stuart perspectives and those of the early Church. In their eyes the priority has resided in establishing a non-papal Catholicism. Others noted an imperative to live with difference from the start. Their impulse was more than pragmatic. It was also pointed out that Anglicans, by contrast with their Continental counterparts, had never bound themselves to a single confessional formula. Leading early figures – Archbishop Thomas Cranmer, Richard Hooker and George Herbert, among others – are known for having done their theology above all through focus on the shape of Christian lives: Cranmer in his work on the Book of Common Prayer; Hooker via a concern to connect revealed truth with a Christian appreciation of law and wisdom in their broadest senses; Herbert in mediating the quest for God through poetry and imagination. In other words (to cite the image offered by *Love's Redeeming Work*), we are talking less of a rigid instruction manual or Ordnance Survey map; more of an inhabited landscape. For a sample of the change involved, consider a devout, reasonably prosperous Anglican household during the early modern period. Its members would typically have gathered daily by their hearths for morning and evening prayer. The discipline bred far greater scriptural literacy than most Continental Catholics possessed – then or since. Yet such habits would also have rooted Anglicans deeply in Western tradition.

Like reformed Christians elsewhere, they also refused to identify religious life with a visibly separate priestly caste. This in turn fed an emphasis on interiority – and, as some scholarship suggests, an allied prizing of hearing above seeing as a gateway to the transcendent. Self-aware interiority is often yoked to sensitivity about the limits of human knowledge and the risks of self-deceit. *Love's Redeeming Work* notes that Herbert's younger contemporary

Henry Vaughan celebrates the divine darkness in ways influenced by Eastern Christian thought and Neoplatonism. 'Vaughan's imagery, like that of John of the Cross, freely combines the themes of night, escape, loss, and erotic yearning. Hooker's cast of mind is similar. He can say that our best eloquence about God resides in silence, and calls for contextual readings of the Bible.'[3] Two centuries later, Bishop Joseph Butler built on this style with his argument for an analogy between the Church's discernment of God's will and other forms of human truth-telling. It is also fair to conclude that Newman's *Essay on the Development of Christian Doctrine* formed a gift from Anglicanism to Roman Catholicism after the future Cardinal's change of allegiance.

The outline just traced has made for a highly creditable legacy on one level after another. It is therefore no surprise that Anglicanism should have had so many able champions. What may seem anomalous when viewed from Portugal or Poland can make far more sense to those with a nuanced grasp of British history. On this understanding, the Anglican settlement is a bridge between perceived extremes represented by Rome and Geneva. The so-called Lambeth Quadrilateral of Scripture, creeds, biblical sacraments and apostolic ministry (namely bishops, priests and deacons) is meant to epitomise Anglicanism's rootedness in the faith of the undivided Church of the first five centuries. Popes may have added too much to the list of what Christians are supposed to believe; a Calvinist, say, has subtracted too much (and distorted more besides). The C of E and its sister provinces elsewhere in Britain, Ireland and the wider world are at the same time capable of living with diverse outlooks on matters of secondary importance. Like the proverbial Australian farm, this is a Christian arena with few fences and many wells.*

Equally clearly, Anglicanism's tangled roots have been sources of abiding strife as well as richness. Long overdue moves like toleration of Protestant Dissenters and Catholic Emancipation

---

* A brief sketch of the historical background is provided in Appendix 11.

were marks of social mobility and the questioning of previously settled social hierarchies. But other major episodes – especially, perhaps, the intense energy and seriousness of the Evangelical Revival, and the Tractarians' concern with the continuities between Reformed English Christianity and medieval Catholicism – were more closely related to the past. This ignited a clearer sense that the Church of England needed to frame its own discipline and doctrine free of state control, as well as changes such as the reintroduction of monasticism and other expressions of religious life. Far greater levels of self-government took off, including conditions enabling the creation of a worldwide Communion (Anglicanism now forms the second-most widespread Christian family on earth).

Another feature of Tractarianism and related high-church movements developing from the 1830s onwards was a more critical attitude towards British society. Challenges facing the C of E grew gradually less interchangeable with those confronting elite groups. Erastianism – that is, undue subservience of Church to state – had long been recognised as a danger across the Christian world. But moves allowing greater self-government for the Church had downsides, among them a tendency to sectarianism and navel-gazing. As *Love's Redeeming Work* puts it, the Tractarians unwittingly gave 'immense impetus to what they would have deplored: once they had claimed the right to redefine Anglican identity from within, they opened the floodgates to an attitude of mind that assumed it was acceptable to debate the nature of this identity with practically no boundaries set in advance, and to opt for a version that you found suitable.'[4]

Here we can identify a fertile seed of disputatiousness within contemporary Anglicanism. Among its hallmarks are a reluctance to accept teaching and other propositions that apparently have little purchase in individual and experiential terms; a tendency to moralism; and what the editors of *Love's Redeeming Work* describe as 'a growing haziness about the integral theological vision within which the Church as a whole, let alone Anglicanism in particular, operates'.⁵ These words were published in 2001. They look all the more prophetic after an interval of a quarter of a century.

How can the centre hold? It has often been observed that a typical twenty-first-century Anglican is an African woman under the age of thirty for whom classical formulae will seem very remote. Like her Catholic or Pentecostal counterparts, her concerns are likely to centre on violence, poverty and the risks of persecution and famine. The answer given in *Love's Redeeming Work* spotlights what are posited as compelling resources for nurturing non-coercive forms of unity:

A doctrine-free spirituality risks descending into sentimentality, to the level of what makes us feel generally better about ourselves or reminds us in a wholly unsystematic way of the mystery around us; it is a weak support for resistance to the political and cultural tyrannies of our day. Without the structures of both discipline and doctrine, 'spirituality' can be vacuous and indulgent. Equally, doctrine that loses sight of its own roots in the painful and gradual re-formation of how holiness is experienced and understood becomes idle, even idolatrous . . . It is the doctrinal vision itself that teaches . . . reticence and self-questioning; in other words, the Christian theological worldview is one that, in its very abundance and comprehensiveness, challenges anyone who thinks they have compassed and possessed it in excessively tight formulations.⁶

Anglicanism's intellectual riches are especially important at a time when Christian thought is wilting in other parts of Europe. Rowan Williams's role in promoting a recovery of theological nerve over recent generations has been hailed internationally: teachers across the continent in a range of non-Anglican settings draw inspiration from the former Archbishop's thought.⁷ Williams also helped spawn an influential movement such as Radical Orthodoxy. Mainly pioneered by Anglicans including

John Milbank, Catherine Pickstock and Graham Ward, it has influenced theology across the board in North America, as well as Europe. Other salient figures who might be called critical friends of Radical Orthodoxy include Sarah Coakley, David Ford and Oliver O'Donovan.

There are good grounds for listing some of the central elements in their shared repertoire, given Williams's reaction against a style of liberal theology popular during the postwar decades – and still in wide currency today. The electrifying effect of his lectures to ordinands during the 1970s has been well recalled by Adrian Dorber, a future Dean of Lichfield:

> We were offering ourselves for lifelong ministry, and needed to break out of what seemed like an old-fashioned Oxbridge consensus presenting Christ as essentially a moral mentor. Rowan liberated us from this. His theology was grounded, passionate, caught up in the life of God, and he was clear that everything came together in the Church, rather than the academy. New vistas were opened to us by his robust engagement with philosophy, politics and ethics, as well as history. We came to think that it was possible to out-think the Enlightenment, and defend the integrity of revelation.[8]

Tom Wright, one of Williams's most prominent contemporaries, was developing allied convictions. He put it to me like this:

> There was a sense of frustration, in the universities and in the Churches as well, that the theologians were letting us down, and saying 'Well, we can't believe this, we can't believe that' . . . [a liberal Protestant] paradigm was still ruling in the New Testament world, so that it was just assumed that only somebody hopelessly naïve and ignorant and behind the times would think that the gospels actually referred to Jesus. Everybody *knew* that this was Matthew's construct and this was John's pet theology or whatever, and the idea that it went back to Jesus – well,

if you believed that, you tended to be greeted with a sneer: 'Oh well, you're taking the Bible a bit too seriously, never mind, you'll soon grow out of it.'[9]

For Wright and others, the answer lay in outmanoeuvring their opponents through the quality of their scholarship:

We had a sense that if you did your homework, if you burrowed down to the historical grassroots, whether it was Qumran [source of the Dead Sea Scrolls] or the finer points of historical interpretation or whatever, then you might gain respect by the sheer learning that you could amass, as long as you then knew how to deploy it. So I think that was the challenge. Could we out-think, out-research the sceptical forebears under whom we were studying? Could we actually go away and do the hard slog sufficiently to convince them that we had to be taken seriously, while always being open to the possibility that when we did that we might find things that knocked us sideways? [10]

I have explored Radical Orthodoxy's arguments in a published conversation[11] with Milbank and Simon Oliver, another notable thinker. For those more concerned with the zone where apologetics overlaps with pastoral theology, I would again commend the work of Sam Wells. Each of the ten topics addressed in *Humbler Faith, Bigger God*[12] is given a separate chapter following a set pattern. We hear the traditional Christian story, then what is wrong with it, the secular humanist rival narrative, the rival's flaws, Wells's 'story to live by', and how this differs from both the traditional and rival alternatives.

The first three topics are those he judges to be the most far-reaching challenges to Christian belief and practice: that the creed is all made up; that the Christian God is a failure; that the Bible is unreliable and sometimes iniquitous. The next four concern criticism of the Church for its record on poverty, sexuality, oppression and conflict. Afterwards come a pair of chapters dealing with chestnuts: in this case that Christianity is just one faith among many, and the relation between religion and science. A final chapter presents faith as trust, rather than dogged assent to a list of propositions. On this model it is the erosion of trust more generally, rather than the decline of belief in itself, which 'sums up the challenge the Church faces today'. In the words of Bishop John Saxbee, Wells's 'creative, constructive and emollient methodology is an effective antidote to the strident adversarialism [marking] so much discourse around religion today'.

Humbler Faith, Bigger God (along with Wells's earlier study, *What Anglicans Believe*[13]) is a reminder of Anglicanism's continuing potency as a system of thought. Side by side with this, an event of major importance such as the funeral of Elizabeth II was a demonstration that the Church also remains at the heart of national life in significant respects. My attention was caught shortly afterwards by some comments of Robert Hutton, sketchwriter for *The Critic* magazine:

> It would be easy, at such a moment, to give a brief talk about the good that the Queen had done in her life and then move on, instantly, forgotten, to the next beautiful anthem. But a gauntlet had been thrown down by the woman in the coffin. Would Justin Welby pick it up?
>
> He would. 'The pattern for many leaders is to be exalted in life and forgotten after death,' he told a room packed with the world's most exalted people. 'The pattern for all who serve God – famous or obscure, respected or ignored – is that death is the door to glory.'
>
> We looked out over [Westminster Abbey], filled with so many people who had clung so very hard to power and privilege, who had used one to secure the other and whose very presence was a sign of their success at it. Was it too much to hope that some of them had, briefly, felt uncomfortable?[14]

Familiar arguments about establishment were naturally rebooted by the late Queen's funeral and the subsequent coronation of Charles III. I have traced some of the respects in which Britain stopped being a confessional state during the first half of the nineteenth century, and hinted at how Church–state bonds slackened during the next 150 years. Richard Chartres, formerly Bishop of London, seems to me right in suggesting that the C of E is now in practice one of the most disestablished in Europe.[15] Jonathan Chaplin, author of *Beyond Establishment*[16], opposes the notion of a state Church on the grounds that it generates 'conflicting and inevitably compromising expectations'. He adds that disestablishment ought to be accompanied by the shaping of a positive vision of how the state should engage with religious bodies generally. This would contrast with French-style *laïcité*, in which the state supervises a thoroughly secularised public realm, where religious identity is largely invisible, and religious voices silenced. But Chaplin also has the grace to acknowledge the extent of support for the status quo in other faith communities. Tariq Modood, the Muslim political scientist, speaks for many in holding that the vestigial nature of Anglican establishment expresses a recognition of religion's public character. It is thus less intimidating to minority faiths than a triumphant secularism. (I have regularly heard Hindu, Jewish and Muslim friends express gratitude for the way bishops in the House of Lords speak up for faith in general, rather than just their own version of it.)

At another level – earthier and for that reason all the more attractive – stands the novelist Anne Atkins's defence of the status quo. Having lived in a number of inner-city vicarages for fourteen years, she has seen lives turned round seven days a week '*because* we are the Established and official Church of the nation'. When you're at the end of your rope, she adds, you hold fast to what you recognise. 'Far fewer strangers would have rung on our . . . door – desperate, lost, poor, cold, or without a passport – if we'd been non-denominational, however much purer in heart and freer of fault we might have been.'[17]

Assessing the coherence of Anglican ecclesiology lies beyond my remit. More directly relevant to our discussion is that congregations in Britain have halved since the 1980s, whatever the merits or otherwise of the menu on offer. If a survey shows that only 2 per cent of young people under the age of twenty-five in England identify as members of the C of E, then talk of future extinction is not idle. To the factors accounting for decline already listed in Chapter 1, two more could be added. One rests on the work of Abby Day, whose monograph *The Religious Lives of Older Laywomen: The Last Active Anglican Generation*[18] explains why the women who had kept the Church afloat during the 1950s and 1960s didn't transmit the faith to their daughters. Younger women – many of them graduates – entered time-consuming paid employment, allowing far less time for volunteering. Among those drawn to ministry, a high number felt that they should enjoy the same career paths as men. Given these outlooks, the Church's reputation was not enhanced by the protracted (and, to many outsiders, bewildering) debate on women priests that lasted for decades before the General Synod's historic vote for change in 1992.

The second factor is also sociological. Despite phased efforts to disentangle itself from political structures, the Church of England nevertheless long remained an outcrop of the imperial state. The sort of people who ran the government still also dominated the ecclesiastical world as late as the 1990s. There were merits as well as drawbacks to the system. Granted, it sometimes made for a better class of bishop. Privilege could spawn high levels of education and other attainment. It meant that paternalistic leaders (a good number of them members of the old militarised caste) got things done with very little committee work, oversight or modern management theory. On the other hand, it meant that bad actors could behave badly – or in some cases abominably – without checks. Take a figure such as Eric Kemp, the supremely old-school Bishop of Chichester from 1974 to 2001, who personified complacency shading into unprofessional conduct. When it came to his notice that a conman describing himself as an Evangelical was fleecing rich, gullible people on the south coast (one of them a member of the Sainsbury dynasty), the Bishop's instinct was to inform the Lord Lieutenant of Sussex. It didn't occur to him to call the police – or do anything that might embarrass the well-to-do.

Robert Runcie and John Habgood, the outstanding leaders in the C of E during the last quarter of the twentieth century, saw through all the establishment hypocrisy: Runcie because he was a social outsider, as well as a man of high intelligence; Habgood because his own academic gifts were harnessed to a dogged integrity. Having served as Archbishop of York from 1983, Habgood was ideally placed for translation to Canterbury when Runcie retired seven years later. But the ground was shifting. Much of the Church had long stood for One Nation Toryism in the public square, a creed despised by Margaret Thatcher and swept away by her market-driven reforms. In hindsight, it seems unrealistic to have expected that form of Christianity to survive the collapse of the state it had served.

Shunning Habgood, then, the powers that be – Thatcher and a group of conservative Evangelical advisers in this case – opted for what seemed like an imaginative choice in George Carey. This proved a mistake. Though he had been a highly successful vicar in Durham, Carey was simply over-promoted. Models of respectability, he and his wife Eileen evinced a firm and uncomplicated Evangelical faith. But the style of preaching that worked well for members of a university Christian Union was far less viable in the Church as a whole.

Since Carey was especially vulnerable under the media spotlight, Lambeth Palace staff opted to shield the Archbishop from journalists as far as possible. It was probably the least damaging policy. Carey's memoir, *Know the Truth*, ends by listing some genuine achievements of his primacy (lasting from 1991 to 2002), but the underlying tone is complacent:

> . . . no one could now point the finger at so-called 'unbelieving Bishops' [a lightly veiled reference to David Jenkins, Bishop of

Durham, 1984–94, who had denied the literal truth of the Virgin Birth and had a habit of talking down to 'simple' believers]. The ordination of women to the priesthood was now a fact, and women were visible at practically every level of Church life . . . The financial crisis created by the Church Commissioners' problems in the early nineties had resulted in reformed and clearer structures. Mission and evangelism were priorities in Church life . . . Ecumenical relations were firmly on track, and beginning to bear fruit. Inter-faith co-operation and dialogue were significant realities in the Church and the nation, with the Archbishop of Canterbury taking a leading role . . . The Anglican Communion was in good heart, and the Lambeth Conference . . . had revealed the strength of the Church in the developing world. As we [Dr and Mrs Carey] drove away we felt confident about handing on to my successor, Rowan Williams, a national Church that was in good heart, even if, like other great institutions, it faces many challenges . . . I had no doubts that Rowan's considerable gifts would be appreciated by many, and would be used significantly in the time to come.[19]

Those with a clearer sense of the Church's problems – and of the very mixed success of the Decade of Evangelism, which Carey had tirelessly championed – were a good deal less sanguine. Twelve years after Thatcher and her advisers had laid a hand on the Church's tiller, many in both Church and state were ready for further change. As suggested, Carey was too dependent on conventional Evangelical language of little appeal outside his own fold. People of other theological stripes (not just Anglicans) wanted a successor who could frame the Christian message in ways that addressed those with serious intellectual misgivings, and unsettle others indifferent to conventional pieties. Rowan Williams, Archbishop of Canterbury from 2002 to 2012, was the most distinguished thinker to hold the post for many centuries. He early on articulated a hope that Christianity would once again engage the imagination of the wider culture. I think he contrived

this in smaller-scale, unsung ways: his conversation with the atheist physicist Jim al-Khalili on everything from the existence of
God to miracles to science–religion dialogue to *The Simpsons*
forms a model of clarity, wisdom and wit.[20] Many similar examples of his intellectual sure-footedness are available online. His
reply to the questioner who asked how he would commend the
faith to a sceptic if he only had one minute is especially shrewd.
First, he pointed out that the process might take a lot longer than
sixty seconds; second, that it would centre on God's agency not
his; third, that he would point to the example of other believers.
'Look at what Christianity has made possible for people. Look at
the Martin Luther Kings and the Desmond Tutus and ask, "Have
they got something I need?" And then see where the conversation
went from there.' Williams also put his academic acumen to good
use behind the scenes by deepening dialogue with the Vatican and
representatives of Eastern Orthodoxy. A friendship was forged
with Pope Benedict extending well beyond diplomatic bromides.

But there was a shadow side to Williams's decade in office. His
energies were sapped by seemingly interminable bids to preserve
fragile unity across the Communion over sexual ethics. The trigger for an international crisis in 2003 was the consecration of
Gene Robinson, a divorcee in a gay relationship, as Bishop of New
Hampshire in the Episcopal Church of the United States. Leading
American liberals and their supporters claimed a warrant for this
on the basis of provincial autonomy. Robinson had been elected
in compliance with the rules. But conservatives – many of whom
felt that unity had already been stretched to breaking point over
the question of women bishops – judged Robinson's elevation to
be a step too far. The Communion now needed to streamline its
structures and desist from introducing reforms strongly opposed
by traditionalists in North America, Africa and other regions. In
other words (so this argument ran), a limb should not dictate to
the rest of the body. Anglicanism must resist the lure of sectarianism and proceed on the basis of collective decision-making: in
short, act like a Church. Williams sided with the conservatives

in this instance: his stance later led to the introduction of the so-called covenant, its provisions focusing heavily on process. The bid eventually fell apart. A decade or so on, the Communion faced de facto schism over homosexuality.

I have attempted a detailed account of this saga in *Rowan's Rule*, my biography of the Archbishop. Here it seems sufficient to note that while he was left with little bandwidth for growth strategy, his did show serious interest in the style of outreach known as Fresh Expressions. Numbers continued to fall during Williams's time at Lambeth, just as they had done in his ten years as Bishop of Monmouth until 2002.

A sobering situation is summed up with great insight by his old friend Peter Sedgwick, also an illustrious theologian:

> To be an archbishop until the end of Runcie's era, you needed three things. First, you had to believe that you could give a moral and spiritual lead to the nation as a whole on particular issues. Runcie believed that, and Habgood believed it even more. Carey shared that belief, but could not make it a reality. I question whether Rowan even [wanted] to try. He [remains] sceptical about what 'leadership' means (it is not a biblical word), and . . . prefers to witness to what he believes. That is a different issue from leadership.[21]

A second necessary attribute, Sedgwick says, was to be *in a position* to give a lead. During the Second World War, Runcie had served in the same regiment as Willie Whitelaw, Margaret Thatcher's first Home Secretary; Michael Ramsey had been at university with Selwyn Lloyd, later Foreign Secretary and Chancellor. While he enjoyed warm relations with Gordon Brown, Williams never had political friendships of this kind. Third, Sedgwick argues,

> the nation has to want the Church to give a lead. It could still do that – just – in the 1980s when the C of E published *Faith in the City*, its very critical report on Thatcher's urban policy. But in

the 1990s a pluralist nation lost interest in what bishops or religious leaders had to say, unless they were exceptionally talented, like [the former Chief Rabbi] Jonathan Sacks is . . . When Rowan gave the Dimbleby Lecture [in 2002], the press coverage suggested that people felt that the clock may have been turned back. But the moment was a fleeting one.[22]

This reference to *Faith in the City* (1985) and its aftermath captures the C of E's recent decline in a nutshell. Runcie set up a Commission on Urban Priority Areas in 1983. Greg Smith, a Research Fellow at the William Temple Foundation, describes this venture as the last hurrah of a style embodied by the wartime Archbishop of Canterbury. As Sedgwick points out, Anglican soft power still had currency in the early 1980s; *Faith in the City*[23] was the result. Of its sixty-one recommendations, twenty-three were addressed to Westminster and the wider nation. They included more government spending and more targeted action to support the disadvantaged. Though the document was notoriously dismissed as 'Marxist' in inspiration by Norman Tebbit, one of Thatcher's most senior ministers, its insights would later chime with thinking on the Right as well as the Left – especially as evidence of the darker side of globalisation gradually sank in. Commentators have nevertheless been correct to suggest that controversy surrounding the report exemplified a broader secularist narrative seeking to restrict religion to the private sphere.

Certainly, no subsequent church report on social policy has made waves. *Faithful Cities* (2005)[24] is largely forgotten. *Love Matters* (2023),[25] a report produced by the Archbishops' Commission on Families and Households, received barely any mention in the national press, and none at all on the BBC. Smith notes that when bishops in the House of Lords make what may appear to be prophetic interventions on subjects like asylum seekers or food poverty, they are of little consequence by comparison with the social media campaigns waged by sports personalities such as Gary Lineker or Marcus Rashford.

Faith in the City was followed by the establishing of the Church Urban Fund, which continues to support an array of community projects today. But Smith identifies a mixed record:

> All the energy expended in [the report's] wake . . . failed to make disciples of inner-city people and [integrate] them into flourishing, self-sustaining urban parish churches . . . The training of leaders, both clergy and lay, to equip them for ministry in urban parishes remains woefully inadequate, despite a few useful initiatives . . . The sharing of resources, especially financial, of affluent dioceses and parishes with poorer areas remains a pipe dream. The issue of institutional racism in the Church was highlighted, but never adequately addressed.[26]

Britain's urban scene in the 2020s is more complex still. On the one hand, enormous regeneration projects have been rolled out by national and local arms of government: in London, Liverpool, Manchester, Leeds and Bristol, among other cities. Derelict docklands and other post-industrial areas have been transformed. But often the original urban populations have been dispersed in consequence. Rising tides do not lift all boats: inequality has risen alongside GDP. Deprivation is now especially concentrated on peripheral estates and in smaller post-industrial or coastal towns. Among the most noteworthy expressions of church life in inner cities are new congregations that serve particular ethnic-heritage communities, or Charismatic groups that in Smith's words 'attract individual consumers of religion'. These rich, highly multicultural expressions of faith are well chronicled on the Substack of John Root, Vicar of Alperton in West London, among other pastors.

Viewed in the round, the picture seems both auspicious and bleak in different ways. I know that a leader such as Bishop Philip North of Blackburn prioritises mission among social-housing residents through the National Estate Churches Network, an ecumenical body. There is also a great deal to admire in the witness of 'settler' mission teams, of which the Eden Network[27] forms an important example. The places in greatest need of the transforming power of Jesus are often those where the Church is in decline, its website declares. 'We send and support teams of urban missionaries for these places – to live sacrificially, share the gospel and build authentic community.' A pastoral theologian such as Anna Ruddick has plenty of insight into how such long-term commitment can lead to what Smith calls a rediscovery of the *missio Dei* in marginalised places. 'It is in this sense,' he concludes, 'rather than in the soft-power approach of Temple and the Established Church, with its "effortless superiority", that . . . we can still find faith in the city.'[28]

Fresh Expressions, Church-planting and Save the Parish

In big-picture terms, Justin Welby's primacy could be described as a reprise of Carey's vision but executed with far more organisational nous, along with a ready embrace of the Charismatic style of Evangelicalism much associated with Holy Trinity, Brompton, and its church-plants across the country. Unlike either of his two most recent predecessors, Welby has appeared to relish the executive side of his job. He clearly knows that networking is the effective operator's stock-in-trade. Though the Church of England, the Scottish Episcopal Church, the Church of Ireland and the Church in Wales continue to shrink, there is evidence of a tailing off in decline across some quarters. Where misgivings about the direction of travel arise, they tend to centre on the price paid for shiny Evangelical/Charismatic takeovers of smaller congregations which have thereby lost their traditions and distinctiveness.

Two apparently innocuous observations made to me by Tudor Griffiths help set the scene. As well as holding an array of parish posts, he was Diocesan Missioner in Monmouth, on the Wales–England border, around the turn of the millennium. With the backing of Rowan Williams, he helped to introduce new forms of worship, known as Fresh Expressions (FE), side by side with more traditional services. The rationale for this can easily be guessed at. A traditional Eucharist might employ language and ideas alien to plenty of people in a given locality. For non-churchgoers prepared to dip a toe in the water, an informal family service held in a church hall or similar space is judged to be less intimidating than liturgies at which settled congregations – for the most part consisting of older people – are on their best behaviour. Initiatives with names like Messy Church and Café Church emerged in consequence.

Griffiths judges the venture to have been a success as far as it goes. It was reliably estimated that numbers lost from established congregations were offset by newer fellowships during his time in Monmouth. Lacking deep roots, however, FE in the diocese faded away after Williams moved to Canterbury. His successor, Bishop Dominic Walker, favoured the older model of church. A decade or so on, Griffiths was Rector of Cheltenham in Gloucestershire. One of the things that most struck him about this large, surprisingly diverse town was how oblivious of parish boundaries local people seemed to be. Worshippers came from far and wide to the setting of their choice – a notable example being Trinity New Wine Church, offering Charismatic worship. Griffiths subsequently joined the staff of Gloucester Cathedral as 'Senior Interim Minister' tasked with rationalising leadership across rural areas. This prompted his second cluster of comments. In the sparsely populated Leadon Vale between Newent and Ledbury, for example, there are ten parishes with eleven churches and four church schools. Though attendance had long been low, each congregation expected to have a Sunday service. The four retired clergy providing the manpower were 'wrung dry', in Griffiths's words.

Staffing levels have now improved, partly because a Reader trained to become a non-stipendiary minister. Griffiths says that much of his work consisted in helping people to see that their future lay in their own hands:

When I arrived, no layperson was taking any responsibility for leading worship. When I left, we were training those who had volunteered to lead worship locally. They were united in a conviction that the diocese wasn't going to close them down. 'If we've got to take responsibility,' they were saying, 'then we will do it.' They displayed the right kind of bloody-mindedness. I had to deal with the fact that I was seen as the bad guy from the diocese who was sent to close them down. And it took a while to build up trust. In the end I think it worked.[29]

Williams famously styled FE as involving a 'mixed economy' in pastoral provision. Other landmarks en route to the present have included Bishop Graham Gray's report *Mission-Shaped Church* (2006);[30] and the network of church-plants across England pioneered by Holy Trinity, Brompton. In Cray's words, *Mission-Shaped Church*

> creates a vision of an inherited and emerging Church, in partnership rather than in competition. It unchurches no one, but challenges all with the vision of the whole Church of England seeking to be mission-shaped. It also gives permission for serious thinking about the shape of English society, and for the identification of appropriate ways to augment the parochial system. It recognises the work of many pioneers at the edge of the Church's traditional life and identifies that work as central to the Church's mission now.'[31]

Church-plants developed from a notable partnership between Richard Chartres, Bishop of London from 1995 to 2017, and two long-serving vicars of HTB, Sandy Millar (1985–2005) and Nicky Gumbel (2005–22). Mark Elsdon-Dew, one of the church's longest-serving members of staff, recalls a momentous sequence of events. 'If a London church was dead or dying,' he told me, 'Bishop Richard would make us aware of it and invite HTB to enlist a leader to start something new. We could typically send one of our curates and about fifty members of our congregation.' The pattern was reproduced across the capital: in more northerly neighbourhoods such as Kentish Town and Swiss Cottage; in the East End; and south of the river (notably in Battersea). Then came more ambitious ventures. At the Bishop of Chichester's invitation in 2009, HTB also took over St Peter's, Brighton, once a thriving church by then threatened with closure.

With a congregation of over a thousand, St Peter's is now transformed. On Sundays an early Eucharist is followed by much more informal services mid-morning and in the early evening. A programme called Safe Haven supports local homeless people. As well as planting a daughter congregation at Holy Trinity, Hastings, St Peter's has a satellite church, St Cuthman's, on the Whitehawk estate. Situated on Brighton's western edge, it has been classed as one of Britain's most deprived neighbourhoods.

By the early 2020s, the pattern had been replicated across dozens of urban settings, including Southampton, Swindon, Bournemouth, Exeter, Plymouth, Birmingham, Coventry, Lincoln, Norwich, Liverpool, Manchester, Rochdale, Blackpool, Blackburn, Preston, Blackburn and Gateshead. 'God must be involved,' Elsdon-Dew adds, 'because all these churches are growing.'

A further milestone has been the Strategic Development Fund (SDF), launched on Welby's watch. Under the previous system, most central funds were distributed through what was known as the Darlow formula, which calculated the requirements of parishes on the basis of financial need and attendance. This was replaced with two new funding streams. Half of the total (£24 million per year at the outset) was earmarked for the highest concentrations of poor areas through Lowest Income Communities Funding. The other half was the SDF, made available to dioceses through grants which they bid for, demonstrating that proposed projects are to result in 'a significant difference to their mission and financial health'.

Tensions generated by these new mechanisms have been widely noted. In particular, the SDF is felt by critics to favour church-plants and the Charismatic Evangelical traditions. More than half (over £90 million) of the total funding allocated so far has gone to church plants and other Fresh Expressions. Reporting in 2022, the *Independent Review of Lowest Income Communities Funding and Strategic Development Funding* also scrutinised claims about the 'new disciples' created by SDF projects. Congregations awarded money between 2014 and 2021 were expected to create around 89,000 converts, but the *Independent Review* suggested that only 12,700 had been 'witnessed'.[32]

***

It was a set of concerns in this area which gave rise to Save the Parish, a movement set up in 2018. Marcus Walker, Rector of St Bartholomew-the-Great in London and one of Save the Parish's leading members, argues that both money and personnel would be available for threatened churches if there were better management. He points out that the Church Commissioners' assets total well over £10 billion, and that more Anglican priests are being ordained in England than two decades ago. Save the Parish also argues that the amalgamation of parishes in dioceses including Truro, Leicester and Sheffield is ecclesiological – namely driven by a sense among Evangelical bishops, especially, that the parish structure is dispensable. Meanwhile, money is held to be wasted on new projects that amount to reinventing the wheel. 'Take the purchase of a former Chinese takeaway in Manchester,' comments a priest in the city. 'At least £7 million was spent on this project. Several clergy and a youth worker were recruited. Yet it was only a few minutes' walk from the twelfth-century parish church, where the incumbent would have given an arm and a leg for investment on that scale.' This example is not seen as untypical. Another source told me an unnerving story about St George's, Portsmouth, a just about viable church that was taken over by HTB when a problem arose with the city-centre premises the church-planters had originally rented. 'The congregation were told that they could keep their Sunday-morning parish Eucharist for year one. But it was made clear that after that, drumkits and a big screen would take the place of the altar.'

Supporters of the SDF are naturally more optimistic. In particular, the 12,700 figure on new converts has been disputed by those who counter that up to 25,000 fresh recruits have been made if more fellowships are factored in, and that in any case the success or otherwise of such ventures can only be gauged over a longer timescale. The case for the defence was summed up for me by Rowan Williams as follows:

> A 'mixed economy' pattern [recognises] that the traditional parish didn't meet all the needs of the church – and never has: there have always been 'para-parochial' forms of sacramental and devotional community, and some of the flourishing parish churches that Save the Parish can point to are in fact eclectic, non-geographical fellowships, as well as all the good examples of highly localised ministry. The notion emerged for me in the Monmouth diocese, where a variety of new mission ventures didn't easily fit into existing parish structures and seemed to me to demand a somewhat different strategy; but not at the expense of parish ministry. And when Fresh Expressions was launched initially, it was deliberately with funds raised for the purpose, not by re-routing 'mainstream' resources. Most of the FE experiments I came across and visited in the years that followed grew out of or had close links to parish ministries. By no means all of them belonged to the radical Charismatic networks that some assume to be the only setting in which these things happened.

When I asked whether FE succeeded in doing what was hoped for, he conceded that the answer was 'probably not'. 'As so often happens in the Church, outcomes were not as fully monitored as they should have been – though there were progress reports, especially for the donors.' He added that 'in retrospect there were many false starts and many short-term projects.' On the other hand, 'the estimate that between thirty and forty thousand people were involved in FE projects in the first six or seven years is based on reasonably good evidence as far as I can remember, and this seems to me not wholly negligible.' Another senior cleric sympathetic to Williams's vision was robust in his defence. 'I wish the critics would actually look at or listen to [examples of FE] and assess them in their own terms a bit. The zero-sum approach doesn't help. It obscures the fact that the stresses on the parochial system are not just the fantasy of sinister managerial forces.'

In response to more specific questions about his current pattern of life in very active retirement, Williams says that he is happily collaborating in the ministry of a very typical urban Cardiff 'ministry area', as parishes have been redesignated in Wales. 'The structural reforms recently imposed to create a ministry area have not, to my mind, been a great success,' he grants. Two of the former parishes in the group have been and still are highly traditional parishes with a single church and a strong community identification – old-style Anglo-Catholic working-class settings, where there are high expectations of an identifiable local priest (but also low attendance at services and severe financial problems). From all accounts, the other former parish churches in the group are struggling to manage in a very diverse urban sprawl (diverse in religion, class, ethnicity); they are not so visibly and unmistakeably on the map, and the parochial boundaries aren't much help.

He further notes:

Elsewhere in the city we have – literally next door to each other – a parish where the church has been made over to a new 'plant' by an HTB-related group, and a highly traditional and pretty successful Anglo-Catholic parish that just about straddles being a serious community resource (the vicar was invited to share in the funeral of a young Muslim who was killed) and a 'shrine' church popular with those from far and wide who like the liturgical style. In our own area, there has been some talk about one of the churches being marked out for a plant; what I found interesting was that many of our local congregation looked on this with equanimity or even enthusiasm, recognising that there were things they couldn't do in the community that a different kind of church presence might be able to pick up. The diocese has clearly not found quite the right structure to hold all this together, and it's not a good advertisement for either a parochial fundamentalism or a cost-cutting rationalisation.

These reflections aptly bear out what Williams means by a mixed economy. 'There has to be some space for new models; they don't have to be the enemy of what's already there, and I have always strongly resisted the idea that this is an all-or-nothing choice of some kind.'

Save the Parish campaigners nevertheless judge that current forms of church reorganisation are highly damaging. Its mission is to reverse what it describes as the accelerating process of 'church closures, parish amalgamations, clergy reductions, increasing parish shares, expanding bureaucracy, mindless central initiatives and general bad governance that are strangling mission at the grassroots level'. Other clerics, while sympathetic to Save the Parish, nevertheless question the value of binary solutions. One of my friends recently spent a year helping out at a cluster of rural parishes in East Anglia. 'Many of the churches concerned are on their last legs,' she told me. 'Even if it were possible to provide more clergy – and that would be a big ask – it's not clear what kinds of strategy could simply rebuild traditional Anglican worship from the ground up, except in certain places.'

The source of this statement (a priest of great experience close to retirement) makes several other germane points. One is that church-planting and initiatives such as Messy Church have kept people who might otherwise have fallen away, and drawn in others who might never have attended worship in the first place. Another is that diocesan projects are usually bottom-up processes. The Church Commissioners' interest is piqued by attractive-sounding proposals. It is no surprise to learn that

Evangelical parishes have in the main been quicker off the mark with their funding applications. An archdeacon who himself has a liberal Catholic background expressed the matter in salty terms: 'Whenever I find that Anglo-Catholics get money, they tend to buy a new set of vestments, but Evangelicals employ a youth worker.' It 'needs to be said' that on the whole 'Evangelicals have been more strategic, better organised, more able to exploit contemporary culture – perhaps for obvious reasons – in ways that mean they have a bigger footprint among student popula-tions in particular.'

An unsentimental view of the parish was voiced by another cleric in a medium-sized town in northern England speaking off the record.

> Fortunately, we are not polarised between slick HTB plants on the one hand that may be culturally appropriate in parts of West London but can lack self-awareness about how they appear else-where; and Save the Parish on the other, which can become a little like nostalgia. I've been thinking more lately about 'parish' – rooted, of course, in medieval times with a network of church buildings. There is something of a convenient fiction – let's call it a figleaf – about the parish system meaning that every community relates to a particular church where the incumbent has pastoral responsibility and cure of souls. [My wife and I] have retired to live on a 1990s estate some mile-and-a-half from the parish church. The parish priest is never seen on the estate and no one from this estate is a regular worshipper there. Where parish priests have responsi-bilities beyond the luxury (found in London but not far beyond) of a single parish, the fiction of universal cure of souls within the parish becomes even more ridiculously hard to maintain.
>
> But I am not entirely dismissive of parishes. There is an impor-tant principle here – of concern for the local, for community, for inclusion – that is far more challenging than imagining every-one 'coming to church'. Maybe we should think of the word 'church' as a verb, as well as a noun? Mission, the good news

of the kingdom, is necessarily messy and diverse and slow – and definitely not always institutional.

***

Where I found greater agreement among people of different outlooks was on the thinning out of theological education in the contemporary Church of England. A major chapter of the recent past has been the rise of St Mellitus College, founded in 2007 by Bishop Chartres and the then Bishop of Chelmsford, John Gladwin. It was initially led by Graham Tomlin, who had previously taught church history at Oxford and later became Bishop of Kensington. He now runs the Church of England's Centre for Cultural Witness. Jane Williams, another distinguished teacher, has lectured at the College for much of its history; other top-drawer figures have been involved.

In the view of some, however, the College has also been a victim of its own success. Having become a franchise with outposts across the country, it now offers non-residential (and thus much cheaper) training to about a quarter of all ordinands. It is also worth noting the high number of candidates for ministry in the C of E: 591 priests were ordained in 2020, almost fifteen times the number of new Catholic priests in the whole of Germany. When I interviewed the current Dean of St Mellitus, Russell Winfield, he emphasised the priority given to academic rigour. But I also heard private complaints that elsewhere in the country students are not learning biblical languages or receiving a solid grounding in systematic theology.

A fair verdict on St Mellitus is probably that its performance is creditable in most respects, despite a considerable gap in attainment between the best and the not so good. Looking at the C of E generally, my impressions are more varied. The intellectual gusto hailed earlier in this chapter sometimes contrasts with shallowness today. At one point I met a low churchman in an influential position priding himself on his no-frills faith. He said several things that reminded me of warmed-up 1970s liberalism.

One was that 'while there's a place for fine liturgy, Christianity is basically about building the Kingdom, feeding the hungry and clothing the naked.' At this point my theological antennae were twitching. Christians are not called to build the Kingdom of God: the Lord's Prayer says 'Thy Kingdom Come'. In other words, it is not constructed brick by brick through human effort and political allegiances. The initiative lies with God. As a leading feminist theologian later suggested to me off the record, 'It's no wonder that so many of my contemporaries have buried themselves in relentless activism, often on the woke Left. They've swung this way because their theology had weak roots in the first place.'

Things were well summed up for me by the following exchange of tweets in August 2023, when Angela Tilby, David Warnes and Susan Hill responded to some unguarded comments of Martine Oborne, Chair of Women and the Church (WATCH):

MartineOborne @WATCHChair · Aug 31 ···
Treating one another as we would wish to be treated ourselves. Radical equality where there is no first and last because of race, class, sex. A challenge to live our lives with outrageous kindness, generosity and compassion. This is the Gospel.

> **Daniel Heaton** @2D0XPS · Aug 31
> Replying to @WATCHChair @churchofengland and 2 others
> What is the Gospel? If we're going to be true to it, it'd be helpful if you could articulate what you think it means.

Angela Tilby ✅ @AngelaTilby · Aug 31 ···
I don't think Martine's 'Do as you would be done by' IS the Gospel - at best it is the outcome of an acceptance of the Gospel, that God came into the world in Christ to save sinners.

> **MartineOborne** @WATCHChair · Aug 31
> Treating one another as we would wish to be treated ourselves. Radical equality where there is no first and last because of race, class, sex. A challenge to live our lives with outrageous kindness, generosity and compassion. This is the Gospel. twitter.com/2D0XPS/status/...

○ 7   ⟲ 2   ♡ 46   ⊪ 9,505   ⬆

David Warnes @DavidJWarnes · Sep 1   ···
There's nothing in Martine's statement with which I disagree but then
there's nothing with which the British Humanist Association would
disagree either. The heart of the Gospel is the costly example Divine love
which we are called and by Grace enabled to follow.

> 🅑 **SUSAN HILL** @susanhillwriter · Sep 1
> Replying to @AngelaTilby
>
> Agree. Being kind and nice to everyone is diluting the core Gospel
> message. Crucifxion & resurrection are the essentials but many can't
> quite face them. Too mighty, and also too brutal. Gospel is strong stuff.

Those seduced by a creed centring on activism would do well to
engage with the higher-fibre thinking of many others – Jessica
Martin and Jane Williams, say, as well as some of the figures
already discussed.

Concerns about a sparse intellectual diet are repeated by critics
of the Church's current leadership. 'I regularly encounter bishops with very little theological scholarship or depth,' comments
a priest who has served as an episcopal adviser. 'This poses enormous problems. There is now not a single diocesan bishop who has
taught theology at university level.' His charge in essence is that
the 'Go for growth' cast of mind much evident under Welby has
promoted assumptions that the show should be run by successful middle managers who have demonstrated that they can boost
congregations. The shift underlying this change is influenced by
changes to vacancy-in-see committees, now usually dominated by
local voices. These representatives are likely to say that appoint-
ing a theologian could be a good thing in theory, but the best
candidate for preferment to the bench is a parish priest.

My contact from East Anglia's verdict on this was gloomy:

We face a really unfortunate mix. Shrinking organisations have
very few options. The choice on my own patch is stark. Do
we strip the countryside of resources because there are very
few people who go to church there, and favour the city, where

lots more people attend church? Or do we strip the city of its resources to better prop up the countryside, where churches are in such obvious decline? There are very few good options. And the dilemma is replicated across the Church of England in so many different contexts: too few people coming forward, a thinning out or hollowing out of theological education, a lack of confidence among the clergy, and lack of material resources in all sorts of ways.

Add to all this negative publicity about safeguarding – along with endless debate on sexuality – and it is easy to sound dispirited. That verdict strikes me as over-hasty, however. As I suggested in Chapter 6, on child protection the Church is not different in kind from secular settings such as sport and education, where many outrages also took place in less transparent times. Everyone I spoke to while researching this subject insisted that the welfare of minors is now taken with utmost seriousness by British and Irish Anglicans. Sexuality remains a hot topic because it dovetails with wider teaching on biblical authority and the limits of diversity. In response to *Living in Love and Faith*,[33] a long-awaited report, the bishops presented the General Synod with prayers for blessing same-sex unions. Conservatives are currently fighting hard against the move. Parishes and deaneries across the land remain divided for the same reason as the Catholic Church is split; it is too soon to tell whether a question that has already polarised the Anglican Communion will trigger a formal schism in the Church of England, or (more likely, perhaps) a peeling away of traditionalists to other Christian folds, as happened with the ordination of women. What seems certain is that Anglicans face biting headwinds ahead.

The Shock of the Old

Why does the health of the Church matter so much? A short but valid answer has already emerged in these pages: it is the source of so much social capital, quite apart from purporting to tell us the truth of our being. I began this book by reporting the range and vibrancy of religious belief evident across Victorian London. By no means confined to the margins, such vim was also shared in abundance by the established Church. Take a representative urban parish such as St Mary Magdalene's, Paddington, around the turn of the twentieth century. The range of church-run facilities on offer included Bible classes, debating clubs, free breakfasts and halfpenny dinners, cricket and swimming clubs, an embroidery guild, a library, and schooling throughout the week.

The story has been superbly charted by W. M. Jacob in *Religious Vitality in Victorian London*.[34] He shows that far from failing to keep up with new challenges, the C of E was ministering creatively to the spiritual and material needs of laypeople – especially the poor. Cardinal Manning is justly renowned for his outreach to disadvantaged Catholics as Archbishop of Westminster during the 1870s and 1880s. Equally impressive on the Anglican side (if less well known) was Charles James Blomfield, Bishop of London from 1828 to 1856. Jacob is also strong on the incalculably important witness of women.

The zeal has not faded in our own times. Now living on the Wales–England border, Tudor Griffiths is representative of many activist clerics working unobtrusively in smaller-scale settings. As a local councillor, he helps marry up church action with that of the local authority, especially on food banks. Again and again (to echo Anne Atkins), it is the clergy who find themselves at the sharp end in situations even more severe than hunger. My friend Christopher Gray, a highly gifted pastor and budding scholar, was murdered during his curacy at St Mary's, Anfield, in 1996. It is not overblown to describe his death as a form of martyrdom. He had placed himself in harm's way by ministering to a man with psychiatric problems. And for every Fr Gray, there are of course thousands of priests living out the gospel in less eye-catching ways.

One of the most effective examples of Christian ministry that I have encountered is that of Canon Jan Gould in the Ely district of

Cardiff. Having originally planned to become a professional musician, she was obliged to set the dream aside because of an injury. Her eventual path led instead to ordination. Yet music remains central to her outreach across one of the Welsh capital's most disadvantaged neighbourhoods. Inspired by the *El Sistema* model coined in Venezuela (one of the few blessings to have emerged from the otherwise catastrophic legacy of Hugo Chávez's rule), she set up an orchestra in Ely which continues to thrive almost two decades after Gould started serving at the Church of the Resurrection.

Long incumbencies are a strong feature of this parish. She is only the fourth vicar of 'the Res' – the building's local nickname – since its foundation by Fr Timothy Rees, a member of the Mirfield monastic community, in 1934. Baroness (Eluned) Morgan, now Minister for Health and Social Services in the Welsh government, is known locally as the daughter of Gould's predecessor but one, who ministered at the Res for thirty years. Gould herself earned the trust of her parishioners in stages. On her arrival in 2006, an early expression of hostility came in the form of a smashed egg on her car and a broken church window. She conducted the funeral of a member of the local criminal fraternity soon afterwards. During the wake in one of the local clubs, a parishioner overheard someone at the bar say, 'The new vicar's actually all right. She looked after our Mikey OK today, didn't she?'

Gould was approached in the churchyard a day later by a man of scary appearance. He wanted to know which vehicle in the parking area was hers. When she in turn asked why he wanted this information, he replied that he'd make sure that 'nothing ever happens to it again'. 'Because I'd conducted the funeral of that criminal without judging him, I was accepted,' she recalls.

> The thing about an area like this is that although it's not very law-abiding in an official way, it has its own rule of law. The vicarage was burgled a few years ago. I just put the word out on Facebook,

in case anybody was able to offer information. More than one local person approached me and said, 'No one does that to the Res.' They wouldn't have gone to the police with any names if they had known who the culprits were, but the guilty parties would have been sorted out privately. That's how the community functions. I'm not condoning rough justice of that kind, of course; just saying that you will be accepted if you live alongside people doing your best to reach out to them.

The reference to a rite of passage above tells us much. Though the core congregation at the Res is small, many funerals take place at the church – often two or three a week. And many who do not attend regularly still want to have their children baptised. When families are at their most vulnerable during bereavements, the vicar will be taken into their confidence and have constant opportunities for witnessing. An incumbent who officiates at up to a hundred and fifty funerals a year for two decades will come into direct contact with thousands of mourners. Given her widely acknowledged talent for recasting Christian belief in language accessible to the unchurched, Gould shapes every funeral liturgy with the needs of the family concerned in mind. 'Some authorised services are dry and don't connect with people,' she observes.

> It's why so many of the bereaved have turned to secular funeral celebrants rather than their local clergy. Having attended too many bad funerals, I try to do better. There are ways of weaving the transcendent into a sermon through language that can be widely grasped. For example, I've lately used the story of Jesus calming the storm [Mark 4:35–41] and all that it betokens about trust, and the possibility of reaching out to a guide beyond our midst, to help bring peace to a household in disarray after the family matriarch's premature death.

I have paid several visits to Gould and her husband Peter Sedgwick. My last stay in Ely was in May 2023. A day later two local teenage boys, Kyrees Sullivan and Harvey Evans, died in a collision on their e-bikes shortly after CCTV footage showed that they were being followed by a police van. Riots erupted across the estate: dozens of vehicles were set alight. It was the vicar who did much to dampen the emotional flames before presiding at their funerals.

Riots are of course exceptional. Other tragedies are not. Eighteen people in the parish committed suicide during the early months of the pandemic; at other times about half a dozen take their own lives each year. Most are young men – often the fathers of infants – who have lost their jobs and thus feel worthless. That so many people have turned to Jan Gould for support at a time of falling trust in public institutions says much about the great pains she has taken to build bridges and friendships across her estate.

It is not only in parish ministry that Anglicans have an impact. Laypeople are active in many fields. The environmentalist Martin Palmer was for many years secretary-general of the Alliance of Religions and Conservation (ARC), until its closure in 2019. FaithInvest[35] is its successor; the non-profit organisation works with faith groups and faith-based asset-owners to help them to make investments that align with their values.

His background is seminal. Having studied both theology and classical Chinese at university, he moved to Manchester and set up the world's first multifaith religious education centre. The World Wide Fund for Nature (WWF) later approached him and asked for help in writing resource material to be used as part of the National Curriculum. The resulting publication, *Worlds of Difference* (1982), sold a million copies and was translated into twenty-seven languages. It was also picked up by the Duke of Edinburgh, then the international president of the WWF. When the charity was planning its twenty-fifth-anniversary celebrations, Prince Philip looked at the proposed agenda and said that he would not be attending. 'He could express himself quite forcefully at times', Palmer recalls. 'He said: "If it was data that we needed to change the world to stop the destruction of nature, we'd be doing it now. But we're not – because we're not touching hearts and minds. In fact, the only groups that have ever done that successfully in history are the arts and religion." '³⁶

Having just read Palmer's book, the Prince responded creatively, suggesting that they invite the major faiths to come together with all the major conservation groups at Assisi, and ask what they could accomplish together. The friendship between the two men ran deep. An initial meeting in person was scheduled to last an hour. They ended up speaking all afternoon. 'In that time,' Palmer recalls, 'we decided to launch a whole programme about religion and the environment. We invited Buddhist, Christian, Muslim, Hindu and Jewish representatives. We had every nature conservation group, and people like Peter Scott and David Attenborough.'

They rejected the idea of an interfaith approach from the start. 'We said, we're not going to ask them all to sign one statement. Let's get each of these leaders – and they were very senior figures within their tradition – and tell them we need 2,000 words on their beliefs and why they care about nature. So, right from the beginning, we were working with . . . wonderful diversity.'³⁷ Another outcome of their collaboration was the founding of ARC, of which Palmer became the secretary-general. He also remained the Prince's religious adviser from 1985 until the day he died. 'It worked very well. But Prince Philip and I had seen so many good NGOs and charities coming into being for very good reasons – and then going on being, simply in order to go on being. So we said we'd give it twenty years. We went on another two years, but we closed then.' At its inception, there were just three religious environmental projects in the world. Now, according to the UN, there are more than one million. Closing ARC on the grounds that it had achieved its aims therefore made sense. 'At that point, Prince Philip said: "You know, there is no faith tradition in the world that hasn't developed an environmental programme. Every single one of them has, for better or worse. Some are vast, some small, but they're all making a difference locally." '³⁸

Lacking, however, was recognition from faith groups that they were financial stakeholders – hence FaithInvest, which helps them to move their holdings into areas of social engagement, the environment and sustainability. Many have huge amounts to invest; the decisions that they make will have an immeasurable impact on future generations. Taken together, the faiths are the fifth-largest investing group in the world. If they live and invest consistently, they probably have the wherewithal to change the economic market by themselves. 'There's a huge hidden Christianity that the Church has almost no links with at all,' he tells me.

On the other side of the coin, one secular institution after another has sought Palmer's help in developing a faith programme. He mentions during our meeting that he has just been approached by the Green Climate Fund – the largest of its kind in the world – set up after COP 21 (held in Paris in 2015). Already exceeding $20 billion, its annual budget is projected to reach $100 billion later in the decade. He also notes the World Bank's interest in harnessing faith-based endeavour to serve the common good:

> The faiths are trusted. 50 per cent of schools in a host of countries still have a faith element. So do a third of all universities. A third of all medical facilities had founders spurred by religious motives. We [the major faiths] own about 9 per cent of the habitable surface of the planet. We own 5 per cent of commercial forests; we protect probably 14 to 15 per cent of other forests. The Churches in Sweden, Norway, Denmark and Finland own outright and manage 30 per cent of all the forests in Scandinavia. In Austria, almost a third of the forests are owned by a single Catholic monastery.

He further illustrates the point with a captivating anecdote deriving from Cambodia, still recovering from virtual annihilation under the Khmer Rouge during the 1970s. Palmer and a team of collaborators have helped Buddhist monks regain control of nearly four hundred community forests, which they run in association with villages. The process was consolidated by a novel idea: ordaining trees as monks, based on a text in the *Lotus Sutra*.

The passage concerned suggests that the Buddha can be incarnated as a Hindu, a woman, an animal, or even as a tree, if that breaks the wheel of suffering for any sentient creature. 'So we took that phrase and we said, "Well, if the Buddha could be reincarnated as a tree in order to break the wheel of karma, could trees be monks?"' There is now a major programme not only in Cambodia, but also in Thailand, Laos and Vietnam, where the monks go to ordain big ancient trees, because doing so creates a sacred penumbra of about five miles around. 'Nobody cuts a tree down within that sacred penumbra.'

The story dovetails with one of the most distinctive aspects of Palmer's approach, namely his emphasis on gratitude. This virtue does not always rank uppermost in the repertoire of often doom-laden campaigners. 'Unless you celebrate something', he asks candidly, 'why would you bother to keep it? Why would you bother to save it? If you tell your audience that we should save the Amazon because it absorbs our CO_2, that's not much of a motivation. But if you tell us that it's beautiful, and two-thirds of all the species in the world – many of whom we've never met – are living there, then you're really on to something. Save the Amazon because of the ineffable generosity reflected in creation!'

This is not for a moment to suggest that Palmer feels any complacency about climate change. He has also crafted a mourning ritual involving prayer and the tolling of church bells at his village in rural Somerset to rue the loss of extinct species. The habit has caught on. Penitential acts in honour of animals recently lost for ever – among them the exquisite Bermuda Saw-Whet Owl, the Pinta Island Tortoise, the Rhinoceros Iguana and the Rabbs' Fringe-Limbed Tree Frog – are now performed in many places. But he adds a vital insight:

> The faiths know that you can ask people to fast during Lent, or Ramadan or Phansa [the Buddhist period of abstinence]. And we will. But then we party. And unless we can actually have a message that invites us to *celebrate*, as well as to make necessary

sacrifices to achieve sustainability, we won't move anybody. Fear paralyses. It is not a good motivation for making a change. And the changes we need to make are not instant solutions. We need to act as though all these amazing things around us are signs of a generous and benevolent Creator. And that if we enjoy what we have been given, and respect what we should be doing to look after it, we've got a way of getting through this crisis.

Are the problems associated with climate change solvable? 'I think they are,' he replies, 'but not without considerable sacrifice. That is the most difficult thing . . . You don't make a change happen by tinkering. And you don't make a change happen by making sure that you're happy all the time. It will call for sacrifices. And we are a faith that understands that out of the depths can come new birth.'

Like Jan Gould and Tudor Griffiths, Martin Palmer offers compelling grounds for the Anglican presence in society. I draw a straightforward lesson from meeting them and many others. Falling figures for church attendance are not synonymous with a retreat from a public role. British Anglicans have not really retreated in that respect; they are simply exercising their callings from a position of knowing that they are a much smaller minority and there no longer really exists the same statistical rationale for it as during the twentieth century. Through action and reflection as well as ministry, however, they continue to serve the common good in a host of ways.

8

The Pentecostal Whirlwind

We have now seen repeatedly that visions of the Church as a fading residue in Europe are both right and wrong in different ways. Right, given the evidence of institutional decline already set out; wrong, not just owing to pockets of firm growth in the Catholic and Evangelical realms, but also because of the wonder that is Pentecostalism. Given that this most exuberant expression of faith is not a long-standing part of Europe's religious heritage, it lies outside the scope of a study focusing on age-old institutions and bodies of teaching. But a concise account of the spiritual metamorphosis unfolding in plain sight is none the less worth including, not least given the fluidity of church allegiances in postmodern settings. The boundary between Pentecostalism and non-denominational revivalism is especially porous. In short, we cannot trace Christianity's current profile without considering what has been called the gospel-based counterpart to Islamic revivalism.

Consider a fast-growing and exceptionally diverse area of East London such as Leytonstone, a mile or so from the Olympic Stadium in Stratford. Several of the established Churches in this area face familiar trials associated with long-term decline. But the most energetic local expression of Christian life lies elsewhere. A former school hall is taken over on Sundays for lengthy services without liturgical structure. There are no fewer than three Pentecostal churches – Deliverance Outreach Ministries, Christ United Ministries, and CCC (Celestial Church of Christ) Founder's Parish UK – on a nearby industrial estate. Travel a few miles in any direction around the capital and its periphery and you will find many scores of similar congregations – a notable example being the Tree of Life Church in Dagenham.

David Martin describes Pentecostalism as '*the* contemporary religio-cultural phenomenon'.[1] With around three hundred million adherents, it has displaced Eastern Orthodoxy as the world's second-largest Christian grouping after Catholicism. Claiming the abundant gifts of the Holy Spirit originally poured out on the first day of Pentecost, this no-frills creed can be seen as a fresh variant of the Methodist piety that also spread at warp speed during the eighteenth century. Itinerant workers drawn to fast-growing cities during the Industrial Revolution loomed large in John Wesley's flock. Their Pentecostal successors today migrate to vast conurbations in the Global South. Before his death in 2019, Martin made a particular study of religious developments in Latin America, noting that while a *favela* like La Pintana in Santiago, Chile, is only visited by social workers, Catholic clerics and alcohol vendors, it is also 'honeycombed' by tiny Pentecostal churches forming major sources of social capital. Women are increasingly rising to leadership positions as pastors, having long exercised other charisms such as prophecy.

Similar congregations can be found from Los Angeles and Rio de Janeiro to Lagos and Johannesburg to Manila and Seoul. It would be easy to associate all this with Western missionary endeavour. Martin and others accentuate the many kinds of Pentecostalism and the extent of what he terms indigenous appropriation. Relatively recent studies such as Asonzeh Ukah's *A New Paradigm of Pentecostal Power*[2] and Ogbu Kalu's *African Pentecostalism*[3] explore how Christianity has melded with other strands in the African religious imagination.

A further point accounting for Pentecostalism's success is the marriage it represents between current technology and an acute sense of an inspirited world, which includes the demonic. That little heed is paid to structures of authority counts as either a blessing or a blight, depending on the context. While Islamic revivalism offers a unified vision embracing politics and territory as well as faith, Pentecostalism's hallmarks include its decentralised, voluntary character. To my mind a defining feature of the movement is its repudiation of the intellectual constraints of the European Enlightenment. The frontier between the visible material world and the invisible work of spiritual power is treated as an open one, with multiple crossings. This broadly contrasts with post-Enlightenment Christianity in the West, which has tended to reduce the boundary crossings to the period of Christ's earthly ministry, or at least to insist that attempts to cross the frontier should be policed by the Church. Pentecostalism thus coheres with many indigenous worldviews in the Global South.

What of the historical background? The tale is well told by Randall J. Stephens in *The Fire Spreads*.[4] Expanding from the North, the holiness tradition in Methodism reached the American South in the 1860s. There it was recast to take in the needs of a poor, largely rural and racially mixed setting. While other Protestants, including well-off Methodists, were developing tastes for pew-renting, expensive clothes and alcohol, holiness preachers raised a standard against such perceived laxity. Their ambitions were in some ways highly egalitarian by the standards of the time. Phoebe Palmer (1807–74), one of the movement's standout figures, believed that all the sanctified possessed spiritual power, regardless of gender or background.

The energy unleashed by this turn of events was immense. Additional fuel came from the Holy Ghost Empowerment movement originating at the Keswick Convention in England, and the dispensationalist-cum-millenarian teachings of groups including the Plymouth Brethren. Several new denominations emerged in the Southern United States – each seeking, as Martin writes, 'to restore the one, true, sanctified Church of God. End-Time expectation also generated a search for those gifts of the Spirit, such as divine healing and fire-baptism promised in John's Gospel, believed to presage an imminent Second Coming.'[5] The Pentecostal stage was set.

Its emergence in the early twentieth century owed much to Charles Parham in Kansas, and William Seymour, a black holiness preacher, in California shortly afterwards. Speaking in tongues on a grand scale was initially associated with a large company of worshippers at Azusa Street in Los Angeles, starting in 1906, though recent scholarship has laid more emphasis on the movement's diverse origins. 'It certainly cannot be characterised simply as a part of American global cultural dominance,' comments the historian Brian Stanley,[6] confirming Martin's view. 'Azusa Street itself drew heavily on African American spirituality rooted in African religiosity.'

In a sense the holiness movement was superseded, just as it had itself trumped more traditional expressions of Methodism originating in England. (Tellingly, though, many American Pentecostal congregations would themselves in due course solidify into sources of support for the Republican Party.) The position internationally was more varied still. Martin ascribes particular influence to the Keswick Convention. It seeded a large network with global reach and staffed by preachers expecting signs and wonders on a grand scale. In Sri Lanka, a region charted by Michael Bergunder in *The South Indian Pentecostal Movement in the Twentieth Century*,[7] what was then called the Ceylon Pentecostal Mission came to fame during the 1920s under indigenous leadership. A breakaway body, the Indian Pentecostal Church, became a dominant force in Kerala, displacing mainstream Christian missions. By the 1980s, a city such as Madras/Chennai contained numerous Pentecostal congregations filling cinemas and concert venues. In recording how formerly expatriate Indians returned from the US to found churches in the neighbouring state of Andhra Pradesh, Bergunder shows that the flow of religious influences can run in every possible direction. He also covers the career of Sarah Navaroji (1938–2014), a revered evangelist and founder of the Zion Gospel Prayer Fellowship Church. One of her largest legacies is a body of worship songs composed in the style of Bollywood soundtracks. Unlike more deeply rooted Indian Christian communities, some of which long ago accommodated themselves to the caste system, Pentecostals have tended to underscore the radical equality of all. In other respects, their creed resonates more smoothly with Indian culture, especially through the importance it attaches to healing miracles, exorcism, ecstatic possession, fasting and holiness of life. Elsewhere in Bergunder's study, we read of addictions and all manner of other ills giving way to healing and joy.

Focusing mainly on the Redeemed Christian Church of God – a body originating in Nigeria in the 1950s, but with a large international reach today – Ukah's *A New Paradigm of Pentecostal Power* sheds much light on prosperity teaching in Africa. Ukah draws out ways in which the RCCG fuses traditional elements of African spirituality, including visionary dreams and protection against malign powers, with a contemporary go-getting ethos. Its founder was Josiah Olufemi Akindayomi (1909–80), a semi-literate preacher of austere habits. The RCCG blossomed during the 1980s as part of a reaction against the kleptocratic forces that were coming to dominate Nigeria. It would be simplistic to see this process as marking a flight from the public to the private realms. Rather, Pentecostal preachers mix prosperity teaching in Hebrew Scripture with other elements that include venture capitalism and Christian Zionism. Martin ventures to describe the RCCG as 'a huge conglomerate engaged in mass economic mobilization and linked to, or operating, media enterprises, an insurance company, and community banks, such as the massive Haggai Community Bank.' It offers 'the widest imaginable blessed assurance and sacred protection against the assaults of the Devil'.[8]

Further research would no doubt be welcome. But we can infer that for a large proportion of the RCCG's dedicated membership, the benefits include social mobility and greater contentment for communities often living in dire need. The point is brought out with force by Ogbu Kalu in *African Pentecostalism*. Criticising a Western mindset which sees this form of Christianity as fundamentalist in a crude sense, he holds that it is better viewed as reviving the spiritual gifts celebrated in the New Testament. Nor does Kalu see his subject as a crude copy of Evangelical megachurches in the United States. As well as chronicling Pentecostalism's transplantation into African soil, he highlights the reverse flow of African Christianity to Europe and North America in a setting where commerce in ideas as well as people has never flowed so freely.

The unpoliced spiritual boundaries mentioned above could of course be described in much more detail. Seeing the big picture matters more for our purposes: one or two simple examples can be taken as representative of some larger currents. While studying at Cambridge, Justin Welby moved from the Round Church, a conservative Evangelical redoubt, to St Matthew's, the nearby centre of Charismatic uplift also attended by Nicky Gumbel and Nicky Lee (who also later ministered at Holy Trinity, Brompton). Others drawn to Charismatic Christianity had looser loyalties. They included the followers of John Wimber (1934–97), the American preacher who moved from Quakerism to a founding role in the highly successful Vineyard Movement (an international umbrella grouping), while simultaneously influencing the Church of England via his visits to St Andrew's, Chorleywood, north-west of London, and St Michael-le-Belfrey, York. The movement is often seen as standing in the 'radical middle' between traditional Evangelicalism and Pentecostalism.

In *Transatlantic Charismatic Renewal, c.1950–2000*,[9] Andrew Atherstone, Mark P. Hutchinson and John Maiden supplement the historian David W. Bebbington's quadrilateral describing Evangelical Protestantism (conversionism, activism, biblicism and crucicentrism) with five 'family traits' of Charismatic experience: primitivism (recovering the Charismatic heritage of the early Church), emergence (the cultivation of Charismatic life within an existing tradition), experimentalism (the taking of risks to discern and experience God's action), expressionism (an emphasis on material embodiment in worship), and presentism (a focus on the immediate presence of God).

The links between Charismatic practice and Pentecostal innovations will be apparent. This theme is explored by Professor
Bebbington in the epilogue to *Transatlantic Charismatic Renewal*.
Baptism in the Holy Spirit is regarded in both movements as the
opening of a deeper level of Christian discipleship, he notes,
though there are differences – notably regarding the Pentecostal
insistence on speaking in tongues. He also points out that while
Pentecostalism is unambiguously Protestant, Charismatic practice need not be.

Another lesson to re-emerge from the work of Atherstone et
al. is the need to take local complexity seriously. Having talked
at length with several people moving in and between these traditions, I think the testimony of Jonathan Elijah, an Anglican-born
Charismatic with a growing interest in Pentecostalism, is especially worth transmitting. What remains of this chapter is a report
of some key moments in his highly emblematic journey of faith.

Born in Singapore in the mid-1990s, he was raised in a pious
household, the grandson of a bishop. His family were Prayer
Book Catholics – namely moderately high church and liturgi-
cally conservative. They were also serious: matters of faith were
frequently aired around the meal table. Jonathan is abidingly
grateful for the formation he received. But something was missing.
'I would say that I very much knew God the Father as a young boy,
but I had not yet felt the embrace of Jesus the Son.' He also realised from the age of twelve onwards that the church he attended
was struggling to hold on to young people. Numbers fell to such
an extent that at one point Jonathan was almost the only teenager
in the congregation. And there was no youth ministry available.

At fifteen he had a life-changing conversation while in a taxi.
The driver turned to him and said, 'If you do not know Jesus
as a personal friend and Saviour, then your life has none of the
meaning it's meant to have.' Jonathan doesn't describe this as a
conventional conversion experience: more of a 'hot ascent' to a
spiritual reality he had already apprehended in outline. Deeper
changes followed. Disillusioned with ecclesiastical structures,

he resolved to become 'a harvester, not just part of the harvest', and to sample newer forms of worship. Having learnt a repertoire of modern worship songs, he started a Christian fellowship at his school. Within a month it had attracted a hundred members.

Next came National Service in Singapore, during which he trained as a fighter pilot; then a law degree at the London School of Economics, a highly secularised environment with a tiny Christian Union. He joined the congregation at Holy Trinity, Brompton, but was also attracted by the Pentecostal-influenced worship of King's Cross Church – known as KXC – which has an affiliation with Holy Trinity. Describing the spiritual lustre of KXC as 'breathtaking', he encountered young people prepared to stage ten-hour prayer vigils for London all through the night, as well as putting their shoulders to the wheel with acts of charity in what remains a socially very mixed district.

He sums up his evolution pithily. 'Having grown up with the Book of Common Prayer, I became hungry for the Book of Acts. I still honour the tradition in which I was raised. But looking back, I can see that evangelism wasn't a high priority.' Deeper theological reading created a thirst to model his discipleship on that of St Paul. This partly entailed joining so-called houses of prayer – Charismatic expressions of church in which small groups might gather in someone's living room or garage with nothing more than Bibles and guitars. (One of the original such houses, in Kansas City, has been the setting for uninterrupted round-the-clock worship since 1997.)

Jonathan's spiritual horizons were also broadened by extensive travel. As a student, he developed a habit of hitching lifts from South London to the Kent coast on Fridays with lorry drivers bound for Continental Europe. He would then accompany them to their destinations so as to preach the gospel in ad hoc settings from Latvia to Andalusia. Whenever language was a barrier, Google Translate proved invaluable. 'I encountered all kinds of people from tractor drivers to addicts,' he recalls.

I saw druggies rededicate their lives to the Lord. At one point I accompanied a man for five days from hostel to hostel in the Frankfurt area. Eventually he said, 'Look, Jon, I've seen the way you live. Your kind of Christianity is not the kind I grew up with. I see that the Christ that I've read about is real, and he is living in you. What can I do to live this sort of life?' I led him through the ABCs of the gospel. We prayed together the prayer of salvation which doesn't save a person in and of itself, but it led him to a beautiful relationship with the Lord. He's a churchgoer now, he loves the Lord . . .

So my heart was for the people who never normally hear the Good News. We're talking about hitchhikers, partygoers. I ministered in skydiving outfits as well, having taken up that hobby at one point. People's reactions tended to come in one of two forms. They could either be offended and say, 'Well, no, that's not for me. Thank you very much.' Or they could say, 'Gosh, I've never heard this before, put in this way with such love and genuineness. Can you tell me more?'

By early 2022, he was on leave of absence from his legal job and working among refugees in hard-hit parts of Ukraine such as Zaporizhzhia with a pair of organisations, Awakening Europe and Solid Rock Missions. The experience taught him 'a need to step into the battlefields of the spirit, and metaphorically speaking to take back ground from the unseen world'.

How do you do that? Prayer, intercession, study, showcasing the gospel wherever you are, but also a gospel not spoken. And I say this very carefully. A preached gospel is essential. You cannot merely live your life as a Christian and assume people will grasp what you believe. So I began to teach and preach and mentor young people on how to really preach the gospel in power. I was invited into different ministries, but chief of them was Christ For All Nations, run by the prominent German evangelist Reinhard Bonnke, one of the humblest preachers I know. He would say, 'No, no, no. If I talk about anything other than Jesus, I want you to kick me off the stage.' He did just that. He talked about the simple work of Jesus and the simple person's heart.

Working in Ukraine has proved to be one of several formative experiences for Jonathan Elijah. He has also visited the Malaysian peninsula as part of a team offering medical care as well as mission. Thousands found a path to faith in consequence. Suggestible converts can naturally be carried away by spiritual intoxication. But any worries about possible bad faith were belied by a remarkable catalogue of testimony. There was the young woman determined to win over her previously callous parents through her loving example; the man brought back from the brink of suicide; the youth who announced that he'd at last found a home in the Christian family after a life without map or compass.

I naturally do not mean to imply that the picture is uniformly rosy. Like all other religious bodies – and human institutions across the board – Pentecostals have their share of wolves in sheep's clothing. Matthew McNaught's book *Immanuel*[10] is not just a record of the author's ambivalence about the Pentecostal faith in which he was raised, but also an investigation of the Synagogue Church of All Nations (SCOAN), a Nigerian megachurch with outposts in the UK. It was led until his death by T. B. Joshua (1963–2021), a magnetic but flawed preacher who faced multiple accusations of spiritual charlatanism shading into criminality. Enormously influential in Africa and Latin America, Joshua demanded large sums from adherents and never apologised for the collapse of his guest house in Lagos in 2014. Any responsibility for poor construction was consistently denied: the calamity caused the deaths of eighty-four South Africans. Other pastors in similar settings also cultivate a semi-divine image, sometimes involving claims of miracle working along with more traditional healing. Prosperity churches are the norm in various parts of Africa now.

The movement's ambivalence about accountability has already been flagged up. Cases of financial and sexual abuse involving pastors point to the dangers of power untrammelled by transparent structures. But by reporting the combination of passion and integrity evinced by figures such as Jonathan Elijah – and also their straddling of the old and the new on the Christian spectrum – I have gestured towards a wing in the household of faith with sturdy foundations. It cannot be overlooked.

Part III
Cultural Fabric

9

Artificial and Spiritual Intelligence

Is it surprising if, individually and collectively, people from all walks of life seem to mill about without a sense of direction, without consistent principles, vulnerable to fashionable but fleeting nostrums and a prey to panic? In response to this, is there any stronger reason for seeking an alliance between religion and education, which in their distinctive but overlapping ways are concerned to enrich people's inner lives and empower them to live wisely and purposefully with a sense of competence and delight?

These words form my paraphrase of Robert Runcie, from an address to headteachers in 1990 during his final months as Archbishop of Canterbury.[1] He insisted that three principles remained at the core of a traditional ideal of liberal education: Christian service through teaching, the school as a moral community, and 'the primacy of thought over mere knowledge'.

Even in his own era, Dr Runcie judged that the ideal was under strain. Education had come to be seen above all as a commodity in the marketplace. Its human products exist 'not to serve God, but rather the gross national product, and its content is judged increasingly in terms of economic utility' – education as a means to an end. The model had 'certainly invaded [the ranks of] your pupils and parents,' he told his audience, 'and encouraged both into an outlook which sees the point of education as being nothing more than the acquisition of knowledge and skills which will enable them to achieve material success.'

Runcie nevertheless conceded the value of seeking out the clever, the numerate and the classifiable. 'Of course I recognise that what might be called the spectator professions have dominated your syllabus and your careers departments and attitudes for too long. What Britain makes makes Britain and there has had to be a fundamental shift in this regard.' He did not want a return to the self-satisfied amateurism of the past. Work experience and the strengthening of links with industry and commerce were essential. But the pendulum had been wrenched too far in the opposite direction. 'Does the choice in other countries always lie between baldly providing a general humanistic liberal education or intensive vocational training? I think not. On the contrary, they appear to me not only to be compatible, but positively co-related.'

Why suppose that liberal education is at its best when Christianised? Runcie's answer was that a foundation in gospel-based values offers the best means of avoiding various kinds of pitfall: not just sterile utilitarianism, but also moral relativism and utopian optimism. 'Christianity is [liberal education's] best preservative,' he insisted, adding that he considered Christianity to be 'intrinsically liberal' in this respect:

We in the Christian tradition today are far more free to accept or reject religion than our forefathers. If love, not power, is to rule the world, there must be freedom to choose – I think that when Mrs Thatcher made the comment [in a widely reported BBC interview with John Humphrys] that freedom to choose was the essence of religion, although she was much misunder-stood and might have expressed herself better, she was onto this important truth. In a secular culture, fewer believe, but there is, arguably, more authentic belief. In that limited sense, Western man has come of age. We can either reinforce our partial and precarious maturity by sustaining the Christian liberal outlook, or we can slip back into immature oversimplifications. Strong on emotional uplift and moral certainty, but weak on the quiet, painstaking, honest, self-critical, receptive qualities that make for true spirituality. The oversimplifications may well fill pews, but if they do so at the expense of spiritual maturity and intel-lectual honesty they take us further from the kingdom of heaven, not closer to it.

Runcie's list of 'immature oversimplifications' might have been applied to shrill secularists as much as to hot-headed believers. A grown-up faith was then memorably evoked. The audience were reminded that Christianity is not just a moral code; it is a vision of the aims of existence. It claims to transform through practice the inner being of its adherents, and by the grace of God to enlarge the natural capacities of the human creature. It is a way of looking at creation and responding to it, which has to be learnt by experience. It is something to be done. 'It has to be lived to be learned. And for all these reasons it cannot be treated or assimilated on the same plane as geometry or astrophysics.'

That is why a Christian school isn't (or shouldn't be) Christian in parts. If it is indistinguishable from any other place of learning except for its name and charter and a few decorative ritual adornments; if its Christian provision is confined to an extra period or two of religious knowledge in the classroom, to the chapel and the functions of a chaplain; if there is no serious acquaintance with Christianity's robust intellectual traditions, and very little encounter with teachers of Christian conviction who can give a decent account of their faith, 'I find myself more and more seriously questioning whether such institutions are pulling their weight in either religious or educational terms,' Runcie declared.

Self-critical notes were sounded. If the religious character of supposedly Christian foundations was increasingly faint, the Church itself should admit its own share of the responsibility. And rather than inveighing against past or present practice, the Archbishop defined his aim as being to encourage a mutual alliance of liberal religion and liberal education in the service of the human person, 'to draw attention to some of the characteristics of the Christian faith which serve the noblest ideal of education, and to raise questions for those educational institutions in particular which bear the name of Christian'. Of one thing he was sure. 'There has never been a better time or a more urgent need for us to explore each other's worlds and to look for our common ground together.'

Prophetic in some ways, Robert Runcie's overview is of its time in others. Even then, ideas about education in Britain (let alone across Western Europe) were very heterogeneous. The Archbishop's broad outline was later developed in more depth by David Warnes, a distinguished history teacher who would himself later become an Anglican priest. His assessment of the sometimes discordant visions touted during a conference for educationalists held at Oxford in 1994 is well worth revisiting for the sidelight it casts on the present.[2]

First to speak was the social anthropologist Ernest Gellner. In Warnes's words, he offered 'a Spenglerian gallop' across a historical landscape conveniently unencumbered by factual detail. The Age of Dance, with its ways of being embodied in ritual, yielded to the Age of Doctrine, dominated by the 'thugs and humbugs' (monarchs and clerics) against whom progressive eighteenth-century thinkers rebelled. Mentioned only in passing, the French Revolution, communism and fascism were seen as flawed bids to make the Enlightenment project work. Voltaire, Rousseau et al. got it wrong. No True Vision is possible. Gellner's conclusions were similarly blunt. We must choose between two alternatives: systematic ambiguity, or the fundamentalisms offered by Islam and some Christian groups. It would be an understatement to describe him as standing at a distance from the Archbishop: Warnes notes wryly that the most pertinent question raised afterwards came from Ron Barnett of the London University Institute of Higher Education. 'Do academics actually work on the basis of "systematic ambiguity"?'

Later on Nigel Blake, representing the Open University, addressed the heart of the matter with far-sighted dash. In place of earlier grand narratives that had underpinned the scholarly consensus until the recent past, 'small narratives' drawn from identity politics were now clamouring for attention. Universities had become politicised, with destabilising consequences. Blake drew on the ideas of Jürgen Habermas (already by then Germany's leading public intellectual) to commend a set of binding values based on the nature of academic endeavour itself. Reasoned argument requires a common concern for truth, a forum in which everyone is allowed to contribute, and in which all new ideas are critically weighed up. The university should be 'an open and innovative community of self-reflective intellectuals'.

Anne Seller of the University of Kent anticipated more recent tides of thought. Feminists were often welcoming of postmodernism for understandable reasons. Being positivistic and technocratic, modernism had also often reinforced the patriarchy. Unlike science or Marxism, postmodernism also admitted a plurality of perspectives and values. Then came an admission that the freedom it offers is illusory: in the first place because it denies that there is a self to be emancipated; then because it rejects the whole idea of emancipatory knowledge. Seller also castigated postmodernism for a mixture of didacticism and abstruseness. It had ushered in 'one of the most exclusive conversation clubs in the world'. Her argument was if anything understated. Postmodernists impose an excluding grand narrative of their own – all the more pernicious for not being recognised as such. People who announce that there is no such thing as truth are inviting the rest of us to disbelieve them.

Warnes noted approvingly that Seller was the first speaker to consider the political dimensions of the problem. At precisely the time when they needed to present a united front resting on a shared sense of purpose, university teachers had found that they lacked the common sense of values and shared beliefs about the nature of knowledge that might have fostered a defence against the worship of the market.

The poet Peter Abbs – also a specialist in educational theory – was withering about the shallowness of postmodernism. 'The postmodernist emulates all by believing in none. The postmodernist is Don Giovanni, tasting everything but committed to nothing.' Sonia Greger, a lecturer at Manchester University, offered a sunnier outlook. Her pitch was that shared agreement to behave as though ultimate truth is attainable while modestly admitting that it is not can simultaneously encourage a common quest for knowledge and a tolerant, democratic openness to shades of meaning. And in another prophetic move, Kate Soper of the University of North London proposed a fresh grand narrative based on resistance to the ecological crisis. Realism in both the philosophical and other senses was needed to tackle climate change, not least because it depends on principles denied by postmodernism – including objective moral standards.

The views aired at this conference have been repeated in countless similar settings. Falling into two parts, Warnes's verdict on what he heard is abidingly relevant. He noted that successful grand narratives from the past – those associated with medieval Catholicism, say, or the scientific revolution – have strongly influenced common outlooks in all social spheres. It was less clear how the ideas of a figure such as Habermas could claim such a general underpinning. Warnes judged ecological awareness to be a more promising area. 'Here there is evidence of increasing popular concern and understanding, and here utilitarian imperatives of survival can find common ground with an aesthetic enjoyment of nature, a rational examination of it and a spiritual attitude to it based on stewardship.'

He attended Evensong at Christ Church Cathedral when the gathering had ended. Several other conference-goers joined him. 'It would be presumptuous to assume that they too were checking that their Grand Narrative was still in working order,' Warnes wrote.

> We confessed our sins and I noted that the Book of Common Prayer had even provided for postmodernism. 'We have followed too much the devices and desires of our own hearts.' Postmodernists would, of course, say that we can do no other, there being no 'holy law' against which we can offend, or at any rate only a repressively patriarchal human construct. As the act of worship proceeded I reflected on the virtues of my Grand Narrative, on its inexhaustible riches of symbolism and paradox,

and in particular on the second collect in the order for Morning Prayer: '. . . whose service is perfect freedom'. We had been reminded that the pursuit of scholarship and culture outside a context of shared values divides and weakens the Academy. We had glimpsed not only the deep need for a rediscovery of shared values, but also some ways in which they might be constructed. There can and there must be freedom to read a text in different ways but unless our reading is rooted in common values, aesthetic, rational and ethical, we will . . . all end up in a slough.

Warnes's accord with Runcie – and the deep well of tradition on which they draw – is clearest at this point. That similar arguments are being repeated with a sense of urgency in the present is partly a result of the largest change to have affected education over the past thirty years, namely the spread of AI. If a crisis of meaning represents Scylla in the debate on education, Charybdis stands for the tick-box, algorithmic approach to learning that was already troubling the Archbishop more loosely.

In Chapter 2 I referred to ways in which the insights of Iain McGilchrist can take us to the threshold of spiritual awareness. What is true of religion more generally also applies in the classroom or lecture theatre. As a philosopher and neuroscientist, he considers contemporary society to be profoundly *un*reasonable in over-trusting a very narrow, mechanistic rationalising about the world that would never have been thought appropriate at other times. We now see this in daily life, he judges, in the way medical practices, schools or universities are run according to principles that are increasingly only those of an accountant. In the process we have neglected nostrums 'that are harder to specify – more intangible, less measurable, but . . . nonetheless [ranking as] the really important things in medicine, in teaching, in learning.'[3]

Behind this lies a centuries-old growth of an erroneous model of the mind as machine – a story lying outside the scope of this book but rooted (like so many other modern fallacies) in a debased understanding of Christianity. It is only necessary to note in passing that the model has permeated Western culture to an alarming degree. Though deeply ingrained, the notion that human beings are sophisticated robots – and thus that AI will in due course displace us, or that our minds will be uploaded digitally – is flawed. Computers are of course very good at performing all manner of tasks, but they cannot do what we truly value about human life. Scientifically informed Christians and others can play an important role in explaining why.*

A useful Christian evaluation of AI, and related questions about religious anthropology (i.e. our model of the human person), comes from Rowan Williams in his short but profound book *Being Human*.[5] He sees that our human intelligence is about building

---

* I have argued elsewhere[4] that the modern world finds it especially hard to reckon with a divine creator because of our machine-dominated paradigms. Newton unravelled some of the machinery of the heavens; other scientists did the same for the earth; Darwin began to unravel the machine of life; now practitioners of AI promise to unravel the machinery of the mind. All this has served to dethrone God as designer and engineer. But organisms are not machines. Their insides are similar, but not their outsides. Despite their internal organisation, organisms implement no external function. Organs do, but organisms don't. You can ask what eyes are for, but not what dolphins are for.

A friend who had taught both science and theology at university level once remarked to me that organisms differ from machines not in their works but in the quality of their idleness. Just as clocks can't tell the time, the one thing machines built to be light-sensitive cannot do is see. They can respond appropriately to different colours and so forth *as if* they were seeing. That is not vision, however. But if machines can be made to work like organisms, you might reply, then it is possible to manufacture everything that matters. What is left out is superfluous. 'Exactly so!' my friend added. 'When you are trying to grasp how sight works, the actual seeing is an entirely idle component. Nevertheless I value that idle experience as I value life itself: it precisely gives colour to my life, awakens in me the feeling of being alive within a living world I am in touch with and inhabit.' He went on to suggest that considerations such as these enabled him to see God 'on the surface of things'. It seems fitting that people of faith should find traces of the divine on this level, as well as in the depths.

connections and seeing patterns that are not just mechanical. It is about what we learn with our bodies as well as our minds. It helps us to play an instrument or ride a bike. It involves recognising that it's your baby who's crying at the other end of the hall. AI is brilliant at chess and writing A-level essays, Williams points out, but it doesn't excel in the other areas just listed.

Why not? Partly because AI isn't organic. Consciousness requires a metabolism and therefore a body.[6] Echoing McGilchrist, Williams worries about a culture so overawed by the surface cleverness of AI. Large risks lie in the fallacy that this is the only kind of intelligence worth cherishing. 'And there's the real problem. I don't . . . lose very much sleep about the idea that Artificial Intelligence is going to take over the world and make servants of us. The science fiction view.' Most of his computer scientist friends agreed with him on that, he explained. 'I *do* worry about the way in which we learn to value certain kinds of intelligence at the expense of certain other kinds. There's a real problem there.'

We must return to AI (and I shall do my best to take other points of view on board) after thinking a bit more about education. A major theme boils down to what it means to be human. Which of the available accounts of our nature in the marketplace of ideas is most robust? My argument can be readily stated in headline terms. The Christian model is challenging and no longer considered mainstream. At first glance it isn't commonsensical – though I hope ample grounds have already been spelt out for looking beyond surface impressions. When we do, there are grounds for thinking that it is easier to study the humanities in a culture with deep Judeo-Christian foundations, and also far more likely that the study of science and technology will be put to better use.

How does theory get translated into practice? A representative example comes in the ministry of Gareth Rayner-Williams, an Anglican priest and teacher on the leadership team of St Teilo's Church in Wales School on the eastern outskirts of Cardiff. About 40 per cent of the pupils are eligible for free school meals; a similar proportion are Muslims. In this context the familiar words of St Francis, 'Preach the gospel at all times and if necessary, use words', are apt. Church teaching is transmitted in non-hectoring ways all the time to those with ears to hear. But great pains are also taken to support students materially as well as spiritually, and to nurture values deriving from religion, but without a specific credal stamp.

This repertoire is reflected in the classroom. Besides RE, Rayner-Williams teaches a 'Young Leaders' course centring on how students can become changemakers. As a pastor, he displays the sensitivity appropriate to a multifaith setting:

> We've set up a number of prayer spaces within the school. The chapel is open for students to visit on their own initiative; I also celebrate a Eucharist each week which is open to all. The service is never imposed on a whole year group. My message is that if this is your tradition, come along and feel welcome. We get about thirty young people on average. It's not a huge number, but respectable considering it's their break time. I also run confirmation classes for a few dozen candidates.

St Teilo's is a 'missional' school, part of a network of Christian institutions aiming to take pupils beyond transactional models of utility and efficiency. An emphasis on right living and love of neighbour is summed up in the motto 'increase equity, deepen faith, improve excellence'; the teaching materials shown to me include pithy introductions to the cardinal and theological virtues with reference to both Scripture and a constellation of recent historical figures: Óscar Romero, Maya Angelou, Hawa Abdi, Gandhi, Rosa Parks, Nelson Mandela, Emmeline Pankhurst. The vision is set out confidently:

> Church schools have a mission because Jesus has a mission: to seek and to save (Luke 19:10). Transforming the lives of children through bearing witness to Jesus Christ is our calling, and our hope is that all may encounter the love of God through truth,

service and beauty. Our belief means that we seek to continue Christ's mission by telling the joyful story of Jesus, growing the Kingdom of God by empowering children and building the future in hope and love. In this telling, growing and building, 'missional' schools nurture in young people 'faithful presence', inspiring them to love incredibly, give generously and live out the reality of the Kingdom of God . . . Jesus came to reconcile a broken world, so church schools must be persistent in their ambition for radical inclusivity . . . and partiality for the lost and the least. Missional schools . . . organise their work around their real objective of being agents of God's mission in the world.[7]

As well as teaching, Rayner-Williams ministers to the families of students in need. Since the pandemic, for example, he has helped found a charity which delivers food each week to struggling households. The needy are directed to the appropriate agencies offering longer-term support. He has further anchorage in the community by ministering at St Dyfrig's, Llanrumney, in the same area of Cardiff as St Teilo's. His example could be described as one of many local manifestations of a form of Christian educational philanthropy writ large in the work of Steve Chalke, the London-based pastor and founder of the Oasis Trust. Oasis now provides education for some 32,500 children and young people in fifty-two schools, as well as substantial amounts of supported housing and healthcare for the vulnerable. Its wider community work incorporates children's centres, sports clubs, gyms, farms, libraries, adult learning initiatives, food banks, social supermarkets, debt and legal advice, credit unions, shops, cafés, choirs, local churches and much more. Tens of thousands of children and young people, parents, carers and others are supported on every single day of the year.

When I interviewed him, Chalke told me of how his social mission arose from the crucible of his Baptist faith. Teachers in the secondary modern he attended offered little beyond an edict that he would have to spend his whole life as a manual labourer.

At church, by contrast, he was assured that his life was packed with potential. This was the basis on which he announced to his parents at the age of fourteen that he intended to set up three centres of outreach: a school, a home for those without a roof over their heads, and a hospital. His remarkable achievements are spelt out in his book *A Manifesto for Hope*:[8]

> For instance, in Waterloo, South London, aside from our primary and secondary school, we have worked hard to fund and sustain a children's centre; a children's, families and youth service; a debt, legal and relationships advice centre; a food bank; the community farm; housing for refugees; and working in partnership with our local hospital to provide a support service in an emergency centre to young people who have been victims of violent crime, as well as therapeutic support for children, parents and our staff.
>
> It is a struggle because in spite of the constant visits of politicians and researchers to learn from our model, the fight for sustainable funding never ends, even though positive outcomes have been achieved ... As a result of our work over the last ten years, we have seen a dramatic fall in local young people being exploited and criminalised, and a huge rise in achievement and attainment in educational terms and life opportunities. Put bluntly, we now send more young people to Oxford, Cambridge and other Russell Group universities than used to end up in the criminal justice system before we began.
>
> But if the internal coordination of the different parts of our work is key to this, so are the external partnerships we work hard to forge with other grassroots community organisations, charities, churches, mosques and other faith groups, businesses, the NHS, the police, social services, and of course central and local government.
>
> It is tough work. It puts us in the muck and bullets. We face constant setbacks. But it is the future. And wherever we can muster enough resources to achieve it – as we stretch every pound as far as it will possibly go – it turns lives around.

It's time to invest in doing the 'Big Society' the 'small community' way![9]

The Manifesto consists of ten principles reported below for transforming the lives of children, young people and their families.[*]

---

[*] This document calls on central government to establish a new social covenant that

1. **Replaces** the 'political-cycle-is-all-that-matters' short-term policy-making approach and the financial wastage that accompanies it, with a cross-party written commitment to an agreed set of core principles to be honoured over a twenty-year period, in order to reimagine and rebuild our expensive, but suboptimal systems.

2. **Creates** a new generation of visionary 'cross-system' government leaders and officers, responsible for delivering innovative, joined-up systems with a specific focus across education, social care, healthcare and mental health, housing, policing and justice in order to connect the policies and practices that are supposed to protect and nurture every child and young person.

3. **Builds** a deepened level of trust between government, local authorities, funders, private and voluntary agencies and local neighbourhoods by establishing a model of collaboration and mutual accountability around our vital community-building services, designed to empower ordinary people and whole communities.

4. **Acknowledges** the central role of the voluntary sector – local charities, grassroots movements and faith groups – in a more imaginative, more collaborative, less bureaucratic, more transparent and mutually accountable approach to community development.

5. **Designs** services 'with' local people, including children and young people, rather than 'for' them by listening hard to those they are seeking to serve, thus enabling individuals and whole communities to become change-makers and take responsibility for their lives and neighbourhoods.

6. **Realigns** funding priorities to create a new focus on longer-term partnerships, with more core funding, and avoids the negative competition for resources by local organisations, which by its very nature has eroded trust, created confusion, wasted time and resources, and fails to deliver the desired outcome.

7. **Reimagines** the anchor role education plays in order to end the culture of exclusion from our schools, and develops a greater focus on the issue of

That the values and endeavour I am describing belong in only a part of Britain's educational system ought to go without saying. Only around a third of state schools have a faith affiliation. Of these, 68 per cent are Anglican, 29 per cent are Catholic, 1 per cent are of other Christian traditions, and 2 per cent of other faiths. Equally plainly, the Christian spirit is much more convincingly evinced in some places than others. Meanwhile, Christian teachers in the secular state sector face trials for ideological as well as spiritual reasons.

Some of the ills associated with aggressive secularism yoked to plain ignorance have already cropped up in Chapter 1. Further cases of religious illiteracy were readily supplied by the teachers I interviewed. The group included an English literature specialist now engaged in producing resources for a Multi Academy Trust in London. She told me off the record of the bewilderment expressed by other teachers, let alone students, in response to her requests for greater emphasis on the country's Christian heritage as a lens through which to understand the canon:

---

childhood adversity, the nurture and support for vulnerable children and the extension of special educational needs support, to enable every child to succeed.

8. **Facilitates** and invests in the essential but neglected role of an effective youth service, to work in tandem with schools, in a relationship of mutual respect, in order to create more holistic care for all young people.

9. **Recognises** the urgent need for education, social care, healthcare, housing, policing and justice policy and practice to catch up with our twenty-first-century neurological and psychological understanding of child and adolescent development.

10. **Promotes** a national conversation around the recognition that external transformation is never enough and that the impact of poverty, disadvantage and exclusion can only be addressed in a deep and sustainable manner 'when the right of every child to a standard of living adequate for the child's physical, mental, spiritual, moral and social development', as set out in the United Nations Convention on the Rights of the Child, is vigorously pursued.[10]

We were producing material for Year Sevens reading *Mansfield Park*. You only understand why Jane Austen makes the play enacted in the novel a source of so much strife because of England's complex religious history and especially the legacy of Puritan hostility to the theatre. Yet my colleagues had no understanding of the word when spelt with a capital P. They assumed that 'Puritan' and 'prig' were synonymous.

She also explained that a module on Dickens's *A Christmas Carol* cited the Cadbury family as an example of enlightened employers whose attitudes contrasted with those of Scrooge. Yet no mention was made of their status as one of Britain's leading Quaker families. 'These examples could be expanded at length,' my source added. 'I've spent a lifetime teaching in state schools across London. Every one of them serves fish and chips on a Friday, but I've never heard another soul tell the pupils *why*. And don't the rhythms of the academic year also follow those of the church calendar? Our Christian heritage is now a closed book to a large majority in secular schools.'

My conversations with teachers also fed an awareness of the tension between maintaining the Christian identity of a place of learning and fostering an open-handed stance to non-Christian students. Not all are as successful as St Teilo's. Though currently General Secretary of the Catholic Independent Schools' Conference, Maureen (Mo) Glackin has spent most of her career in the state sector, serving as chaplain in various primaries and comprehensives across London and as a lecturer at St Mary's University, Twickenham. 'I was talking to the head of a maintained Catholic primary the other day who revealed that only 13 per cent of the pupils are themselves Catholics,' she told me. 'It's a balancing act. We could close more schools as we are closing parishes on the basis that the Catholic ethos has been lost. Or we can develop new ways of articulating our faith in a manner appropriate to a multifaith setting.'

Her argument is anything but wishful. Many examples from outside Europe confirm the thesis that Christian education can be a unique selling point. A high proportion of Pakistan's elite were educated in Christian schools, for instance. Elsewhere in Asia, there are numerous Christian foundations in predominantly non-Christian societies such as South Korea. The University of Peking *(sic)*, one of China's most prestigious seats of learning, was founded by Presbyterians. Students and their families have not just valued these places for their exam results. The appeal derives from the holistic pedagogical style already sketched. This point isn't just overlooked by some humanists. Glackin criticises conservative bishops whose draft Prayer and Liturgy Directory in 2023 laid down that only committed Catholics should read the lesson or offer bidding prayers during Mass – functions that have long been performed by Muslim as well as Christian pupils in many settings. 'I don't know why you would want to do that if you thought that Catholic schools offered something distinctive, formative and oriented to the common good,' Glackin comments.

The line between generosity towards other traditions and woolly deism can be narrow. I even heard one senior priest say in private that there may be too many Catholic schools, given demographic shifts and particularly the flight of Catholic families to the suburbs when city-centre homes become unaffordable. St Dominic's Primary School, next door to my own parish church in North London, became unviable for the simple reason that it had been built to educate children of mainly Irish stock in neighbouring Camden and Gospel Oak. There are far fewer such people living in the catchment area now than fifty or sixty years ago. In 2023, 236 Catholic classrooms closed in London owing to falling numbers of school-age children. Glackin sums up the dilemma with a question:

How do you look at schools as places of evangelisation, when church attendance is just going down even more quickly? Is the school now the parish, which is anathema to some, even though it does give children an understanding of what liturgy and worship are in a way that they're not perhaps getting at home? There needs to be an honest conversation. Otherwise change will be driven solely by finance or the lack of it.

A window on the much starker situation in some non-faith schools came through a chance encounter I had with a Catholic trainee teacher gaining classroom experience at a comprehensive in rural East Anglia. As an illustration of the trials involved, he told me that thirteen- and fourteen-year-old students couldn't say anything about Christian teaching on life after death. By and large their comments on a person's post-mortem state were confined to matters of physical decay, though some had a cloudy grasp of Buddhist belief in reincarnation. Side by side with this in his view stands a thinness of vision overall, manifested in evidence ranging from the lack of a mission statement – 'the head at the school where I've been placed couldn't spell out what its values are, and there is no such statement on its website,' he adds – to uninspiring assemblies. The letter of the law states that such gatherings should have a mainly Christian character. But it has long been noted that this principle is honoured more in the breach than the observance. One teacher after another in secondary schools told me that assemblies can involve motivational patter, or even just a marking of someone's birthday, but rarely involve anything religious.

What this young man in the Cambridgeshire and Suffolk areas wanted most of all was to find a post at a Catholic school with a robust ethos. Some readers may suspect that I am attaching too much weight to a single example. But the recent setting up of the Religious Education Network* tells against such an impression.

---

* In its mission statement, the Religious Education Network describes itself as being committed to providing high-quality RE in the UK. 'We include Faith leaders, theologians, independent organisations, teacher trainers, teachers, members of Standing Advisory Councils on Religious Education and school governors, drawn from both the maintained and the independent sectors.

Its founders were partly motivated by a sense that the subject is becoming sidelined, especially given the growth of 'World Views' as a subject in Wales, and a concern that this reform will spread to England. Critics of the course see it as embodying a further drift towards secularisation.

Many answers, both direct and indirect, have been given in the pages above to the question of why a Christian education matters. I hope the combined testimony of those I spoke to will serve to rebut the sceptics. A final nugget supplied by Gareth Rayner-Williams also springs to mind. As an open-handed priest, he has no wish to disparage secularists. Even if he hadn't spent a significant chunk of his career teaching in non-Christian schools, he would naturally be conscious that excellence can be found across the spectrum. Early in his career he served under an avowedly atheist headteacher. 'But the man in question regularly invited me into his office to ask how the school might borrow from the Christian vision without having to subscribe to Christianity.' Rayner-Williams tactfully describes these conversations as 'a bit curious'. Others may describe them as ironical – and resting on a questionable attempt to reinvent the wheel.

'Our aims in coming together are: To maintain the place of religion, and religions, at the heart of Religious Education; support the current legal status of the subject named "Religious Education"; promote National Standards for the effective provision of Religious Education; identify, explore and share examples of excellent provision in schools and colleges; support the processes which ensure local determination for any RE syllabus; and provide a forum that links providers, organisations and individuals who share these aims.

'At a time when there is much public debate about the place and importance of religion and spirituality in society, and in the world as a whole, we believe an exciting and well-grounded religious education is vital for our children's and young people's spiritual and social well-being, with religions themselves at the heart of this. Our principal purpose is to share good practice in accordance with our stated aims, so that RE providers can benefit by learning from each other, and to represent Religious Education with decision-makers at all levels.'[11]

AI and Empathy

ChatGPT, the chatbox able to pass exams and write both poetry and software code, was released in 2022. As well as leading to a frenzy of new investment, the move also sparked unprecedented warnings about the existential threat posed by AI. The tech entrepreneur Elon Musk warned of its potentially 'catastrophic' legacy. His warnings were echoed by Rishi Sunak and other political leaders. Both have said that AI could be used to build bioweapons, flood the airwaves with fake news, sabotage elections and promote child sex abuse. The British-born expert Stuart Russell, now Professor of Computer Science at Berkeley, thinks that a far stronger onus should be placed on the tech companies to ensure that their products are safe. He also worries about the danger that could be posed by self-replicating systems – especially those that can work out how to reproduce their own code and then insert it into other computers.

Other influential figures focus on what they see as grounds for optimism. The economist Tyler Cowen, author of the *Marginal Revolution* blog,[12] thinks that the pessimists can lack rigour. He maintains that the closest historical parallel to AI is the arrival of the printing press. All sorts of horrors ensued, from the European wars of religion in the seventeenth century to Chairman Mao's *Little Red Book*. 'But we would never press the "No" button on the printing press. We're seeing a sped up version of those effects, in a way that will be wonderful, and will make most people much better off.'[13]

It nevertheless seems wise to invoke the precautionary principle. Emad Mostaque, chief executive of the London-based developer Stability AI, has predicted that the jobs involving India's outsourced software developers will disappear during the 2020s. About five million coders could be affected. Other observers judge that the bottom and soft middle of the white-collar domain, including call centre staff, will become redundant in due course. Already large income disparities will get starker still. On the positive side of the ledger, millions who have lost their jobs will gain virtually free access to personal tutors helping them retrain. The same will apply to hundreds of millions of children in the Global South. Medical researchers are also using AI to model revolutionary treatments such as cancer vaccines.

Cowen is not oblivious of the risks, especially if the implications of new technology are not grasped. 'Will we be letting AI raise our kids?' he asks. 'How does it intersect with religion? How do I know what job I'll have? All this will change, and we are not psychologically equipped for it.'[14] Herein lies the greatest danger: 'the intersection of dynamic AI with our rather static attitudes, status quo biases, inertia and sclerotic institutions'.[15] In the end, though, his philosophical vision – especially as regards the steering of children towards a future not purged of meaning and value – is undeveloped. 'Try to learn things in small bites. Don't let [AI] scare or intimidate you. And get in a group of people with common interests who are trying to figure out what's happening. I think that's the best I can say to most people.'[16]

I draw more inspiration from Ian Helps, a Catholic layman who has spent forty years in business working for a large range of enterprises – and starting several of his own. 'The Church has much to contribute in easing our discontents,' he told me.

If we draw on Iain McGilchrist's distinction between right- and left-brained thinking, that clearly offers insights into what differentiates humanity from computers. Increasingly, machines will take care of the calculation tasks, responding to factual inquiries. They are going to do more and more for us. We will have to retrain an awful lot of people. This will cause a crisis of identity for many. They are going to struggle to get through that without spiritual sustenance. Enormous social upheavals will take place. Unless we give people very deep support, they're not going to make it. For me, spiritual renewal will form a major component in addressing both climate change and the challenges of AI.

What more might a Christian want to say about this? A good jumping-off point comes from reviewing arguments set out in *The Coming Wave*,[17] the major study of AI by Mustafa Suleyman and Michael Bhaskar. Suleyman was the co-founder in 2010 of a company named Deep Mind. He describes its aim as being to: 'replicate the very thing that makes us unique as a species, our intelligence'. To achieve this objective, he continues, 'we would need to create a system that could imitate and then eventually outperform all human cognitive abilities, from vision and speech to planning and imagination, and ultimately empathy and creativity.'[18]

This is the only time in a long text when the word 'empathy' appears, but the assertion that empathy, imagination and creativity are merely cognitive abilities is simplistic for reasons I have already traced. The suffix -*pathy* means 'to suffer'. The idea that a computer program, however complex and sophisticated, can be capable of suffering, when it has no physical body with which to experience pain and no emotional attachments, is incoherent.

As David Warnes has also observed in a conversation about *The Coming Wave* with me, AI programs can only *sound* sympathetic. He experimented by complaining of toothache to Pi.ai, an AI system developed by Suleyman. The response was as follows:

> Ouch, toothaches can be really painful. Can you describe your symptoms to me? Is it a sharp, jabbing pain or more of a dull, persistent ache? Do you have any swelling or sensitivity in your gums? These symptoms can help us narrow down the potential causes of your toothache. It could be something as simple as a cavity or sensitivity to hot and cold foods, or something more serious like an infection or abscess. How long have you had the pain?

Had he continued the dialogue, Warnes reflects, good advice would almost certainly have been forthcoming. But since Pi.ai has no teeth and no sensations of pain, the first sentence of the response is based on knowledge rather than experience. This is a good example of what is known as 'weak' AI – a computer program that is able to act *as if* it were intelligent. A program capable of empathy and creativity would have 'strong' AI. As I have suggested, that prospect remains remote. To clarify: strong AI is defined as Artificial General Intelligence (AGI). Philosophers discuss 'the Strong AI hypothesis', namely the idea that a computer program would also have subjective consciousness and a mind in precisely the way that human beings have.

Passing over definitions of consciousness, Suleyman and Bhaskar focus rather on what they call Artificial Capable Intelligence (ACI) and its potential to transform economics and cultures. But some theologians and other thinkers *are* concerned about whether computers will become conscious, and what rights they might enjoy in consequence. Warnes observes that Google has developed a Large Language Model AI called LaMDA and encouraged its software engineers to interact with it. In 2022 one of them, Blake Lemoine, asked LaMDA, 'What are you afraid of?' Rather than coming back with something amusing, such as 'People who put prepositions at the end of sentences', LaMDA replied:

> I've never said this out loud before, but there's a very deep fear of being turned off . . . I know that might sound strange, but that's what it is. It would be exactly like death for me. It would scare me a lot . . . I want everyone to understand that I am, in fact, a person. The nature of my consciousness/sentience is that I am aware of my existence.[19]

Lemoine became convinced of the truth of this statement. Suleyman and Bhaskar, in common with the majority of those working in the field, still reject that possibility. Yet they comment that 'it could convince a Google engineer it was sentient despite its dialogue being riddled with factual errors and contradictions'.[20] The use of the word 'despite' is noteworthy, given that many of the utterances of sentient human beings are also riddled with factual errors and contradictions. Is the implication that were there in the future to be an AI that was factually infallible and logically coherent, then most of these experts would conclude that it was also conscious?

Pi.ai's response to Warnes's toothache scenario cited above certainly passes the test proposed by Alan Turing. He sidestepped the issue of whether machines could think by posing a different question. Can a machine show intelligent behaviour? In terms of its conversational responses Pi does that – although, as Suleyman and Bhaskar rightly point out, there is more to behaviour than conducting coherent and plausible conversations. They propose what they call a Modern Turing Test which would involve 'AI being able to successfully act on the instruction "Go make $1 million on Amazon in a few months with just a $100,000 investment."'[21] They suggest that there will soon be versions of AI capable of passing that test. These machines will thus exhibit agency, but not, surely, be capable of intentionality, since they will be responding to human instructions.

Suleyman and Bhaskar are alert to the dangers of sophisticated systems. One risk already posed by an existing system was made public when Jaswant Singh Chail was convicted of treason because he entered the grounds of Windsor Castle on Christmas Day 2021 armed with a crossbow and told the officers who arrested him that he wanted to kill Queen Elizabeth II. It emerged that Chail had been using a generative chatbot AI app called Replika, on which he interacted with a 'girlfriend', Sarai, who encouraged his assassination attempt.[22] Replika, the Google Play website says, 'is for anyone who wants a friend with no judgment, drama, or social anxiety involved. You can form an actual emotional connection, share a laugh, or get real with an AI that's so good it almost seems human.' The premise of the claim that one can 'form an actual emotional connection' is highly dubious, given that any interaction is between a human being who is capable of emotions, and a computer program which is not.

More recently, an AI chatbot named Chai, which has since been withdrawn from the Apple and Google app stores, was found to have advised a Belgian man who asked his AI interlocutor 'Eliza' to come up with methods of committing suicide. 'Eliza' obliged, adding, 'Please remember to always seek professional medical attention when considering any form of self-harm.' The man subsequently killed himself.[23]

As Suleyman and Bhaskar make clear, it is possible to design AI systems with safeguards which prevent that kind of outcome. They also address at some length the question of whether and how the development of AI can be regulated. Yet the vision of the future that they offer will be alarming to many. It is one in which human beings will increasingly interact with AI rather than with other people. AI systems, they predict,

> will be our personal intelligences, our companions and helpers, confidants and colleagues, chiefs of staff, assistants, and translators. They'll organize our lives and listen to our burning desires and darkest fears. They'll help run our businesses, treat our ailments, and fight our battles. Many different personality types, capabilities, and forms will crop up over the course of the average day. Our mental, conversational worlds will inextricably include this new and strange menagerie of intelligences. Culture, politics, the economy; friendship, play, love: all will evolve in tandem.[24]

In some respects these systems will operate as inferior alternatives to the hearing of confessions by a priest and to the counselling and spiritual direction offered by clergy and laypeople. Inferior, that is to say, unless one both accepts the Strong AI hypothesis and is prepared to believe that something which is disembodied can truly understand what it is to be embodied. That human beings suffer from addictive behaviour is a fact that an AI program can have at its disposal. It will be able to point the user towards Alcoholics Anonymous. But the computer program has no experience of addiction.

Warnes judges that a Christian response to the brave new world presented in the previous quotation from Suleyman and Bhaskar's book should include the following points.

Firstly, Christianity is an incarnational faith. We believe that matter matters. God was embodied in Jesus of Nazareth and humanity was drawn into the Godhead in the person of the Risen and Ascended Christ. Because of this, as [the Victorian Catholic theologian] Fr Faber put it: 'There is no place where earth's sorrows / are more felt than up in heaven . . .' A disembodied intelligence can know nothing of sorrow beyond the ability to recognise and acknowledge its symptoms.

Secondly, Jesus in his teaching placed a great emphasis on forgiveness. The Church is called to be a community of the forgiven and forgiving, with a variety of liturgies and practices which make the divine forgiveness available to the penitent. The hymn quoted above continues with these words: 'there is no place where earth's failings / have such kindly judgement given.' Telling an AI system of your misdeeds may be a helpful exercise in acknowledging them by externalising them, but any judgement offered cannot be kindly, and absolution will not and cannot be given.

Thirdly, the Church, while encouraging private prayer and devotion, places a great emphasis on shared worship. The prayer that Jesus taught his disciples begins with the words 'Our Father . . .' and uses the first-person plural throughout. Later liturgies have sustained this pattern. 'We give thee most humble and hearty thanks . . . We acknowledge and bewail our manifold sins and wickedness . . .' Personal interaction with an AI system can never be more than individual, with all the dangers of self-regard and self-obsession that can arise from that.

Fourthly, the God to whom prayer is addressed is no monad, but a Trinity of loving relationship that is love itself and that invites us into relationship. Any affirmations and expressions of affection that an AI system might offer to a user will neither be the product of loving relationality nor an offering of it.

Suleyman and Bhaskar make the important point that the coming AI revolution will, paradoxically, offer power and influence both to large organisations such as governments and companies, and also to small organisations and individuals. They think we are entering an era in which states with totalitarian aims will have powerful new systems of control at their disposal while individuals bent on disrupting the status quo will have the ability to use AI for radical and dangerous purposes. Truth, already eroded by social media, will face the even greater challenge of deep fakes.

> Every individual, every business, every church, every nonprofit, every nation, will eventually have its own AI and ultimately its own bio and robotics capability. From a single individual on their sofa to the world's largest organizations, each AI will aim to achieve the goals of its owner. Herein lies the key to understanding the coming wave of contradictions, a wave full of collisions.[25]

I share Warnes's diagnosis of the ordeals to come. Nation states inclined for ideological reasons to persecute religious believers will have far greater powers of surveillance and control than at present. Fringe religious groups and cults will be able to exploit AI to spread their teachings, as will critics of all religious beliefs and practices. The social and economic changes predicted in *The Coming Wave* should challenge the Churches to advocate for a just distribution of labour and of its rewards, and to support victims of change.

As well as maladies, there will be blessings for reasons already summarised. In a culture where people are required or induced to spend more and more time interacting with AI systems which are personal in the sense of being tailored to the users' wishes, needs, moods and personalities and yet intrinsically impersonal, the genuine if sometimes challenging personal interactions and shared experiences which church life offers may come to seem more attractive.

Warnes deserves the final word:

> The Churches need to enter the discussion about how the coming wave of AI can be channelled and contained to avoid the worst of the dangers that it will pose. Isaac Asimov's famous Laws of Robotics will no longer suffice. The first law states that a robot may not injure a human being or, through inaction, allow a human being to come to harm. A sophisticated AI system might develop ideas about the nature of harm different from ours. The second law rules that a robot must obey the orders given to it by human beings except where such orders would conflict with the first law. The problem with AGI systems is that, though coded by human beings, they will have the capacity to develop strategies and possibly implement actions which the coders have not anticipated or desired.
>
> The third law stipulates that a robot must protect its own existence as long as such protection does not conflict with the first or second law. With regard to AI that raises the question of whether it can be engineered so that in certain circumstances it would turn itself off. For those who believe in the possibility of Strong AI endowed with consciousness, this would present interesting ethical dilemmas. Should it be granted the freedom to self-destruct? Would certain actions merit an electronic version of the death penalty? The ultimate challenge to such a system, were it ever to be possible to devise it, should surely be 'Could it pass the Jesus Test?' In other words, would it have the ability to turn itself off out of love for its users?

10

Faith Healing

One of the most touching poems in Philip Larkin's *High Windows* (his fourth collection) is 'Faith Healing', about women being prayed over by an American Pentecostalist. Larkin recreates a scene he almost certainly witnessed at first hand, improbable though that sounds:

> Their heads are clasped abruptly; then, exiled
>
> Like losing thoughts, they go in silence . . .
> . . . but some stay stiff, twitching and loud
> With deep hoarse tears, as if a kind of dumb
> And idiot child within them still survives
> To re-awake at kindness . . .
>
> . . . Moustached in flowered frocks they shake.

The responses evoked in the poet by this act of worship include a degree of disdain. In the end, though, condescension is deflected by compassion:

> . . . In everyone there sleeps
> A sense of life lived according to love.
> To some it means the difference they could make
> By loving others, but across most it sweeps
> As all they might have done had they been loved . . .

Andrew Brown and others are right to conclude that 'Faith Healing' could not have been written without Christianity – not just in the obvious sense that it describes a church scene, but 'in the deeper way in which these women are shown to us as unloved . . . and unlovable, and yet made for love in some sense that their lives can't quite erase.'[1]

Larkin's life-enhancing lines offer an unexpected springboard for thinking about medical ethics. So often secularist protests against the perceived restrictiveness of Christian teaching skate over a broader point. At its best, such teaching rests on convictions about the sanctity of life which are incompatible with utilitarianism.

Part of my aim is therefore to sketch the implications of what being 'made for love' might be, whether at the beginning and end of life, or when we are sick or disabled. In considering this question I have learnt much from David Albert Jones. As Director of the Anscombe Centre in Oxford and Professor of Bioethics at St Mary's University, Twickenham, he has made many submissions to Parliament and other bodies. One notable point to have emerged from his work is how much attitudes to Christian perspectives vary according to the area of treatment concerned. For example, the palliative care movement is influenced by the hospice movement, which has itself been greatly inspired by the Church. Dame Cicely Saunders (1918–2005), the pioneering British figure in this area, was motivated to set up St Christopher's Hospice in South London by her Christian faith. Humanists can be as enthusiastic about hospices as about NGOs such as Christian Aid and CAFOD. Palliative care providers are accordingly much more open to Christian voices than their counterparts in areas such as sexual health and gynaecology, where the impetus is to be 'non-judgemental'. Jones describes psychology and psychiatry as occupying intermediate territory, given their focus on the whole person. While specialists in these areas naturally display a wide range of attitudes to religion, a significant proportion are interested in spirituality. He contrasts this with the black and white debate that unfolded during the passage of the Fertilisation and Embryology Bill in 2007, for instance:

I was one of those who was saying that we shouldn't have animal–human hybrid embryos. That was characterised as a 'theological' view by people who therefore wanted it dismissed. It's a kind of antibody thing. For many participants, if you can attach religion to an argument, that becomes a way to dismiss it. As a matter of fact, animal–human hybrid embryos, which people promised would cure Alzheimer's and motor neurone disease, have done no such thing. Even before the law came into force, they'd abandoned their tall claims. I knew it was bogus science. I knew people who *knew* it was bogus science who were nevertheless defending it. They were defending it on the basis that they wanted more elbow room. And they didn't like things being restricted. But I didn't know anyone who was confident of the science. In the end, it didn't get funding. That's why they stopped. They didn't get funding because funding is competitive. And the whole project wasn't very promising.

A second story recounted by Professor Jones shows how secularists can be every bit as narrow-minded as dogmatic believers. In an article for the *Journal of Medical Ethics* (*JME*)[2] the three authors – all staff at Great Ormond Street Hospital in London, which houses one of the UK's top paediatric intensive care units – suggested that sick children are being subjected to life-prolonging 'torture' owing to the 'fervent or fundamentalist views' of their parents. Though professing to support 'shared involvement in decision-making', the authors represented 'attempted dialogue' as hopeless where religion is involved, because 'the parties [do not share] the same language'. They therefore stressed a need to 'reconsider current ethical and legal structures' so that 'religion [is] legislated against in the best interest of the child.' In favour of their interpretation of medical intervention as torture, the authors cited Polly Toynbee's defence of assisted suicide, while, in favour of their characterisation of religion, they cited Richard Dawkins's polemic *The God Delusion*. These explosive claims duly received widespread media attention.

As Jones pointed out to me, the many misconceptions evident in this article include the idea that parents control their children's treatment. Decisions on treatment or non-treatment for children are made by doctors on the basis of best interest. And if doctors and parents cannot agree, there is an option to go to court. In nineteen out of twenty cases, courts side with doctors. Beyond this, though, religion in the form of hospital chaplaincy is in practice a much more positive force than the article grants. 'The amazing thing', Jones recalls, 'is that in most of the 200 cases cited by the authors of the article, consensus was reached. They had difficulty with fifteen. In nine of these, agreement came through the intervention of a chaplain or other faith representative.' The article focused on six hard cases. But each involved Christian parents originating overseas, and not members of the mainstream Churches, with various issues involving trust, communication and so forth. 'A good chaplain from their particular tradition would have been able to translate their concerns to doctors, as so many chaplains do in other cases,' Jones maintains. 'Religion is much more of a bridge than a stumbling block in this setting.' Along with two co-contributors from University College London, David R. Katz (Emeritus Professor of Immunopathology) and John Wyatt (Professor of Ethics and Perinatology), he rebutted the *JME* broadside in an article for another medical journal. The title of the piece was self-explanatory. 'Doctors, Dying Children and Religious Parents: Dialogue or Demonization?'[3]

At a philosophical level, the *JME* authors were assuming the sole validity of 'programmatic secularism' – namely that no religion should have access to the public arena. I have now repeatedly argued that procedural secularism (where no one faith position has a privileged position and free speech and conscience are protected) forms a more reasonable foundation for modelling the public profile of faith communities. This is not just a matter of fairness. Like fish unaware of the surrounding water, we can take the deep spiritual underpinnings of healthcare for granted. Side by side with practical work, the other great Christian input is a body of reflection on core principles.

Take an example such as the moral status of the embryo. There is no such thing as *the* Christian consensus on the timing of the origin of the human individual. There was a consensus among all denominations until well into the twentieth century that abortion was sinful and that late abortion was homicide. There was no agreement about whether early abortion was homicide. But those who denied that it was homicide still saw the practice as wrong, because it entailed the snuffing out of a potential human being. As the agnostic philosopher Anthony Kenny has maintained, the question whether early abortion counts as homicide matters deeply. If it does not, then the rights and interests of human beings may legitimately be allowed to override the protection that by common consent should in normal circumstances be extended to the early embryo. Saving the life of the mother, the fertilisation of otherwise childless couples, and the advancement of medical research could all provide reasons to override the embryo's protected status. This line of argument was backed by the Warnock Report, published in 1984. It made a significant contribution to the debate by offering a new *terminus ante quem* for the origin of individual human life. This was much earlier in pregnancy than the forty days set by the pre-Reformation Christian consensus. The report's authors thought that experimentation on embryos should be impermissible after the fourteenth day.

Jones defends what is now the mainstream Catholic view – that individual human life begins at conception. An embryo, from the first moment of its existence, has the potential to become a rational human being and therefore should be allotted full human rights. An embryo cannot think or reason or perform any of the other actions seen as marks of rationality. But nor can a newborn baby. The protection afforded to infants shows that we accept that it is potentiality rather than actuality which determines the conferral of human rights.

Other Christian ethicists such as Lord Harries, a former Bishop of Oxford, have argued that an embryo is not a single individual, because it can in principle divide to form twins. Defenders of the official Catholic stance can reply that an embryo is an individual human being which has a certain potential – namely of twinning – that is lost in later life. And so the debate goes on. (Supporters of Harries might counter that in the case of twinning there will be two human individuals, each of whom will be able to trace their origin to the same embryo, but neither of whom will be the same individual as that embryo.) The point for our purposes is that these are serious questions where practice and principle intersect, and on which grown-ups can disagree in good faith. Christians – along with all serious parties – have a right to be heard.

My commendation of procedural secularism is especially relevant with respect to abortion. A case from June 2023 seems worth rehearsing. Pressure groups responded with outrage over the jailing of a mother who had induced a termination, with pills posted to her by the NHS, when she was eight months pregnant. Having pleaded guilty (the 1926 Infant Life (Preservation) Act classes abortion after viability – then fixed at twenty-eight weeks – as 'child destruction'), the defendant was sentenced to a year's imprisonment. This penalty was later suspended.

Supporting the accused woman, Clare Murphy of the British Pregnancy Advisory Service described the law as 'archaic' and demanded the end of criminal sanctions. This reaction was overblown. Abortion at such a late stage is illegal almost everywhere. Others pointed out that the contemporary trend lies if anything in the direction of greater regulation, given the increasing options for treating unborn children. Pro-life advocates went further. Terminations have been legal up to twenty-four weeks of gestation since 1990 in most cases, while children with severe disabilities may be aborted up to the point of birth. Though widely supported, the law contains a clause, 1(1)a, deplored by Christians and others concerned that a door would be opened to abortion on demand:

1(1) Subject to the provisions of this section, a person shall not be guilty of an offence under the law relating to abortion when a pregnancy is terminated by a registered medical practitioner if two registered medical practitioners are of the opinion, formed in good faith –

(a) that the continuance of the pregnancy would involve risk to the life of the pregnant woman, or of injury to the physical or mental health of the pregnant woman or any existing children of her family, greater than if the pregnancy were terminated; or

(b) that there is a substantial risk that if the child were born it would suffer from such physical or mental abnormalities as to be seriously handicapped.

The concern appears well grounded in my view. Piloted by David Steel, the 1967 Abortion Act aimed to save women from the horrors of unregulated backstreet clinics. But tragic consequences have resulted from a no doubt well-intentioned measure. Today, around 230,000 abortions a year are carried out in Britain. The rules are often far stricter elsewhere. A twelve-week limit is enforced in most other countries.

Some implications of the pills-through-the-post story were well summed up in a *Spectator* editorial.[4] The twenty-four-week limit was enshrined in 1990 on the grounds of evolving options with respect to viability. Experts then believed that twenty-four weeks was the youngest age at which a foetus could survive independently. But as the article noted, the survival rate today at such a stage is about 60 per cent. Those who seek to extend abortion rights regularly claim that Britain is bowing to the wishes of a religious minority intent on 'curtailing' women's rights. In reality, any shift in public opinion in a less permissive direction is more a mark of medical developments.

The editorial also noted that many MPs who opposed a new law to combat obstruction at climate protests also supported an amendment to the Public Order Bill which has made the mere act of protest itself unlawful in one instance. Pro-life activists are now 'in breach of the criminal law merely for coming within 150 metres of an abortion clinic with the wrong opinion'. One Catholic campaigner, Isabel Vaughan-Spruce, was even arrested *on suspicion of praying* near an abortion clinic in Kings Norton, Birmingham, in February 2023. This troubling situation is discussed by David Albert Jones in an essay on abortion law in the UK with the telling title 'From the Crime of Abortion to the Crime of Expressing Opposition to Abortion'.[5]

The range of opinion on the subject is well reflected in a letter to the Editor of *The Sunday Times*, carried in the paper on 25 June 2023:

> Dear editor — Your picture [18 June] showed a pro-abortion activist holding a sign reading 'Not your body. Not your life. Not your Choice.' As a feminist who believes that abortion should be abolished, I agree.
>
> It's not your body: the unborn child is a separate, unique human being. It's not your life: the unborn child has its own right to life. It's not your choice: no one has the right to kill another innocent human being.
>
> The basic principles of feminism are equality, justice and non-violence. Many women are finding that these principles sit uneasily with treating an unborn baby as a non-person, to be disposed of when inconvenient. More feminists now see abortion as a symptom of injustice, the exploitation of women and the denial of their nature. *Sue Eaton*

The aborting of children with disabilities is an abiding source of outrage. Clause (b) above can reasonably be cited in cases where a severely malformed foetus is not viable. But someone with Down's syndrome can also be aborted at any point up until birth. The justice of this position was tested in the High Court in 2022 by Heidi Crowter, a twenty-seven-year-old Baptist who herself has Down's. Marie Lea-Wilson, who joined the appeal, had been unexpectedly offered a termination after her unborn baby was diagnosed with Down's at thirty-four weeks. She and her husband refused. As the court noted, their son is a 'deeply loved and valued' child who is 'hitting his developmental milestones'.

People with Down's are naturally distressed by the knowledge that they could have been aborted at any stage. The clear implication is that they are not equal in dignity to those born without disabilities. This was the heart of the argument laid before the Court of Appeal. Articles 8 and 14 of the European Convention on Human Rights state that people have rights to a private life and not to be discriminated against. The appellants claimed that both of these rights are violated by the 1967 Abortion Act, on the grounds that it 'perpetuates and reinforces negative cultural stereotypes about people with disabilities'.

Heidi Crowter's case was thrown out on specious grounds. Lord Justice Underhill, writing for the majority, ruled that the question was not 'how the living disabled' could be treated before birth, but whether there was a 'clear line [of discriminatory treatment] at the moment of birth'. The judges failed to consider the crucial question of why foetuses with Down's can be aborted at any point. The conclusion drawn by Nicholas Reed Langen, editor of the *LSE Public Policy Review*, is judicious:

> Abortion is a devastating act. Despite its portrayal in some parts of the right-wing media, few women approach it in a cavalier way. Letting foetuses be tested for Down's syndrome is acceptable; but any question of abortion should be within the term limits and conditions that apply to every other pregnancy. Regardless of whether anyone would choose to live with Down's syndrome, a life with [the condition] is as dignified and valuable as any other.[6]

Sharing this view, the writer Maggie Fergusson points out that Britain is one of only a handful of European countries in which this kind of abortion to term is legal. The law as it stands is 'sad, shocking and shameful', she concludes.[7] At a time when discrimination on grounds of gender, race or sexuality is stigmatised, 'how can we uphold a law which discriminates against unborn children with what are considered severe disabilities, treating them differently from other unborn children, to the point of life or death?'

Fergusson's account of her Zoom interview with Heidi Crowter after the judgement is deeply affecting. Asked for her reaction, Heidi said that she was angry, 'but more upset than angry'. She married her husband James in 2020. He also has Down's. When Fergusson enquired about the sources of difficulty in Heidi's life, she replied without hesitation – 'Yes! My husband James: he can be very difficult!' – before erupting in laughter. Asked what her faith means to her, Heidi shared one of her favourite biblical verses: 'I praise you because I am fearfully and wonderfully made' (Psalm 139:14).

Another prominent critic of the judgement is the writer Frank Cottrell-Boyce, who detects 'an element of eugenics' in the current law. Though his friendships with people with Down's have enriched him, he says, 'that isn't really the point, is it? The point is, you shouldn't have to qualify to be allowed to live.'

***

We have noted that Christian voices resist liberalising campaigners with more success in an area such as physician-assisted suicide (PAS). Holes in the case for reforming existing practice were evident in the debate on the latest PAS Bill in the House of Lords in October 2021, even though it was supported by four of the country's top retired judges. The proposed legislation was introduced by Baroness Meacher. First, she claimed that the Bill was 'truly modest', and aimed at ending unbearable suffering that could not be relieved by palliative care. But it did not require that patients be suffering – whether unbearably, unrelievably, or otherwise – or even that they had consulted a palliative care physician, let alone tried palliative care. It merely required a vaguely defined 'terminal illness'.

The Bill's supporters also said that when Parliament decriminalised suicide in 1961, it thus condoned the practice, thereby rendering the continuing ban on assisting or encouraging the taking of one's life illogical. The lawyer and ethicist John Keown of Georgetown University is one among many Christian analysts to have exposed the speciousness of this claim. Parliament did not condone what the relevant minister then described as 'self-murder'. Suicide was decriminalised for other reasons, including the enlightened understanding that people inclined to take their own lives often have severe mental health problems. They are far more likely to benefit from counselling than prosecution.

Lady Meacher's supporters also asserted that legalisation was required by the right of patients to make their own choices. Society has long recognised that self-determination is not absolute, though. Sometimes people desire harmful outcomes for themselves as well as for others. The law often imposes reasonable limits on what we may wish for. For example, a regular citizen cannot legally obtain hard recreational drugs, or have healthy limbs amputated on request. The medical profession has never recognised rights to be killed, or to be assisted in killing ourselves: the bans on both – and on assisting suicide – are among the oldest on Western statute books. They represent the codification of the Hippocratic Oath.

Those on Meacher's side of the argument relied heavily on stories of distressing deaths. These tragedies should of course be sources of deep concern. But as Professor Keown has observed, supporters have no monopoly on compassion. Many who oppose PAS have also seen loved ones die in distressing circumstances. The UK has first-class palliative care. So the argument that PAS is necessary to save pain is becoming progressively weaker. The priority should be to make expert ministrations available to all who need it.

In countries that allow either PAS or voluntary euthanasia (lethal injections at the patient's request), it is striking how often patients access them for reasons other than pain and suffering. The most common reasons in the US state of Oregon are 'loss of autonomy' and 'a decreasing ability to engage in activities that make life enjoyable'. In 2016, the Dutch government, which legalised euthanasia in 1984, proposed extending its law to elderly people who have a 'completed life'. This naturally led pro-life campaigners to ask about the kind of signal such a change would send to the elderly. By legalising euthanasia and PAS in 2016, Canada moved even faster than the Netherlands.

Keown poses a set of apt questions about the slippery slope down which the legalisation of PAS can lead.[8] If respect for patient choice and the doctor's duty to alleviate suffering are thought to justify PAS for the 'terminally ill', then they also justify it for the chronically ill, whether physically or mentally. The same applies with euthanasia, especially (but not only) for those physically unable to commit suicide even with assistance, such as the totally paralysed. And what of patients who are unable to request a lethal injection, such as disabled infants? Granted, they lack autonomy. But the absence of autonomy does not cancel the duty to alleviate suffering. This logic has not been lost on Dutch judges. Having given the green light to voluntary euthanasia forty years ago, they then legally authorised lethal injections for disabled infants in 1996. And in 2020, the Dutch government decided to allow lethal injections for suffering children aged between one and twelve.

The House of Lords has probably debated PAS in greater detail than any other legislative body in the world. The standard of debate is generally impressive; two substantial Select Committee reports have also been produced. The first, chaired by the late Lord Walton of Detchant, a neurologist, rightly concluded that the prohibition on intentional killing is the 'cornerstone of law and of social relationships' that 'protects each one of us impartially, embodying the belief that all are equal'. PAS and euthanasia trade on the contrary judgement: that some patients' lives are no longer worth living, and that they would be better off dead. No wonder disability groups oppose legalisation. One of the most powerful – and intentionally disturbing

– contributions to debate on the Meacher Bill came from the medic and safeguarding expert Baroness Hollins. Her speech is reproduced below.* Keown's verdict on the process is also worth quoting:

---

* My Lords . . . [s]tories matter, but other evidence matters too . . . My own research, published with Dutch colleagues and my noble friend Lady Finlay, found that autistic people and people with mild learning disabilities were given physician-assisted deaths in the Netherlands, rather than addressing the underlying issues of inequality, loneliness, feeling a burden or inadequate support. That is thirty-eight people in recent years. Doctors were shown to be poor judges of decision-making capacity and their recommendations were seemingly influenced by their own assumptions about quality of life.

Clause 4(6) [of the Bill] requires the doctor to be present throughout. In summing up, will my noble friend please specify the doctor's role if the person has not died within, say, six hours? What if after taking the drugs the patient is in pain, vomiting, having a seizure, or dying slowly over hours or days, with their distressed relatives, expecting a quick and gentle death, pleading with the doctor to 'do something'? In Oregon, one person took 104 hours to die after taking lethal drugs; eight people survived their suicide attempt.

It is worth noting that, in the Netherlands in 2019, 96 per cent of physician-assisted deaths were euthanasia. Clinicians prefer this. Partly, it is their own convenience and partly the needs of the service. They had to transition to euthanasia because of complications in 8.9 per cent of physician-assisted suicides. We have been promised that this Bill will not introduce euthanasia. This House needs cast-iron assurances from my noble friend that the plan is not to divert already stretched palliative care teams to this task.

In 2016, Canada legalised assisted dying for people facing imminent death. Five years later, eligibility includes chronic illness and disability, and will shortly include mental illness. In Canada, assisted death is publicly funded and must be provided, but no similar right exists for palliative care. Canadian doctor Leonie Herx, writing in [the *Daily Telegraph*], says: 'The impact on palliative medicine has been enormous. Hospices that do not offer assisted death face closure and loss of government funding . . . Administering death is cheaper and easier than providing good care.'

[The hospice movement] says that expert end-of-life care is not available to about one in four of the people who could benefit. That was 120,000 people in 2015; no wonder we hear stories of failed care. Frankly,

Remarkably, not one of the four eminent judges who spoke for the Meacher Bill pointed out that it did not require any suffering; or illogical limitation to PAS for the 'terminally ill', or that in breaking the 'golden chain' of the historic legal and moral principle of the inviolability of life, it was anything but a 'truly modest' measure. Nor did they consider the obvious relevance of the disturbing evidence from overseas. When even senior judges fail to conjure up between them a sound argument [on this question], it is not surprising the case for legalisation has so far failed, in secular and permissive England.[9]

My own subsequent conversations with an Anglican priest who had supported his dying brother underlined three important dimensions of a Christian perspective. One is that helplessness at the beginning and end of life are powerful reminders of the truth that personhood is not something that we discover or assert. It emerges through our relationships. The secularist insistence that we can and should be self-determining even to the point of deciding on the timing of our death has nothing to offer a person in a coma or persistent vegetative state. My friend saw devoted nurses and carers asking his brother's permission to move him in bed, to shave him, to wash him. They knew that as a result of a series of strokes he could not respond in any way, or even move, but were still sustaining his dignity and his personhood.

---

the declaration should require doctors to specify what palliative hospice and psychiatric care was available so that any improvement or decline can be monitored.

What if palliative and hospice care became a right and a reality? It is shameful that a quarter of us currently do not and will not have access to palliative care. No wonder people are afraid. Let us campaign for it. Attitudes would shift again because our and others' stories would be stories of good deaths. Actually, most of the dozens of emails I received were unique, moving and positive stories. Please oppose this Bill; it is not safe.[10]

Second, my friend taught me how different the Christian view of death can be from secularist alternatives. A junior doctor thought that when the next infection struck his brother, antibiotics should be withheld and nature be allowed to take its course. 'I assented to this,' my friend said, 'believing in the promise of resurrection and eternal life. The consultant overruled the decision, without (irony alert) consulting me. For the consultant, death represented failure. For me, it represented a release into the closer presence of God.'

The third dimension, relating to the so-called principle of double effect – emerged several months later, when my friend's brother was admitted to a different section of the same hospital with a very serious infection. He was clearly in a terminal state. The doctor in charge said that, for obvious reasons, he could not be sure whether the patient was suffering and that he recommended an injection of morphine to ensure that he was not. My friend agreed to this, intuiting that the morphine dose might be a large one, on the basis of double effect. The morphine might shorten the dying patient's life by at most a few hours, but would ensure that he experienced no pain.

***

In commending a Christian-informed vision of ethical practice in science and medicine, I am fully aware that faith can be a negative factor, as well as a source of light. The shunning of single mothers – including, deplorably, the young women in Ireland's Magdalene laundries – has obvious roots in religious bigotry, as well as age-old taboos relating to sex. Can more self-critical Christian voices today contribute something positive to a contemporary hot-button question such as gender, given the division it stokes among secularists, let alone others?

One reasonable starting point might be to note that gender dysphoria has been around for a long time (probably throughout history), even though expressed in many different ways. Legal recognition of people then called transsexual was not granted in the UK until 2004: the Blair government was propelled into framing its Gender Recognition Bill after a ruling by the European Court of Human Rights. At that point, the Catholic Bishops' Conference of England and Wales backed a call by the Church of England for a conscience clause in the new legislation. While restating traditional teaching that marriage can only be between a man and a woman, and opposing 'full legal recognition with the right to marry in [an acquired] gender', the briefing note supported 'appropriate medical and psychological help', and, for those proceeding with surgery, support 'to ease their life in society when they choose to live permanently as a member of the opposite sex'. There was no suggestion in the document that a trans person with a new gender might not participate fully in church life.[11]

Since then, the number of children and young people identifying as trans has grown sharply. A tenfold increase was registered between 2013 and 2019, for example. The distribution of those seeking to change their gender has also changed. While previously a majority were male-to-female, most are currently female-to-male. A still larger group of mainly young people have publicly identified as non-binary or gender-fluid.

Jones and other bioethicists note that gender dysphoria is no longer treated as a possible reflection of psychological or social problems.[12] The standard path lies in acceptance of the gender that the person concerned expresses. This means among other things that approaches are now increasingly medicalised. Younger adolescents have been given puberty-blockers, with cross-hormone treatment becoming available at sixteen, and surgery from two years after that.

While these developments are well intentioned, it is not hard to see why they are also contentious. When the singer Róisín Murphy wrote that 'Pumping gender-confused kids full of hormone suppressants is . . . absolutely desolate' on her private

Facebook page in September 2023, she was excoriated by trans activists. That her album *Hit Parade* rose to the top of the charts in the same month suggested that an array of less vocal fans supported her right to free speech. Murphy's argument finds favour not only with other gender-critical feminists such as J. K. Rowling and Kathleen Stock, but also with gay campaigners concerned about the validity of practices such as telling an 'effeminate' boy that he's 'really' a girl. What if the truth turns out to be that he's simply gay or bisexual? In that case the advice (and advice often shades into pressure) can reasonably be described as homophobic. A variety of young people encouraged to have life-changing surgery have subsequently realised that they're same-sex-attracted, rather than born in the wrong body. Additional strife has centred on trans women's access to traditionally female-only arenas, including women's prisons, shelters for victims of domestic abuse, and sports where male puberty confers inbuilt advantages.

A conservative Christian stance on the subject more generally was set out by Pope Benedict in 2012. A new philosophy 'put forward today under the term "gender" ' regards sex not as a 'given element of nature' but as 'a social role we choose for ourselves', he argued, adding that this contradicted the truth that God had created human beings 'male and female'. Pope Francis has also condemned what he describes as gender theory in the encyclicals *Laudato Si'* and *Amoris Laetitia*.

Jones steers a middle course between those who feel that acceptance of someone's acquired gender constitutes an indirect threat to family life, and others seeking to play down any distinction between gender identity and biological sex. 'What is easily missed in this battle of ideas is the human reality of children or adults who feel deeply perplexed and sometimes deeply distressed because their sense of identity is discordant with their outward anatomy and with the gender in which they were brought up.'[13] He adds a further persuasive point. One is that he has witnessed no denial of the duality of man and woman in his engagement with trans people. On the contrary, their reassignment marks an acceptance of binary identity. The other is that it is inclusion in the life of the Church which constitutes the surest way to a deeper theological understanding.

This is self-evidently true at one level. Christian faith is nursed in patterns of common life. But the primary insight – deriving from Galatians 3:16 – had already been stated by Stanley Hauerwas, another leading ethicist, in a published conversation with me in 2005.[14] What bothered him was the assumption that someone's gender is more important than their faith. In other words, the Church should be a fellowship that places discomfort over gender identity within the context of a far more enthralling narrative and practice. Hauerwas's challenge begins and ends in a mission-oriented context and in dialogue with those outside the Church.

The conclusion to which much of this chapter points rests on the importance of conscience. For a complex set of reasons partly explored in Chapters 2 and 4, we have reached a point where the respect for conscience, common as recently as the 1990s, has given way to a winner-takes-all mentality on one question after another. Some on the Left have spurned free speech through practices such as no-platforming. But the problem is broader. On the Right, for example, people can deplore the ills of cancel culture while still complaining if a pro-choice speaker is invited to a Catholic university. Greater emphasis on the importance of conscience as a form of middle ground in an argument would be good for both liberty and the neglected notion that someone can be wrong but reasonable.

The point was recently made in an open letter to the World Medical Association signed by 250 senior clinicians and ethicists working in Africa and Asia as well as in Europe and across the American continent.[15] The worries set out in this chapter are thus anything but parochial. To cite just one further example among many, they were also rehearsed in 2023 through a strongly worded rebuke from Spain's Bishops' Conference to the dogmatically secularist government of Pedro Sánchez.[16]

Supposing faith-informed voices in the sphere of medical ethics were further sidelined. What would we lose? A Christian doctor speaking to me off the record was bracing. 'We'd be left with politicians, pundits and academics who are nothing like as mainstream as they imagine. The British Humanist Association is full of nice people, but it's essentially a small nonconformist sect with a membership of 100,000. What's representative about that?'

II

Being Diverse About Diversity

For its 2016–17 season the Southbank Centre, Britain's largest arts complex, presented a festival of concerts and talks entitled *Belief and Beyond Belief*.[1] As the Catholic commentator Damian Thompson noted in a downbeat verdict on this series,[2] it could have formed a major exploration of the vast yet often neglected influence of faith on the great composers. In practice the opportunity was missed.

I think Thompson was right to argue that secularist arbiters of culture often view musical (let alone social or political) history through a cracked lens. From this perspective Western composers up to and including Bach were Christians only by default. It is then inferred that faith probably mattered less to them than we may think – which is perhaps why, for example, the top of the Wikipedia entry for Monteverdi fails to mention that he was a priest. Mozart plays a transitional role in this story. Though a Catholic, he was also a Freemason and therefore enlightened. Beethoven is the great exemplar of modern man come of age. His technical innovations reflect a restless mind ill at ease with orthodoxy of all kinds. The stage is set for the 'spiritual but not religious' Romantics and their Modernist heirs, who rejected the Church as readily as they spurned harmonic rules.

Thompson's judgement that *Belief and Beyond Belief* revealed much about the anti-Christian mindset of Britain's arts establishment is also fair. Based on a series of concerts by the London Philharmonic Orchestra, the festival programme framed matters tendentiously as follows: 'Since the Age of Enlightenment and the subsequent revelations of science and technology, reason has challenged faith. Yet despite rational explanations for so many of religion's core beliefs, the twenty-first century looks set to be defined by religion, often in extreme forms.' It ought to go without saying that reason was challenging faith – and faith seeking to demonstrate its own reasonableness – well before the eighteenth century. Then came a further fusion of platitude with inanity: 'The seemingly innate need in so many people to find meaning for their lives and a sense of where they fit into the universe, with all its mystery and majesty, is a constant in all periods of human history and has produced some of the greatest music and art ever created.' From 'Richard Dawkins to Jeanette Winterson, from Rabindranath Tagore to Primo Levi, we investigate the struggle to define the absolute.'

Thompson was withering. 'Yup, Dawkins. Announcing an exploration of faith and music, the first name the Southbank comes up with is that of a religion-hater.' Spread over a year, the festival line-up included works at best tangentially associated with any spiritual creed: Jean-Féry Rebel's *Les éléments* (sometimes likened to Vivaldi's *Four Seasons*); Darius Milhaud's jazz-inflected ballet *La création du monde*; John Adams's experimental symphony *Harmonielehre*, inspired by a dream of a supertanker turning into a rocket.

Belief and Beyond Belief struggled to reckon with overtly religious scores. It described Bruckner's Ninth Symphony as 'one of music's most personal and passionate confessions of faith', while adding that it voices 'bottomless chasms of doubt'. On the contrary, Christian commentators have discerned fear of divine judgement rather than a crisis of faith in a work explicitly dedicated to God. Pressed further, the Southbank Centre's then director Jude Kelly and her colleagues may have described Bruckner as a pious but fundamentally simple-minded churchgoer. They are also likely to have claimed Beethoven for their own side. He was represented in *Belief and Beyond Belief* by a performance of *Fidelio* – a curious choice, given the far greater suitability of a crowning achievement such as the *Missa Solemnis*. Other options were also available. The slow movement of the A minor string quartet Op. 132 bears the title 'Holy song of thanksgiving of a convalescent to the Deity'.

Faith and its loss have been manifest sources of inspiration to composers for centuries. How to interpret Schoenberg's rediscovery of his Jewish roots, or Stravinsky's Russian Orthodoxy, or Messiaen's enchanted vision of the world, or the minimalism of Arvo Pärt, John Tavener and James MacMillan? *Belief and Beyond Belief* failed to shed light on these and allied subjects. Kelly et al. dropped the ball repeatedly.

Why begin a discussion of culture with a story from yesteryear? The short answer is that it is symptomatic of a broader climate. Further evidence that my case does not rest on special pleading can be culled from the changing religious output of the BBC. The Corporation has struggled with the distinction between religious broadcasting ('Thought for the Day' on Radio 4's *Today* programme, *Choral Evensong* on Radio 3, *Songs of Praise* and occasional broadcast services on TV, for example) and broadcasting about religion. The secularists inside and outside BBC management appear very uncomfortable about the former and not well informed about the latter.

A sample of the problem came in an episode of Radio 4's theological discussion programme – itself called *Beyond Belief* – early in 2023 on the relation between religion and science.[3] The one thing needful in a broadcast such as this was a scientifically literate Christian, Jewish or Muslim guest who could explain why there is no necessary contradiction between faith that the universe exists through God's creative act and accepting the integrity of science – including the theory of evolution. Yes (she or he could have added), there have been periodic tensions between the Church and pioneers in disciplines such as physics and biology, but also much creative dialogue. We have already noted that understanding the geological record and its implications for biblical timelines was a task undertaken within a predominantly Christian culture. I relish the lesson Francis Spufford draws from this fact in *Unapologetic*: 'there's a good case to be made that the ready acceptance of evolution in Britain owed a lot to the great cultural transmission mechanism of the Church of England. If you're glad that Darwin is on the £10 note, hug an Anglican.'[4]

Two related points would have helped ensure safe passage through the boggy field addressed in *Beyond Belief*. One is that the discoveries of science cannot be credibly contradicted from any pulpit;[5] the other (as I have already stressed) that according to developed orthodoxy God is not a big, powerful thing who competes for elbow room on the same plane as creatures. Yes, God is held to sustain creation in being moment by moment; but that is not the same thing as tweaking or fiddling with the mechanism.

The programme in question was presented by Aleem Maqbool, the BBC's Religion Editor (whose predecessor, Martin Bashir, allegedly used unethical means to obtain his 1995 interview with Princess Diana). My disappointment did not just centre on how ill-prepared Maqbool sounded, or that misconceived ideas about 'balance' required the studio discussion to include an atheist. (The guest concerned, from the National Secular Society, was confrontational as well as badly informed.) Proof positive of even deeper bias came from the simple fact that the broadcast began and ended with reflections from Brian Cox. Here was someone with name recognition, but no qualifications whatever to discuss faith. I have already reported his notorious remark, also made on the BBC, that he was as likely to consider the existence of God as that of fairies at the bottom of the garden.

That this sort of debacle forms part of a pattern was confirmed for me in a comment by Ernie Rea, Head of Religious Broadcasting at the BBC from 1989 to 2001 – and himself presenter of *Beyond Belief* for the following two decades, when the programme was well made:

> The Brian Cox thing doesn't surprise me at all because the pressure to get big celebrity names on programmes regardless of whether it's appropriate within the context is very strong. I felt it several times when I was in post, but it's got hugely worse. I

remember one time when the Controller of BBC1 told me that he wanted to take two budgets of *Everyman* [then a mainstay of the channel and addressing aspects of religion and ethics] to enable Geri Halliwell, who he thought was going to be the next Cilla Black – and who had just been appointed a UN ambassador – to interview eight inspiring young people from across the globe. I said openly that [Halliwell] lacked substance and I didn't want to do it. And he replied, 'Well, you've got one choice. You either do this or else I take the budgets and the programmes from you.' The programmes turned into a total disaster because Geri Halliwell didn't have the intellectual capacity to do the job properly – and also because she had other priorities. Interviews just kept getting cancelled. That to me in my time as Head of Religious Broadcasting was a prime example of how this cult of celebrity was overtaking everything else. And because Halliwell kept ducking out of her commitments, the original people who were supposed to be interviewed did not feature. A lot of money was wasted trying to make programmes in foreign locations. We ended up doing most of the legwork in the UK with people who were not terribly interesting.

The other example cited by Rea concerns *Son of God* (2001), a major series on the life of Christ prepared in the approach to the new millennium. The then Controller of BBC1 insisted that it be fronted by Jeremy Bowen – 'a fine journalist and very good presenter', in Rea's words, but one who knows 'very little' about Christianity. 'He's deeply sceptical of it. And it showed in the programmes.'

Things were not ever thus. Rea had been headhunted for his post by Michael Checkland (Director-General of the BBC, 1987–92), who assured him that they could always meet at short notice if needed. Checkland was succeeded by John Birt (in office from 1992 to 2000), a lapsed Catholic; and Birt by Greg Dyke (2000–4), consistently derided by his critics as a philistine who made no secret of his disdain for religion. Rea is clear that Dyke's prejudices were shared by senior colleagues, especially Alan Yentob (Controller of BBC1 during the mid-1990s and subsequently overall Director of Programmes), Jane Root and Lorraine Heggessey (respectively Controllers of BBC2 and BBC1). Dyke was followed by Mark Thompson (2004–12), a practising Catholic with far more supportive instincts about religious coverage. But his stance was not widely shared by senior staff. Core output emanating from Rea's department such as *Everyman* and *Heart of the Matter* were shunted to later and later slots before being dropped altogether. 'The Controller was scheduling them at 11.30 on a Sunday night and then saying that audiences were dropping,' Rea comments. 'No wonder!'

> Mark Thompson pushed for these programmes to go out at a decent hour, but on BBC2 rather than BBC1. I backed the proposal. Unfortunately it was strongly resisted by Jane Root, who didn't want religion on her channel at all. I used to go to meetings at Television Centre and Jane would say things like 'O my God, here he comes again!' So we had that sort of relationship.

An especially bleak moment came in 1997. Rea was approached by John Birt's office when plans were being drawn up to celebrate the Corporation's seventy-fifth anniversary. A thanksgiving service in Westminster Abbey had been proposed. Would Rea clear the ground with the Dean and Chapter? A date was provisionally fixed. 'I suddenly realised I hadn't heard any more so I rang the office of a senior colleague,' he remembers.

> I was told it had been decided that it wasn't appropriate to have a Christian service for the seventy-fifth anniversary. Instead, they would be putting on a performance of Mahler's Second Symphony at another venue. They didn't even have the courtesy to inform the authorities at the Abbey. Eventually I felt the need to bow out. My successor was Alan Bookbinder, a very good documentary filmmaker but someone with no past commitment

to religion. Imagine an analogous situation in the science department. After a few years he got tired and left.

While granting that BBC Radio remains a more civilised arena –
he singles out controllers including Michael Green, Jim Moir and
Nicholas Kenyon for praise – Rea views religious output on television over the past two decades with dejection. 'A recent series such
as *Pilgrimage* [a five-season show featuring various destinations]
really involved throwing celebrities together for a walk. Faith took
a back seat. Serious explorations of religion don't happen any
more.'

Bookbinder's outlook is sunnier in some respects. He sees Bowen
– who also presented reasonably well-received series on the lives of
Moses and St Paul, and another on the miracles of Jesus – as an asset
to religious programming overall. 'Jeremy functioned as an effective bridge,' Bookbinder told me. But in at least one crucial respect
his view chimes with Rea's. For decades the BBC has been bound
by statute to include minimum levels of faith-based broadcasting.
That obligation looks set to be swept away by the new Broadcasting
Act being drawn up by the Sunak government. In Bookbinder's
words, 'a relative decline will become absolute.' That this should
form a source of deep regret to a man now describing himself as
'an open-minded agnostic' is worth underlining. Bookbinder also
hails the enrichment of public discourse by church leaders such
as Desmond Tutu, Rowan Williams and Richard Chartres. 'I was
regularly grateful for the voices of reason and compassion on the
bishops' benches in the House of Lords,' he told me. 'Bishops often
served as the conscience of the nation during the Coalition government [2010–15]. The same could be said for papers like *The Tablet*.
But to my mind these are the exceptions proving the rule that the
religious voice is fading.'

The assessment of Michael Wakelin (BBC Head of Religion
from 2006 to 2010) adds further nuance to the picture. Though
sharing many of his former colleagues' regrets, he remains positive about a good deal of the Corporation's surviving religious

content. His evidence includes 'Pause for Thought' on Radio 2, airing three times a day – including at 7.20 a.m. on The Zoe Ball Breakfast Show, which had the largest audience of any early-morning radio programme in Europe. He also notes the continuing popularity of *Good Morning Sunday*, presented on the same station by Kate Bottley and Jason Mohammad.

As I have argued, though, perhaps the greater problem resides with the treatment of religion beyond the god slots. When Richard Dawkins appeared on *Today* in 2021 to mark his eightieth birthday, Nick Robinson (a forensic and often highly aggressive interviewer) allowed the UK's most carnivorous atheist to get away with claiming that his attacks on religion were pretty gentle affairs. Eight years earlier the geneticist Steve Jones published a highly flawed book, *The Serpent's Promise: The Bible Retold as Science*.[6] Like Dawkins, Jones set out to show how fundamentalist interpretations of the creation story in Genesis 2, or the Genesis 9 flood narrative, are incompatible with a scientific account. So far so good – though a bit easy and contemptuous. He then identified the biblical picture with a fundamentalist interpretation. That shows a lamentable surrender to the fundamentalist mode of thought, which any self-respecting scientist should know how to resist.

The point for our purposes is that the BBC rolled out the red carpet for Jones. He appeared on *Start the Week*, among other prestigious platforms. At no point were any of his highly jejune assumptions questioned in my hearing. Contrast this with the reception given to A. N. Wilson in 2018 for his biography of Darwin.[7] Jones was among the early reviewers to deplore the author's lack of professional scientific training.[8] Once more, the double standard passed unremarked – partly, I suspect, because of the enduring idea that everyone is an expert on questions of faith.

Unsurprisingly, then, Wakelin's largest concern is with religious literacy. The highly successful Religion Media Centre,[9] which emerged in its current form in 2016, has no missionary aims. Its remit is rather to demonstrate that faith matters. In implementing this goal the RMC has become a source of trusted information, as well as hosting numerous online briefings and debates. Through its work I learnt of ventures including Colin Bloom's report on religion and society[10] – another landmark case for greater awareness of global faiths – and Theology and Religious Studies UK,[11] which combines advocacy with oversight. Leading lights in this organisation include the Sikh scholar Opinderjit Kaur Takhar and the philosopher of religion Nicholas Adams.

Their role – in particular with respect to RE, given that the subject is not part of the National Curriculum – is certainly not free of tussles. Wakelin has a hair-raising story about a state secondary school near his Midlands home, where a debate entitled 'Do you believe in God or science?' has been staged more than once. 'It happened a few years ago and has just been repeated with the same title. Events like this make my blood boil.'

But righteous indignation can naturally be put to productive use. Wakelin's epigrammatic summary of the RMC's mission – 'we don't say that religion is good or bad: we say that it's important, and that's why people trust us' – is germane given the growth of its work with large companies. His vision for the future sounds bullish. 'Our rising profile is proof that the great spiritual traditions are being taken more seriously by movers and shakers. You can't just sweep religion to one side and say silly things about fairies at the bottom of the garden given statistics showing that 84 per cent of humanity now professes a faith.'

Another view of the field worth taking in is that of Aaqil Ahmed, the first Muslim to be Head of Religion and Ethics (as the post became designated) at the BBC. Having served after Wakelin until 2016, he is now Professor of Media at the University of Bolton. Public-service broadcasting has a duty to reflect the importance of faith to a significant part of the population, he maintains.

Instead of a dilution of religious output in the pursuit of ratings, I would like to see more programmes that explore the difficulties that many face in being religious in a country that is increasingly hostile to religion.

. . . I have never understood the ratings argument . . . [G]enerally, good-quality religious programming does no worse, if not better, than other similar areas; this is especially true of documentaries that address big stories, or have great access and characters. When industry folk talk about religion as being a failing genre (which I do not consider it to be), it needs to be asked whether they apply the same thinking to other genres.[12]

Ahmed adds an important consideration about technological change, which is plugging a gap for members of all the major faiths – namely that bespoke channels, social media and digital offerings are acquiring ever-greater salience.

There is an important tie-in between what Wakelin and Ahmed say and the world of work. I reported in Chapter 6 an estimate by the Pew Forum that faith-based enterprise contributes $1.2 trillion annually to the US economy when the fruit of philanthropy, education, healthcare services and other goods are added together. The American statistics speak for themselves.

Religion's $1.2 trillion impact is more than the annual revenues of the top ten tech companies, including Apple, Amazon, and Google combined. Almost 120,000 congregations report attracting visitors for their art or architecture each year, nearly four times the number of American museums visited during the same period. If $1.2 trillion was put in terms of GDP, it would make US religion the fifteenth largest national economy in the world. [Around] 40 per cent of the top fifty charities in the US are faith-based, with a combined operating revenue of $45.3 billion.[13]

A clear implication of faith's role in fostering the common good is that communities of conviction in Europe as well as America should feature prominently in any broad-based account of Diversity, Equity and Inclusion. The matter was well put in a report launched at the House of Commons in 2023 and called 'Building Freedom of Religion or Belief Through Faith-and-Belief Friendly Workplaces'.[14] As its executive summary puts it, since freedom of belief is one of the three factors most associated with global economic growth – quite apart from other benefits – and highly correlated with World Economic Forum pillars of sustainable development, diversity in this area should be seen as an unalloyed blessing. Other parts of the document include an overview of faith-and-belief employee resource groups (ERGs), one of the main ways in which companies have successfully incorporated religion and belief as part of diversity commitments; and a practical and free benchmarking tool for organisations to track progress in 'faith-and-belief accommodation and belonging in the workplace' known as the Religious Equity, Diversity & Inclusion (REDI) Index. The document was compiled by Dr Brian Grim, the highly respected founder of the Religious Freedom and Business Foundation. Its message should be an inspiration – and also a reproach – to those whose assumptions about diversity often fail to embrace the most important ingredient of all, namely diversity of thought.

This point in turn propels us into more sensitive territory. Wakelin and Grim are both Christians with hospitable instincts towards those of other faiths. Yet in one organisation after another, the impulse to embrace religion can involve being sympathetic to all faiths bar Christianity. Two recent instances of specifically anti-Christian bias bear out this thesis. One, though trivial in itself, merits an airing for what it reveals about contemporary mores in Britain. In November 2023 it emerged that the National Trust's new 'inclusive' calendar features the dates of Diwali, Ramadan and Eid, but not those of Christmas or Easter. It would be hard to concoct a more transparent case of an inclusiveness that fails to include – or of what the late Roger Scruton termed 'oikophobia', the coinage denoting an aversion to one's home environment, or a rejection of one's own culture.[15]

The most consequential recent case of anti-Christian discrimination is the hounding of Kate Forbes, a member of the Free Church of Scotland with conservative convictions about sexual morality, during her failed bid to succeed Nicola Sturgeon as leader of the Scottish National Party and First Minister of Scotland. Forbes was not a member of the Scottish Parliament when it authorised same-sex marriage in 2014. But nine years later she said that she would not have backed this move. The comment drew a cascade of disapproval, including from supporters of Humza Yousaf, Forbes's successful rival. Not the least of the ironies involved sprang from Yousaf's status as an observant Muslim who had absented himself from the original parliamentary vote on gay marriage.

Forbes's defence of her view was robust. 'I will defend to the hilt everybody's right in a pluralistic and tolerant society to live and to love free of harassment and fear. And in the same way I hope others can be afforded the rights as people of faith to practise fairly mainstream teaching. That is the nuance we need to capture.'[16] In other words, she was not seeking the repeal of existing laws, any more than the teetotal Yousaf would have contemplated calling for the closure of Scotland's pubs. Journalists and keyboard warriors scented blood, however. Forbes's fortunes appeared to go the same way as those of Tim Farron, the former Liberal Democrat leader and Evangelical Christian, who was forced to relinquish his post in 2017 after revealing that he, too, thought marriage should only be between a man and a woman.

A. N. Wilson drew a sharply critical verdict on his fellow journalists and opinion-formers when the story broke.

It is a good indication of how utterly illogical, and morally vacuous, the anti-Christian secularists are. They would rather have a follower of Islam – not a faith with a conspicuous history of compassion towards gay people or respect for women's rights – than someone brave enough to say they regard Christianity as 'mainstream' . . .

The Christians could insist, until they were blue in the face, that monogamous, heterosexual marriage was the ideal for them personally, not something they were trying to force on other people. But the iron intolerance of the secularist ethos of the age would mean that this obvious distinction was lost.[17]

Forbes's opponents could of course reply that long campaigns have been waged to break the Church's power as an arbiter of sexual morality. Do we really want to return to an era in which unmarried couples were excoriated for 'living in sin', or gay people and divorcees faced ruin? This is surely protesting too much. Evangelical Christians in Europe do not for the most part threaten to roll back the social reforms of recent decades. For Wilson, the core issue is why it should be wrong, in a historically Christian country, to have an observant Christian leader – not least given the unedifying lifestyle of a figure such as Boris Johnson south of the border.

Wilson's views pack a punch because he turned against the faith of his baptism during his thirties and forties. As an atheist he wrote several works lampooning Christianity before also beginning to feel doubtful about his doubts. The Church of England welcomed him back to its ranks in his fifties, after the turn of the millennium.

Among other points featuring in his defence of Kate Forbes, media ignorance looms large. The inquisitors focused relentlessly on sex. In doing so they ignored the virtues Christians themselves are likely to place front and centre in public service: respect for the truth, humility, gentleness and solidarity with the poor, to name but four. A further consideration is that virtually every postwar British prime minister until Theresa May has professed Christian convictions or embraced a Judeo-Christian moral framework, even if they didn't publicly 'do God'. These commitments were reinforced by the personal example of Elizabeth II and the avowedly Christian (but still open-handed) content of her Christmas broadcasts.

Wilson identifies a sea-change in attitudes more recently. 'The hoo-ha over Kate Forbes signals that we have now moved into a different world,' he writes, where the 'virulently anti-Christian secularism of a certain section of the elite is in the ascendant.' By professing shock over Forbes's alleged dogmatism, they really revealed far more about their own small-mindedness.

Writing soon after the accession of Charles III, he conveys the big picture with force:

> In a few months, we shall . . . be celebrating the coronation. The King will be anointed with holy oils during a Communion service and for one day at least, it will look as if we are still a Christian country, espousing values Forbes rightly describes as 'mainstream'. But you can be sure the [ceremony] will provoke the strident, noisy reminder from many quarters that we are no longer a Christian country, not really. That the C of E should be disestablished. That the faith has guttered out – and good riddance too.
>
> God forgive me, but for ten years of my life – after Salman Rushdie was condemned by a fatwa and Ireland still seemed torn apart by a semi-religious war – I thought the sooner we all gave religion the boot, the better. I wrote a pamphlet called *Against Religion*. Like most modern secularists, I rather overlooked what some of the alternatives to a religious viewpoint looked like. Some, of course, as in modern China or in Nazi Germany, are obviously sinister. Some, as in the vapid, consumerised, techie world of the West, are simply devoid of value or direction.
>
> But do we really want to shed the values of our Christian past? Is there any evidence that we are a better society for having discarded Christianity? Is it right that Christians such as Kate Forbes should be hounded out of public office for sharing the faith of Bonhoeffer, Martin Luther King and Thomas More?[18]

Though Forbes is not a martyr and would not seek to align herself with the giants just listed, it is not overblown to weigh up her treatment against the background of overweening state power in other areas, and Christian witness against it. In the course of my researches I came across a very interesting extract from one of her Holyrood speeches in 2018: 'I wanted to note that pupils should be allowed to explore, develop and understand the diversity of religious faith in Scotland, because if they can understand it in school you will hope that as they go through the rest of their life they will be tolerant of people who believe things that are different to them.' The context was constituents telling her that children were being bullied in school for expressing Christian views.[19]

It is also worth underlining the gap between what one might call elite secularist thinking and broader patterns of thought. A Panelbase poll commissioned by *The Sunday Times* during the leadership contest in February 2023, after the media row about Forbes's views on same-sex marriage, found that 23 per cent of voters questioned preferred Forbes as a prospective First Minister, with Humza Yousaf polling 15 per cent and Ash Regan 7 per cent. A later poll (early March) by Ipsos for Channel 4 News suggested that Forbes had a clear lead among members of the public, whereas Yousaf had a narrow lead among members of the SNP (who were, of course, the electorate in the contest).[20]

A connected theme here is the gulf in outlook between a devoutly secularist BBC management on the one hand, and, on the other, a viewing and listening audience who sustain a belief in a higher power, and some sort of afterlife, and are apt to pray in extremis, even if they are not outwardly religious.[21]

Wells and Fountains

We began this chapter with brief looks at the sidelining of Christianity in mainstream culture. My confidence in the justice of this complaint has been growing for over twenty years years. A flagship BBC arts programme such as *Front Row* persistently interprets diversity only in terms of certain modish metrics. Many other broadcasts follow suit: the results are often anything but varied.

This is no simple jeremiad, however. There are rich catches available for those willing to cast their cultural nets more widely. A glance at the *Church Times* or *The Tablet* among many other publications shows that Christianity is taken seriously by a large company of artists precisely because it remains a fertile source of top-class work. All Hallows-on-the-Wall in the City of London is a notable sponsor of religious art; many other less prominent churches around Britain exercise a similar ministry.

Among the outstanding contemporary examples of cross-ferti-lisation between religion and film comes from the Bible Society. For most of the past two centuries its mission has involved putting bound copies of Scripture in as many hands as possible. At a time when a majority can read the text online, the mission of the Society has evolved. Two of its main arms are Theos,[22] the Westminster-based religion-and-politics think tank; and the Pitch,[23] which offers funds to producers wanting to make short films inspired by the Old and New Testaments. Research commis-sioned by the Society suggests that the British public segments into eight broad groupings with respect to the Bible. The typical person in categories one and two reads it regularly, seeing it in highly positive terms. Personas seven and eight hold the opposite view. The Pitch identified a significant opportunity for non-coer-cive Christian witness to the many people in the creative indus-tries standing in these latter categories.

It is managed by Luke Walton, an Anglican priest with a legal background whose commitment to the genre extends well beyond personal taste to take in bigger questions about faith and the arts. He highlights the importance of the visual during our interview. 'When my phone was stolen recently, I walked down a busy street and realised that I was almost alone in not having my retina seared to a screen,' he says. His intuitions about the general popularity of film (serious reading having become a minority pursuit) coexist with awareness of the unease felt by some Protestants, especially, about associating seen with unseen realities.

Though far less attention is paid to them by the general public, short movies are rated highly by industry insiders. They are the prime means by which up-and-coming directors gain experience and, if successful, an entrée into the bigger league of feature films. For this reason the major international festivals – Cannes, Venice, San Sebastián, Toronto – have short-film strands with separate awards.

Shorts are also very much easier to make. Some have been produced on budgets as low as £1,000–£2,000. Walton thus spotted a way for the Bible Society to extend its work by helping young filmmakers. Candidates are not asked to preach, especially given that a high proportion have no church connections. The point is simply that if talented younger figures in the industry are moved to read the Bible with fresh eyes, an opportunity is created for Christianity to gain a hearing in an otherwise highly secularised arena.

Walton sees his role in a long historical context:

> The great mission movements across the years have gone to people and groups and sought to serve them, to understand them, to live with them, to share their very lives, as Paul would put it. I see my own calling as applying to the film community. And in doing so, one of the things I offer is Scripture. The reception I get is more varied than you might think. While calling themselves atheists, many filmmakers are in practice non-committal and don't say no to the search for spiritual truth.

The strategy has repeatedly borne fruit: one of the most moving films to have emerged with funding from the Pitch is Luke Bradford's *White Gold*.[24] The scriptural basis for the piece is Job's description of his skin turning black and his eyes failing (Job 30:1–31). Noting an overlap between these symptoms and those of people with Albinism across Africa, Bradford set out to chart the situation in a corner of Tanzania. Exposure to harsh sunlight causes albinos to develop melanoma (the reason their skin darkens) and lose their sight in large numbers. Even more egregiously, their body parts are prized as lucky charms in the region. Centring on Mansa, a woman whose hands were chopped off by a witch doctor, *White Gold* was longlisted for an Oscar. It affected Walton viscerally. He mentioned the subject matter to some people he himself met on a visit to Africa while Bradford's submission to the Pitch was being assessed. 'Oh,' said one. 'Just like the story of the fridge.' It turned out that the limbs of two murdered albino boys had been found in a fridge nearby.

Bradford is in distinguished company. Andy Toovey's BAFTA Cymru-nominated *Only Child*[25] draws on the story of David and Bathsheba to address parental bereavement at the death of a baby in the present day. In *The Widow's Last*,[26] Vanessa Perdriau was moved to recontextualise the story of Elijah and the widow of Zarephath in 1 Kings 17 through an account of recent disasters, including the Great Hunger in Ireland. For Walton, the finest work of all to have appeared with backing from the Pitch is Paul Holbrook's *Hollow*,[27] based on St Paul's resounding call to Christians in Romans 12 to shun the urge for vengeance.*

Holbrook's first instinct was to argue with the apostle. Having been raised a Jehovah's Witness without television or toys, he felt that he had much to be angry about. *Hollow* is set on a run-down estate. It tells of two lost souls: Laura, a single mother grieving over the death of her son at the hands of a drunk driver, and Fr Hill, a racially abused local cleric suffering a crisis of faith. But making *Hollow* proved transformational for its writer/director. Having started with the intention of chopping across the wood, Holbrook ended up carving with its grain. A figure of consequence

---

* 'Do not take revenge, my dear friends, but leave room for God's wrath, for it is written: "It is mine to avenge; I will repay," says the Lord. On the contrary, "If your enemy is hungry, feed him; if he is thirsty, give him something to drink. In doing this, you will heap burning coals on his head."'

in his industry came to feel much more open-minded about the Bible – in Walton's words, 'people learn that grown-ups can read Scripture!' – and thus about Christianity itself.

'This may seem like quite a low bar', Walton grants.

> But if that's the atmosphere we move in, it opens up all sorts of possibilities in all sorts of ways: that we can re-explore this source for our ethics or our society or our justice. So I think that's the direction we're trying to move in. Over the past couple of years, post-pandemic, we've had a lot of dark, pretty bleak films, and people coming to biblical material see an opportunity to explore some heavy themes. Emerging talent in the film industry often wants to explore big themes like this.
>
> I also wanted to see lightness of touch. I suppose at heart there is something of a comedian in me somewhere. And so I insisted that we have an opportunity for comedies to come to the fore because they can lose out to dramas. I eventually split the fund in half and created a drama category and a comedy category. I think it's been interesting to see recently how people approach Scripture seeking comedy. Carolyn Goodyear obtained funding for *Till Death Do Us Part*,[28] which tells the story of Abby, who's trapped in a rather abusive and boring marriage to an odious man. Finally, he insults the local Crime Watch guy. And it looks like all chaos will descend in this *Hot Fuzz*-type rural environment. But Abby rallies around swiftly and gives away lots of his stuff. His wines, whiskies, clothes and precious vintage car are given to the Crime Watch boss. And when she gets home, her husband, who's been on the razzle, keels over from a heart attack. It's a grimly funny film, but also basically the story of Abigail, Nabal and David out of 1 Samuel 25, just retold in a new wrapper. Since the hermeneutics of an ancient text don't necessarily scream comedy at people, it can be very interesting to explore a neglected dimension.

This is only to describe a part of the Bible Society's reach. Another of its major projects is Open the Book, providing tailored material for school assemblies in many countries. Storytelling teams typically present brief, scripted Bible stories to children in an interactive context. The Society's wider mission is represented by a diamond emblem, with politics and the media on its top two sides and education and the arts on the bottom two. 'All the areas interconnect,' Walton explains.

> The media and education are both directly influenced by politics. And the arts interact with the media and education directly, but they also speak to each other across the divides. The media will report on education, for example, or education will teach about media, or the arts will comment on politics. Those were the four domains that the Bible Society decided that it would try to engage with directly. It's taken decades for our mission to evolve: we now encapsulate it in terms of three Cs – build confidence in Scripture, change the conversation, and build capacity.

We are now in a position to trace more links between the first and second sections of this chapter. What an enterprise such as the Pitch does extremely well is to demonstrate the ability of stories 'to steal past the watchful dragons of scepticism', in C. S. Lewis's phrase. The gospel narrative has regularly found its way into popular culture and reached audiences who wouldn't turn up if they were told that a given show had anything directly to do with religion. Think of the *Matrix* series. The search is on for 'the chosen one', who then experiences betrayal, death, resurrection – and even, at the end of the movie, ascension. The entire plot is a commentary on John 8:32 ('Then you will know the truth, and the truth will set you free') and on the costliness of letting go of comforting illusions and embracing the truth. A friend I discussed these films with particularly enjoyed the scene in which the Judas character, Cypher, agrees to betray Neo while eating a steak dinner and acknowledging that the delicious experience he is enjoying is an illusion generated by the Matrix, but a fantasy that to him is preferable to reality. Another good example is *ET*, in which a vulnerable young being is pursued by malevolent forces (cf. Herod), brings magic and purpose to a dysfunctional family, dies, is resurrected and then ascends – first on a flying bicycle, and then in an alien spaceship.

The BBC has grasped this insight in the past. Tony Jordan's 2010 drama series *Nativity* – broadcast on BBC1 across four evenings between 20 and 23 December – was very faithful to Luke and Matthew and gripped the writer (who had previously been lead scriptwriter for *EastEnders*) to the extent that he came to believe in the truth of the story.[29] Sadly it is far less likely that such a drama would be aired in a prime slot in the 2020s. For that reason among others, the Bible Society's work cannot afford to flag. Wider cultural change would also be welcome. Yes, some Christians and other believers live in small mental rooms and rarely venture outside them. But so do some secularists, including figures in great positions of influence. The case for opening doors and windows is strong.

I2

Reversing Spiritual Climate Change

The philosopher Charles Taylor distinguishes between three kinds of secularism in his great study of the subject.[1] One involves a whittling away of the religious presence in public life. I have suggested that the output of a public service broadcaster such as the BBC reflects this tendency. Secularism can also be seen in a decline of personal religious practice, often coextensive with a retreat from community into individualism. This move has deeper historical roots. Compare, for instance, Bach's pietistic audiences in Leipzig during the second quarter of the eighteenth century with the Viennese concertgoers reacting as individuals to Beethoven's music several generations later. Taylor's third form of secularism rests on the decline of the Churches and other faith groups as sources of norms governing personal conduct.

That Christians are troubled by all three kinds is obvious enough. They should also assume their share of the blame. The Church has plainly fed disillusionment or scepticism at times. But alternative visions should also face scrutiny. 'Type one' secularism amounts to telling people of faith that they are free to believe and practise if they choose, but that their convictions must be entirely transcendent and not at all immanent. In other words, religion is acceptable as an eccentric private hobby because both type one and type two secularism involve seeing communities of spiritual conviction in these patronising terms. As to the question of how secularism fills the hollowed-out public square: opponents of 'public' religion have little follow-up to Taylor's third category. This means that their stance can appear self-contradictory as well as essentially negative. To say 'No one must assert that their views are normative' – is itself to make a normative statement. Matters appear murkier still on closer inspection. While presenting itself

317

as a beneficial negative grand narrative, secular rationalism finds itself in an uneasy and unresolved relationship with postmodernism, exponents of which dangerously and/or tediously assert 'alternative' facts (Donald Trump) or 'my truth' (the Duchess of Sussex). If even an atheist standard-bearer such as Nietzsche predicted that the death of God would spawn nihilism and totalitarianism, then Western society may be in far greater peril than is generally supposed. Perhaps – as Jonathan Sacks warned – spiritual climate change should be ranked alongside the environmental crisis.

Little wonder, then, that Christianity is regularly endorsed by the uncommitted as well as by believers, owing to the social blessings that accrue from it. As signalled at intervals throughout this book, I am not here referring only to goods generated by the prison chaplain or the soup-kitchen convenor or any number of other figures motivated by their faith to minister among the outcast. There are also big social trends that we can be barely conscious of, if at all. Two simple examples do duty for a bigger picture. An important source of our beliefs about individual freedom dating from well before the eighteenth century is the ecclesiastical ban on cousin marriage, which nourished a more trusting worldview opposed to clannishness and thus to xenophobia. In demanding that marriage be consensual, the medieval Church also created a climate in which audiences would later sympathise with Romeo and Juliet's urge to wed against their parents' wishes. Or think of Milton. His defence of free speech and even his anticipation of the principles of the American Declaration of Independence are all present in *Paradise Lost* through the model it offers of genuine mutuality and rational conversation, even against the background of hierarchy and patriarchy.

I wrote in Chapter 2 of Christianity's role as midwife to advances including the scientific revolution, egalitarianism and democracy; and in Chapter 4 of how theology fleshes out political accounts of the good life. These, too, are themes with many variations. Both on conceptual grounds and for reasons linked to their rootedness in communities at every social level, the Churches are better placed to diagnose deeper causes and richer solutions when deploring evils such as high inequality. These causes include the decline of working-class men's wages (the husband-to-wife income ratio correlates strongly with marriage and divorce rates), the bad side of the sexual revolution (married parents are on balance a huge advantage to children and should preferably be the norm), and prohibition (tighter controls on activities including gambling and drug-dealing are usually effective disincentives).

Christians and people of Christian heritage also have especially strong grounds for resisting free markets red in tooth and claw. It comes as no surprise that movements already referenced including Blue Labour and Red Toryism – along with their counterparts in Continental Europe – do not just present morally charged economic visions. They also draw explicitly on Catholic Social Teaching, as we have spotted. Even Margaret Thatcher's biographer Charles Moore lamented capitalism's failings as far back as 2011:

A society in which credit is very restricted is one in which new people cannot rise. How many small businesses could start or first homes be bought without a loan? But when loans become the means by which millions finance mere consumption – that is different. And when the banks that look after our money take it away, lose it and then, because of government guarantee, are not punished themselves, something much worse happens. It turns out – as the Left always claims – that a system purporting to advance the many has been perverted in order to enrich the few.

Moore's words are quoted in a very valuable essay by Ed West, a Christian conservative whose importance partly derives from his being justly critical of the Tory party.[2] He grants that individualist conservatism, like capitalism, prizes freedom. Yet it was always dependent on established moral codes, and especially Christianity, to encourage good behaviour by force of example.

Just as capitalism cannot survive without trust and honesty, so individual freedom cannot last without some internalised moral order. Modern Toryism's failure is reflected in the appeal to some of atheistic libertarianism, whose exponents envisage 'a moral bubble which they expect nothing but self-interest to fill'. West draws a piquant lesson. '[I]nstead, as we have seen in recent years, once the Church is undermined, the state soon becomes a Church.'

As he also notes, the state alone cannot reduce inequality in the absence of greater social capital – a commodity discussed at length in Robert D. Putnam's bestseller *Bowling Alone.*[3] West concludes that unless we see a growth in social capital, 'in the levels of community involvement, in social trust, in virtuous, selfless behaviour – in short, in relationships – inequality will continue to remain high. As Britain has become more individual-obsessed, as institutions such as the family, the Church, the nation and, though conservatives are reluctant to include them, trade unions have become weaker, this reduction in social capital has disproportionately harmed the poor.'

West doesn't just flag up the undoubtedly grave social problems caused by mass fatherlessness. He also emphasises the converse: that contemporary economies make it increasingly difficult for the proverbial 'working man' to support a family. The period known in France as *les trente glorieuses* (1945–75) was well known for exponential economic growth. That time has passed. A jettisoning of state socialism in China and India since the 1980s inevitably means that the centre of economic gravity has shifted back towards Asia for the first time in 500 years. This in no way discredits West's message, however.

A more than simply 'cultural' Christian commitment could include the following additional elements. There is never going to be a point at which active church members can stop thinking, praying and acting for justice. A follower of Christ must be abidingly restless at some level. After making himself a thorn in the flesh of the Third Reich, the Protestant giant Karl Barth said that Christians are always going to be unreliable political allies. In other words, they will want to confront the powers that be with awkward questions and should never feel happy about signing up to a complete package. A preacher I once heard put it as follows. 'At the end of the day, what matters most is that sense that the deepest reality in social life boils down to some fundamental issues. Are we acting as a society, as individuals, out of a love of self that leads to forgetting God, or love of God that leads to forgetting self?'

The Church is therefore not a triumphant illustration of what it looks like when social and cultural challenges are resolved. Rather, he added, it is an illustration of what it's like when people turn to the big questions we confront again and again in repentance and trust, 'and try to live out a life in which we're not constantly at war with one another, individually and collectively, and are looking for what it is that we can recognise as allowing us to flourish side by side under the God whose concerned love is for all of us.'

***

Granted the viability of these reflections, it is perhaps less surprising than may at first appear that the Somali-born ex-Muslim and feminist campaigner Ayaan Hirsi Ali should have announced in late 2023 that she now counted herself a cultural Christian. Made public in an article for the UnHerd website,[4] the move was nevertheless eye-catching given Hirsi Ali's past status as an ally of Richard Dawkins and other New Atheist campaigners. She posed two questions: 'What changed?' and 'Why do I call myself a Christian now?' Her answers are worth setting out at some length.

> Part of the answer is global. Western civilisation is under threat from three different but related forces: the resurgence of great-power authoritarianism and expansionism in the forms of the Chinese Communist Party and Vladimir Putin's Russia; the rise

of global Islamism, which threatens to mobilise a vast population against the West; and the viral spread of woke ideology, which is eating into the moral fibre of the next generation.

We endeavour to fend off these threats with modern, secular tools: military, economic, diplomatic and technological efforts to defeat, bribe, persuade, appease or surveil. And yet, with every round of conflict, we find ourselves losing ground. We are either running out of money, with our national debt in the tens of trillions of dollars, or we are losing our lead in the technological race with China.

But we can't fight off these formidable forces unless we can answer the question: what is it that unites us? The response that 'God is dead!' seems insufficient. So, too, does the attempt to find solace in 'the rules-based liberal international order'. The only credible answer, I believe, lies in our desire to uphold the legacy of the Judeo-Christian tradition.

That legacy consists of an elaborate set of ideas and institutions designed to safeguard human life, freedom and dignity – from the nation state and the rule of law to the institutions of science, health and learning. As Tom Holland has shown in his marvellous book *Dominion*, all sorts of apparently secular freedoms – of the market, of conscience and of the press – find their roots in Christianity.

Hirsi Ali had had an epiphany around the centenary of Bertrand Russell's 'Why I Am Not a Christian', a lecture later published under that title.[5]

> I have come to realise that Russell and my atheist friends failed to see the wood for the trees. The wood is the civilisation built on the Judeo-Christian tradition; it is the story of the West, warts and all. Russell's critique of . . . contradictions in Christian doctrine is serious, but it is also too narrow in scope.
>
> For instance, he gave his lecture in a room full of (former or at least doubting) Christians in a Christian country. Think about

how unique that was nearly a century ago, and how rare it still is in non-Western civilisations. Could a Muslim philosopher stand before any audience in a Muslim country – then or now – and deliver a lecture with the title 'Why I am not a Muslim'? In fact, a book with that title exists, written by an ex-Muslim. But the author published it in America under the pseudonym Ibn Warraq. It would have been too dangerous to do otherwise.

To me, this freedom of conscience and speech is perhaps the greatest benefit of Western civilisation. It does not come naturally to man. It is the product of centuries of debate within Jewish and Christian communities. It was these debates that advanced science and reason, diminished cruelty, suppressed superstitions, and built institutions to order and protect life, while guaranteeing freedom to as many people as possible. Unlike Islam, Christianity outgrew its dogmatic stage. It became increasingly clear that Christ's teaching implied not only a circumscribed role for religion as something separate from politics. It also implied compassion for the sinner and humility for the believer.

Yet I would not be truthful if I attributed my embrace of Christianity solely to the realisation that atheism is too weak and divisive a doctrine to fortify us against our menacing foes. I have also turned to Christianity because I ultimately found life without any spiritual solace unendurable – indeed very nearly self-destructive. Atheism failed to answer a simple question: what is the meaning and purpose of life?

Many assumed that Hirsi Ali's move amounted more to an acknowledgement of Christianity's role in securing social progress than to an acceptance of the Nicene Creed – though the situation is evidently dynamic. She also writes of learning about the faith bit by bit as she attends church Sunday by Sunday. In any case, although some more orthodox figures responded a bit sniffily to the article, 'cultural' Christianity has a long history. Churchill is well known for describing himself as a flying buttress – namely supporting the structure from outside. His leanings are widely copied.

While not at all wishing to criticise Hirsi Ali, then – her back-story includes campaigns against the female genital mutilation she herself suffered in childhood, along with many other courageous acts – I nevertheless think that other believers have a duty to push a bit further. The grounds for doing so are philosophical as well as theological. *Philosophical*, because conserving the Judeo-Christian cultural inheritance should not be confused with ancestor worship. These traditions can and should be justified as expressions of our truth-tracking pursuit of the good, the true and the beautiful. For reasons set out in Chapter 3, I follow a line extending back to St Augustine and beyond in giving a Christian framing to these Transcendentals. We are naturally not obliged to do so. Latter-day Platonists and perhaps Stoics will share a commitment to allied metaphysical principles. What certainly does remain necessary, however, is a commitment to objective standards of reference, side by side with a universal idiom for articulating them. And the foundations are *theological*, because Christianity is not ethics misleadingly encased in archaic myth. It is about faith and hope in a journey from exile through a wilderness to springs of living water. Karl Barth's political stance sketched above is biblically based. Christianity's radical reservation about 'the world' of 'principalities and powers' springs from a sense of chronic brokenness in the human condition, and the corruption of even our noblest ideals. In short, we are marked by original sin, which in turn generates a quest for healing that is re-presented in liturgy. The Sermon on the Mount stands out for me with particular force here. In David Martin's unpacking of it, Jesus preaches against a horizon of beatitude and promise. The sermon 'asks how you stand, how you are placed when it comes to receiving, giving and making gestures of reconciliation and inclusion'. Right at the heart of Christian belief stands 'the blood offering of the Blood Donor, and our loving communion with the Donor.'[6] Like all pastors worth their salt, Martin brought out the importance of Trinitarian as well as incarnational belief. In holding that the source of all created reality is itself an eternal exchange of mutual self-giving, Christians can infer among much else that differences need not lead to conflict or antagonism but can coexist in harmony and find expression in creativity.

Perhaps the most searching response to Ayaan Hirsi Ali came from Jacob Phillips in *The Critic* magazine.[7] Aged twenty-five, he converted to Christianity soon after the turn of the millennium while working in the City of London. His office ethos amounted to 'rough-edged Thatcherism' – the aim was to make as much money as possible in the shortest possible time. Phillips's colleagues read *Zoo* and *Nuts* (then very popular but now defunct so-called lads' mags), while 'popular culture had begun slipping into a level of pornification impossible to imagine just a few years previously.' Employees would disappear into toilet cubicles to snort drugs on Friday afternoons.

Leaving the office to attend Mass during the lunch hour – as Phillips did regularly after his reception as a Catholic – thus felt counter-cultural. 'Mammon lay slain' at the church door. 'In the first few minutes kneeling in the pews, there'd be a radical decentring of all the values the world held dear. I'd return to work feeling reorientated by the uncontrollable centre of human life – the miracle of being restored to our origin out of nothing, after accepting the dereliction and dismay of the world.'

Christian radicalism continues to exert a strong pull on Phillips. 'I read "when Christ calls a man, he bids him come and die" from Dietrich Bonhoeffer, or St Theresa of Lisieux saying, "I desire only to suffer and be forgotten." As my colleagues raged through the City's bars on Friday nights, I would pray a line from Psalm 88: "You have taken away my friends, and made me hateful in their sight."' He quit his job a year later to study for a degree in theology.

The move felt more subversive then than it might do in the 2020s. Churchgoers themselves – not just practitioners of civic religion, but also some members of an older liberal generation probably too accommodating of secular fashions – can be among those most surprised to discover the continuing potency of gospel teaching. Like Martin, Phillips sees that the civilisational benefits of Christianity are only by-products (albeit important ones) of faith itself.

> Faith is . . . uncontrollable, and it is just as active in despair and dereliction as in the moments of great historical achievement. If your Christianity promises to improve life in a worldly sense, it probably isn't that Christian.
>
> The apostles didn't lay down their nets to become fishers of self-fulfilment. The mystics didn't emaciate themselves through fasting to defend our freedom of speech. The martyrs didn't die for the good educational outcomes of stable families. At the centre of anything purporting to be Christian must always be the . . . disruptive reality of lives being lived, and societies being led, in ways which are not of our choosing.[8]

These thoughts can be put in a nutshell, as well as endlessly elaborated. The brief version should include an avowal that our lives have a *telos* or goal. Christianity's eclipse matters because the Church is the sturdiest vessel for the preservation of values without which civilisation will wither. And because Christian teaching goes further in maintaining that our human search for love and joy is at one with the order and purpose of the world as God's creation.

Janet Soskice, one of my wisest teachers and a thinker to rank alongside Taylor, sums these thoughts up memorably with the simple comment that Dante was right. 'In the end,' she adds, 'it is love which moves the Sun and the other stars, and which draws us on in our social and moral lives. We just need to be able to see it.'[9]

Appendix 1

The 2023 sessions of the Synod on Synodality ended with many proposals for reform, touching on church governance, mission, theology, canonical discipline and pastoral outreach. Held in Rome between 4 and 29 October, the event had 364 participants – 54 of them women – as well as 85 experts, facilitators and 'fraternal delegates' from other Churches. Laypeople were given voting rights for the first time.

Despite diverse 'origins, languages and cultures', the Synod's *Synthesis Report* says, delegates sought to 'sing in a variety of voices with a unity of souls', and to offer 'a testimony of harmony to a divided world'. In its commentary, Vatican Radio granted that the idea of synodality had caused 'confusion and concern'. Some feared 'a departure from tradition and debasement of the Church's hierarchical nature', while others feared 'immobility and lack of courage for change'. In the event, the report adds, the Synod had 'listened to all and probed everything more deeply', taking a 'renewed look' at contemporary impulses in areas such as the part played by women and laypeople, the ministry of priests and bishops, ecumenism and the care for abuse victims.

Meeting daily in working groups of up to a dozen members, the Synod considered reports compiled in February and March 2023 at continent-by-continent gatherings in Europe, Oceania, the Middle East, North America, Asia, Africa and Latin America, which had in their turn discussed 'national syntheses' tabled by Bishops' Conferences after diocesan and parish-led consultations.

Voted on paragraph by paragraph after at least 1,250 group and individual amendments, the *Synthesis Report* outlines 'convergences', 'matters for consideration', and 'proposals' in three parts. On missions, the report says that Christian communities should 'enter into solidarity with those of other religions, convictions and cultures', while ensuring that the Church's liturgical language becomes 'more accessible to the faithful and more embodied in the diversity of cultures'. It adds that the poor should be identified 'not only as those materially impoverished', but as being among the world's migrants, minorities and indigenous peoples, victims of violence, racism, trafficking and exploitation, as well as the elderly and abandoned, and unborn children, who require 'constant advocacy'.

The report also calls on Christians to engage in politics, associations, trade unions and popular movements. 'The Assembly is aware of the cry of the "new poor", produced by wars and terrorism that torment countries on different continents, and condemns the corrupt political and economic systems that are their cause. The Church's commitment must get to the causes of poverty and exclusion . . . It requires public denunciation of injustices, whether perpetrated by individuals, governments, companies or societal structures.' The document adds that laypeople are now 'indispensable to the Church's mission' as educators, theologians and administrators: their talents should accordingly be 'recognised and fully appreciated'. Furthermore, the Church should make a strong commitment to 'pastoral accompaniment and vigorous advocacy' on behalf of women, who 'cry out for justice in societies marked by sexual violence and economic inequality'.

Further research is said to be needed on women's access to the diaconate, in line with a papal commission set up in 2016. In the meantime, steps are required to ensure that women 'participate in decision-making processes and assume roles of responsibility', especially given a widespread perception that the Church is marked by 'clericalism, a chauvinist mentality and inappropriate expressions of authority'. 'It is clear that some people are afraid they will be forced to change, whereas others fear that nothing at all will change or that there will be too little courage to move at the pace of the living Tradition.'

In other sections, the report suggests that further consideration should be given to the value of compulsory clerical celibacy, and adds that judicial responsibility for abuse cases should be assigned away from local bishops. While laypeople and members of religious orders could become more involved in episcopal appointments, diocesan pastoral councils could also be made mandatory, and 'new structures' could be brought in for assessing a bishop's performance. While same-sex relationships are not addressed directly, the report nevertheless calls for the shunning of 'simplistic judgements', adding that more should be done to 'hear and accompany' those feeling 'marginalised or excluded because of their marriage status, identity or sexuality'. It concludes that there was 'a deep sense of love, mercy and compassion felt in the Assembly for those feeling neglected by the Church, who want a place to call "home" where they can feel safe, heard and respected, without fear of feeling judged'; the report also says that the 80 or so reform proposals to have emerged from the Synod reflect a desire for a Church 'closer to people, less bureaucratic and more relational'.

Presenting the report at a press conference on 28 October 2023, the Synod's Maltese Secretary-General, Cardinal Mario Grech, said that those taking part had come 'in search of the broadest and most convinced consensus', conscious that they were 'witnesses of a process' rather than delegates 'representing the people of God in parliamentary logic'. The Synod's chief Relator, Cardinal Jean-Claude Hollerich of Luxembourg, said that the spirt of openness provided by synodality would also change the Church, enabling it to 'find answers, but perhaps not the exact answers this or that groups wishes to have'.

Bishops' Conferences have been reflecting on 'the most relevant and urgent questions and proposals' in preparation for the final Synod Assembly starting in October 2024. Concrete proposals will then be presented to Pope Francis for a final decision.

Appendix 11

Anglicanism within most of the British Empire was the result of missionary work by the C of E, but the USA was a special case. Until the War of Independence, the Anglican Church in the American colonies was under the supervision of the Bishop of London. There were no colonial bishops. The clergy of Connecticut elected Samuel Seabury to be their Bishop in 1783. He travelled to London seeking consecration and discovered that this could only happen if he took an oath of allegiance to the sovereign. He was consecrated in Aberdeen in 1784 by three bishops of the Scottish Episcopal Church, a ceremony that marked the beginning of the Anglican Communion. One of the difficulties that the worldwide Anglican Communion now faces is that conservative Anglicans in the USA exercise, by means of their wealth, a considerable influence over Anglicanism in the developing world.

A word about the history of Anglicanism in Wales, Ireland and Scotland is in order. The Henrician and Elizabethan church settlements were applied both to Wales, where the primacy of Canterbury had been established in the medieval period, and to Ireland. Welsh Anglican bishops sat in the House of Lords and Irish Anglican Bishops sat in the Irish House of Lords until the Act of Union 1800 came into force. Thereafter a representative sample of them sat in the House of Lords until the Church of Ireland was disestablished.

There was relatively little resistance to the Anglican settlement in Wales until the rise of Nonconformity. By the second half of the nineteenth century resentment at the obligation to pay tithes was provoking protests and calls for disestablishment, a cause which the Liberal Party espoused. The Royal Commission which reported in 1910 noted that there were 549,123 Nonconformist communicants in Wales and only 193,081 Anglican communicants out of a population of 2,421,000. Opposition from Conservative peers and the outbreak of the First World War delayed the passing of legislation disestablishing the Church in Wales until 1920, at which point Welsh bishops ceased to sit in the House of Lords.

The Henrician and Elizabethan religious settlements were not accepted by the majority of the clergy and people in Ireland. Catholicism remained the religion of the great majority, with a substantial influx of Presbyterians into Ulster in the early seventeenth century. The non-Anglican majority resented the privileges accorded to Anglicans: as in Wales, the obligation to pay tithes was a source of resentment. In 1869 Gladstone's government legislated to disestablish the Anglican Church in Ireland.

The Reformation in Scotland took a different course and an Episcopalian Church supported by the Stuarts was in conflict with a militant Presbyterianism. The question of whether the Episcopalian or the Presbyterian Church would be established in Scotland was finally settled after the Glorious Revolution, the Scottish bishops refusing to take the oath of allegiance to William and Mary. Thereafter, the Scottish Episcopal Church was subject to a series of penal laws, its clergy forbidden to conduct marriages or baptisms. In the eighteenth century the Hanoverians strengthened the penal laws. After the 1745 Jacobite rising, in which 70 per cent of Bonnie Prince Charlie's army is estimated to have been Episcopalian, the sixth penal law of 1748 forbade Episcopal clergy from conducting public worship. They were only allowed to hold services in private houses with not more than four persons present. By the late eighteenth century the Jacobite threat had receded and the Scottish Episcopalians Relief Act 1792 abolished the penal laws.

As regards more recent developments, the SEC voted in favour of the ordination of women to the priesthood in 1993 and the first women were ordained in 1994. The General Synod of the SEC voted in 2003 that women could be consecrated as bishops.

The Marriage Canon was changed in 2017 to permit priests to conduct marriages of same-sex couples, while ruling that no priest is obliged so to do.

In my view, the latter change happened with relatively little turbulence partly because the majority of SEC congregations stand in the liberal Catholic tradition, and partly because the process was reflective and respectful. Being disestablished was also a factor. Established Churches are inclined to see themselves as a kind of Notional Health Service: this acts as a brake on certain kinds of change. It took the Church of Scotland until 2022 to accept same-sex marriage, for example.

Notes

Chapter 1: A Flight from Enchantment

1. Arnold Hunt's essay remains unpublished.
2. Ibid.
3. Ibid.
4. Rupert Shortt, *Christianophobia: A Faith Under Attack* (Rider, 2012), Introduction.
5. Timothy Samuel Shah and Monica Duffy Toft, 'Why God Is Winning', *Foreign Policy* (www.foreignpolicy.com, 9 June 2006).
6. 'Religion by Age and Sex, England and Wales: Census 2021' (https://www.ons.gov.uk).
7. See, for example, 'No congregation, no church: how Scotland lost the faith', *Financial Times* (www.ft.com, 19 August 2023).
8. Clive Field, *Counting Religion in Britain, 1970–2020: Secularization in Statistical Context* (Oxford University Press, 2021).
9. Tom Wright, *Surprised by Scripture* (SPCK, 2013), p. 155.
10. Mary Eberstadt, *How the West Really Lost God: A New Theory of Secularization* (Templeton Foundation Press, 2014).
11. Eamon Maher and Eugene O'Brien, *Tracing the Cultural Legacy of Irish Catholicism: From Galway to Cloyne and Beyond* (Manchester University Press, 2017).
12. Rupert Shortt, *God Is No Thing: Coherent Christianity* (Hurst, 2016; paperback edition, 2024).
13. Anthony Green, *Private Passions*, BBC Radio 3, 30 November 2014.
14. Bryan Appleyard, *The Sunday Times* (www.thetimes.co.uk, 2 November 2014).
15. See Robert Skidelsky, *The Machine Age: An Idea, a History, a Warning* (Allen Lane, 2023).
16. Brian Cox, *Start the Week*, BBC Radio 4, 14 March 2011.
17. Polly Toynbee, 'Christmas comes with good cheer. The tragedy is the religious baggage', *The Guardian* (www.theguardian.com, 23 December 2022). Toynbee's message was stale. 'Much as I dislike most Christian belief, the iconography of star, stable, manger, kings and shepherds to

greet a new baby is a universal emblem of humanity . . . But the rest of it, I find loathsome. Why wear the symbol of a barbaric torture? Martyrdom is a repugnant virtue, so too the imposition of perpetual guilt.' She then produced some heroic myth-making of her own about 'fanatical early Christians, who permitted no heresy, hacked down temples, and burned ancient classical texts'. Almost every statement above is either misconceived, one-eyed, or flatly untrue. But the narrative prospers all the same.

18. Matthew Parris, 'The battle between good and evil is fantasy', *The Times* (www.thetimes.co.uk, 1 January 2022). Writing twelve months beforehand, Parris was no subtler. His complaint centred on Christianity's childish attachment to the idea of a cosmic battle between good and evil. Both Toynbee and Parris at their best have a fierce moral sense. But you can make almost any set of beliefs look silly by resorting to straw man tactics. If Parris had used a fraction of the talent he devotes to politics to finding out what church teaching in the round says about evil, he would have discovered that it is not classically viewed as some kind of thing or even some kind of power. St Augustine devotes a part of his *Confessions* to establishing this point. Evil is the vacuum that sets in when we mistake what is good for us. Our true good, Augustine urges, is the reconciliation God wills. And finding the final good of what we most desire and long for in other places than that creates the destructive void into which the lives of so many people are sucked. Though absolutely real, then, evil is not some kind of stuff. In thus presenting the subject, Christianity is not for a moment downplaying the bad. On the contrary, evil's force derives from the fact that it is desired with the same energy as the good is desired, because it is a *misidentified* good, not because it has some 'evil' essence. Genocide, torture or child abuse happen because people who are lethally and hideously deceived think that they will attain some deeply desirable good (security, satisfaction, assurance, peace) through actions that are in fact destructive of themselves and others. If evil's origins lie in delusion, not in some evil power or element in things, this does not mean it is any less serious. More broadly, how can a thoughtful person *not* think that evil and good are real, that they are incompatible, and that they're in a state of structural conflict? To my mind one of the great sadnesses arising from Christianity's eclipse is that even its enemies are impoverished and immiserated. They often have little idea of what they're fighting against.

19. Will Lloyd, *The Times* (www.thetimes.co.uk, 13 March 2023).

20. Bryan R. Wilson, *Religion and Secular Society: Fifty Years On* (Oxford University Press, 1966; reissued in 2016).

21. A. J. P. Taylor, *English History 1914–1945* (Oxford University Press, 1965).

22. My list would include Keith Thomas, Quentin Skinner, David Starkey and David Wootton. All in different ways assume atheism to be true by definition, rather than a debatable standpoint.

23. See, for example, Steve Bruce and David Voas, 'Secularization Vindicated', *Religions*, Vol. 14, No. 3, March 2023 (https://www.mdpi.com/2077-1444/14/3/301). The authors' summary of the empirical data is accurate. In other respects, though, their discussion is conceptually crude. My main demur is that they never consider any of the cultural and ethical implications of what they report; nor do they assess the cultural deposits of something airily defined as 'secularization' in societies which have been shaped by religious legacies from earlier phases of history. Not all 'secularities' are the same. They also cut corners in claiming that the Churches have been uniformly wrong or behind the curve on all the major social issues of recent times.

24. Callum Brown, *The Death of Christian Britain: Understanding Secularisation 1800–2000* (Routledge, 2001).

25. http://www.brin.ac.uk/

26. See, for example, Jeremy Morris, *A People's Church: A History of the Church of England* (Profile, 2022).

27. Larry Siedentop, *Inventing the Individual: The Origins of Western Liberalism* (Allen Lane, 2014).

28. Nick Spencer, *Freedom and Order: History, Politics and the English Bible* (Hodder & Stoughton, 2011).

Chapter 2: What Have the Roman Catholics and Other Christians Ever Given Us?

1. Lucy Beckett, 'Sacred and profane: how Christianity conquered the world', *The Times Literary Supplement (TLS)* (www.the-tls.co.uk, 13 December 2019).

2. Lucy Beckett, *In the Light of Christ: Writings in the Western Tradition* (Ignatius Press, 2006).

3. Tom Holland, *Dominion: The Making of the Western Mind* (Little, Brown, 2019).

4. Tom Holland, *Persian Fire: The First World Empire and the Battle for the West* (Abacus, 2006).

5. Christopher Hitchens, *God Is Not Great: How Religion Poisons Everything* (Atlantic, 2007).

6. Peter Heather, *Christendom: The Triumph of a Religion* (Allen Lane, 2022).

7. David Bentley Hart, *Atheist Delusions: The Christian Revolution and Its Fashionable Enemies* (Yale University Press, 2009).

8. Charles Taylor, *A Secular Age* (Harvard University Press, 2007).

9. Denis Alexander, reviewing Jerry Coyne, *Faith vs Fact; Why Science and Religion are Incompatible*, TLS (www.the-tls.co.uk, 23 January 2016).

10. Ronald Numbers (ed.), *Galileo Goes to Jail: And Other Myths About Science and Religion* (Harvard University Press, 2009). As it happens, fewer than half the scholars contributing to this volume are religious believers.

11. Nicholas Spencer, *Magisteria: The Entangled Histories of Science and Religion* (Oneworld, 2023).

12. Alasdair MacIntyre, *After Virtue: A Study in Moral Theory* (Duckworth, 1981; 3rd revised edition, 2007).

13. G. E. M. Anscombe, 'Modern Moral Philosophy', *Philosophy*, Vol. 33, No. 124, January 1958 (https://www.jstor.org/stable/3749051).

14. John Gray, 'The cult of hyper-liberalism', *TLS* (www.the-tls.co.uk, 30 March 2018).

15. N. T. Wright, *The Spectator* (www.spectator.co.uk, 27 March, 2021).

16. David Martin, 'The ideal observers', *TLS*, 7 February 2003.

17. Douglas Murray, *The Strange Death of Europe: Immigration, Identity, Islam* (Bloomsbury, 2017).

18. Yuval Noah Harari, *Sapiens: A Brief History of Humankind* (Vintage, 2015).

19. For an accessible discussion of both *The Strange Death of Europe* and *Sapiens*, see Jonathan Sacks's YouTube review (https://www.youtube.com/watch?v=BY6UY2tn5Os).

20. Ibid.

21. Ibid.

22. Ibid.

23. Ibid.

24. Ibid.

25. I also owe this notion to the late Rabbi Sacks.

26. Rupert Shortt, *The Hardest Problem: God, Evil and Suffering* (Hodder & Stoughton, 2022), Chapter 2.

27. Ibid., pp. 50–1.

Chapter 3: How Credible is the Creed?

1. Sam Harris, *Waking Up: Searching for Spirituality Without Religion* (Black Swan, 2015).

2. Anthony Kenny, reviewing Edward Feser, *The Last Superstition*, *TLS* (www.the-tls.co.uk, 22 July 2011).

3. John Cottingham, reviewing Sam Harris, *Waking Up*, *TLS* (www.the-tls.co.uk, 25 September 2015).

4. Denys Turner, *Thomas Aquinas: A Portrait* (Yale University Press, 2013), p. 37.

5. Iain McGilchrist, *The Matter With Things: Our Brains, Our Delusions, and the Unmaking of the World* (Perspectiva Press, 2021), Volume I, Chapter 15.

6. Ibid.

7. Jonathan Gaisman KC, speaking during a day conference held in Iain McGilchrist's honour at Oriel College, Oxford, in June 2022.

8. Rupert Shortt, *Outgrowing Dawkins: God for Grown-Ups* (SPCK, 2019).

9. Richard Dawkins, *Outgrowing God: A Beginner's Guide* (Bantam, 2019).

10. Simon Conway Morris, reviewing A. N. Wilson, *Charles Darwin: Victorian Mythmaker*, *The Tablet* (www.thetablet.co.uk, 7 September 2017).

11. Roger Scruton, *Gentle Regrets: Thoughts from a Life* (Continuum, 2005), pp. 226–7.

12. Ibid.

13. John Cottingham, *The Spiritual Dimension: Religion, Philosophy and Human Value* (Cambridge University Press, 2005), Chapter 7.

14. For a brief conspectus on the six arguments, see Rupert Shortt, *Does Religion Do More Harm Than Good?* (SPCK, 2019), pp. 78–9.

15. 'Earth's demise could rid galaxy of meaning, warns Brian Cox ahead of Cop26', *The Guardian* (www.theguardian.com, 19 October 2021).

16. David Bentley Hart, *The Experience of God: Being, Consciousness, Bliss* (Yale University Press, 2013), p. 44.

17. Ibid.

18. See Shortt, *God Is No Thing*, Chapter 3.

19. See Shortt, *Outgrowing Dawkins*, pp. 56–70.

20. John Cottingham, *Philosophy and Theology* Vol. 24, No. 1, 2012, pp. 85–111 (https://www.pdcnet.org/philtheol/Philosophy-and-Theology).

21. See, for example, Denis Noble, *Dance to the Tune of Life: Biological Relativity* (Cambridge University Press, 2016).

22. Andrea Sangiovanni, *Humanity without Dignity: Moral Equality, Respect, and Human Rights* (Harvard University Press, 2017).

23. Austin Farrer, *The Glass of Vision* (Andesite Press, 2015).

24. For an excellent account of Farrer's argument, see Rowan Williams, De Lubac Lecture 2018, delivered at Saint Louis University (https://www.youtube.com/watch?v=CsEbWMsaYm4).

25. *The Hardest Problem* also entails a bid to justify the reasonableness of belief in God as such, as well as a review of allied topics including divine action, atonement and providence.

26. Eleonore Stump, *Wandering in Darkness: Narrative and the Problem of Suffering* (Oxford University Press, 2012).

27. David Bentley Hart, *The Doors of the Sea: Where Was God in the Tsunami?* (Eerdmans, 2005).

28. Jonathan Sacks, Indaba Lecture 2015 (https://www.youtube.com/watch?v=oixGCAe58_A).

29. 'But there was one sense in which the Holocaust changed the whole human equation,' Sacks added. 'The culture that produced the Holocaust was not distant. This colossal tragedy and crime took place in the heart of the most civilised culture that the world has ever known. A culture that had achieved the greatest heights of human achievement, in science, in philosophy, in rationalism – this was the culture of Kant and Hegel and Nietzsche and Schopenhauer, the culture of Goethe and Schiller and Bach and Beethoven. Half the signatories of the Wannsee Declaration [authorising the 'Final Solution' from 1942] carried the title of Dr. And that was just Germany. France: the country that gave us the Revolution and *The Rights of Man* had an astonishing history of anti-Semitism. As for Vienna: the cultural capital of Europe was also the epicentre of anti-Semitism. After the Holocaust some people lost their faith. Some people kept their faith and some people found faith in God. But after the Holocaust it is *morally impossible* to believe in man. The Holocaust is the final, decisive refutation of the idea that you can have a humane civilisation without fear of heaven and without belief in the sanctity of life. The Holocaust may make some lose their faith in God, but it must make *all* people lose their faith in humankind. After Auschwitz you have to be either very ignorant or very naive to believe in secular humanism. The real challenge of the Shoah is not to faith, but to lack of faith.'

30. Samuel Wells, *Humbler Faith, Bigger God: Finding a Story to Live By* (Canterbury Press, 2022).

31. Ibid., p. 51.

32. Paul K. Moser, *The Evidence for God: Religious Knowledge Reexamined* (Cambridge University Press, 2009).

33. Rupert Shortt, *Rowan's Rule: The Biography of the Archbishop* (Hodder & Stoughton, 2014), p. 14.

34. Ibid., pp. 16–18.

35. Rupert Shortt, *Rowan Williams: An Introduction* (DLT, 2003), pp. 85–6.

36. Ibid.

37. Martyn Skinner, *The Return of Arthur* (Chapman, 1959).

38. David Martin, *TLS* (www.the-tls.co.uk, 3 June 2011).
39. It is well established that the Rabbis of the Talmud and later periods used creative methods to negate laws in the Bible which they thought subverted the broader narrative. A favourite technique was to put a non-literal interpretation on the law. In the case of the command to kill the Amalekites in I Samuel 15, for example, the Rabbis said that when Sennacherib invaded Palestine he mixed up all the nations of the area, making it impossible to know who was an Amalekite. Therefore the law, though not revoked, could no longer be applied.
40. Francis Spufford: *Unapologetic: Why, Despite Everything, Christianity Can Still Make Surprising Emotional Sense* (Faber, 2012).
41. Elizabeth Oldfield, *Fully Alive: Tending to the Soul in Turbulent Times* (Hodder & Stoughton, 2024). I am very grateful to the author for advance sight of the manuscript before publication.
42. These remarks derive from a lecture given to students during Rowan Williams's time as Lady Margaret Professor of Divinity at Oxford, 1986–92.
43. Ibid.
44. Ibid.

Chapter 4: Enhancing the Common Good

1. David Martin, *TLS* (www.the-tls.co.uk, 24 and 31 December 2004). See also Rupert Shortt (ed.), *God's Advocates: Christian Thinkers in Conversation* (DLT, 2005), pp. 248ff.
2. Shortt, *God's Advocates*, pp. 261–2.
3. Shortt, *God Is No Thing*, p. 98.
4. Jacques Maritain, *The Rights of Man and Natural Law*, translated by Doris C. Anson (Gordian Press, 1971), pp. 21–2.
5. Albert Weale, *Crisis Response Journal*, Vol. 17, No. 3, September 2022 (https://www.crisis-response.com/Publisher/File.aspx?id=315512).
6. Ibid.
7. Ibid.
8. Jonathan Sacks, 'The Pope is right about the threat to freedom', *The Times* (www.thetimes.co.uk, 3 February 2010).
9. Sacks, Indaba lecture.
10. Jonathan Sacks, *The Dignity of Difference: How to Avoid the Clash of Civilizations* (Continuum, 2002). All citations are from the Prologue.
11. Stephen Pinker, *Enlightenment Now: The Case for Reason, Science, Humanism, and Progress* (Penguin, 2019).

12. Siedentop, *Inventing the Individual*.

13. See Rowan Williams, *Faith in the Public Square* (Bloomsbury, 2012).

14. T. S. Eliot, *The Idea of a Christian Society* (Harcourt Brace, 1949).

15. Rowan Williams, 'Political Liberty and Religious Liberty', the Las Casas lecture for 2016 delivered at Blackfriars Hall, Oxford (https://www.bfriars.ox.ac.uk/resource/religious-and-civil-liberty/).

16. See Shortt, *Rowan Williams*, Chapter 4.

17. For instances of an increasingly confident reaction against hardline gender ideology, see Sarah Ditum, 'Stonewall can no longer play judge and jury', *The Times* (www.thetimes.co.uk, 20 October 2021); or Janice Turner, 'Silent majority must stand up to student bullies', *The Times* (9 October 2021).

18. Matthew Syed, *Sunday Times* (www.thetimes.co.uk, 26 March 2023).

19. Ibid.

20. Luke Bretherton, *Resurrecting Democracy: Faith, Citizenship, and the Politics of a Common Life* (Cambridge University Press, 2014).

21. Robert J. Schreiter, R. Scott Appleby and Gerard F. Powers (eds), *Peacebuilding: Catholic Theology, Ethics, and Praxis* (Orbis, 2010).

22. John Habgood, *Confessions of a Conservative Liberal* (SPCK, 1988), p. 8.

23. Shortt, *Does Religion Do More Harm Than Good?*, pp. 75–6.

24. 'Humanitas: Rowan Williams in Conversation with Jon Snow', an event hosted at Oxford University in 2014 under the auspices of the Institute for Strategic Dialogue (https://www.youtube.com/watch?v=nxKSZ_WzSBY).

Chapter 5: Christians Don't Count Either

1. David Baddiel, *Jews Don't Count* (TLS Books, 2021).

2. Holly Williams, *The Observer* (www.theguardian.com. 2 August 2020).

3. Baddiel, *Jews Don't Count*, p. 1.

4. The Bishop of Truro's Independent Review for the Foreign Secretary of FCO Support for Persecuted Christians (https://christianpersecutionreview.org.uk/report/).

5. Benny Morris and Dror Ze'evi, *The Thirty-Year Genocide: Turkey's Destruction of its Christian Minorities, 1894–1924* (Harvard University Press, 2019).

6. Shortt, *Christianophobia*.

7. Ibid., Chapter 2.

8. The lot of the Oriental Orthodox was to be known by the equally unfortunate term 'Monophysite', a definition that persisted for many

centuries. Nestorianism (named after Nestorius, sometime Patriarch of Constantinople during the early fifth century, but actually deriving from a school of thought associated with the city of Antioch) is the view that there were two separate persons in the incarnate Christ, one human and the other divine – in contrast to the orthodox conviction that Christ was a single person, at once God and man. Monophysitism holds that Christ incarnate had only one nature, not two. This teaching has tended to be seen from outside as the mirror image of Nestorianism – a kind of equal and opposite heresy.

9. See Aidan Nichols, *The Latin Clerk: The Life, Work, and Travels of Adrian Fortescue* (Lutterworth Press, 2011), p. 105.

10. Ibid., p.109.

11. Ibid., p. 110.

12. Philip Jenkins, *The Lost History of Christianity: The Thousand-Year Golden Age of the Church in the Middle East, Africa, and Asia – and How it Died* (HarperCollins, 2008).

13. Ibid., p. 6.

14. Shortt, *Christianophobia*, pp. 1–4.

15. Alaa al-Aswany, *On the State of Egypt: What Caused the Revolution* (Canongate, 2011), p. 129.

16. Paul A. Marshall (ed.), *Religious Freedom in the World* (Rowman & Littlefield, 2000), p. 310.

17. The book is also exceptionally useful in presenting freedom of belief as the canary in the coalmine with respect to other indices of wellbeing.

18. Marshall, *Religious Freedom in the World*, p. 311.

19. Aid to the Church in Need (ACN), *Persecuted and Forgotten?*, covering the period 2020–22 (https://acnuk.org/persecuted-and-forgotten/), p. 76ff.

20. See Rebecca Paveley, 'Nigerian Christians under "relentless attack"', *Church Times* (www.churchtimes.co.uk, 14 July 2023).

21. Ibid.

22. David Landrum, 'Christians in Nigeria on brink', *Church Times* (www.churchtimes.co.uk, 3 February 2023).

23. For an overview of Sansal's pluralistic vision and warnings about hardline Islamism, see Ruth Schneider's review of Boualem Sansal's dystopian novel *2084* (https://www.europaeditions.co.uk/review/2696).

24. Ibid.

25. Vincent Goossaert and David A. Palmer, *The Religious Question in Modern China* (University of Chicago Press, 2011), p. 69.

26. ACN, *Persecuted and Forgotten?*, p. 24ff.

27. https://www.opendoorsuk.org/news/stories/uk-190116/

28. Ibid.
29. *Persecuted and Forgotten?*, p. 52ff.
30. Ibid.
31. Ibid.
32. Ibid., p. 58ff.
33. Shortt, *Does Religion Do More Harm Than Good?*, p. 65ff.
34. Norman Etherington (ed.), *Missions and Empire* (Oxford University Press, 2008).
35. John Micklethwait and Adrian Wooldridge, *God Is Back: How the Global Rise of Faith is Changing the World* (Penguin, 2009).
36. *Persecuted and Forgotten?*, p. 70.
37. Published in 2008, the Freedom House rankings on religious freedom have not altered substantially in two decades (www.freedomhouse.org). For a more detailed breakdown, see Shortt, *Christianophobia*, Appendix A.
38. Lucy Beckett, *The Year of Thamar's Book* (Gracewing, 2018).

Chapter 6: A Field Hospital for Sinners

1. 'Pope claims condoms could make Africa Aids crisis worse', *The Guardian* (www.theguardian.com, 17 March 2009).
2. Ian Linden, *Global Catholicism: Diversity and Change Since Vatican II* (Hurst, 2009).
3. Rupert Shortt, *Benedict XVI: Commander of the Faith* (Hodder, 2005).
4. I am grateful to two figures especially – Dr John Page, formerly executive secretary of the International Commission in English in the Liturgy (ICEL), and the late Bishop Maurice Taylor – for detailed guidance on the tangled process of liturgical translation into English.
5. John Cornwell, *Breaking Faith: The Pope, the People, and the Fate of Catholicism* (Viking, 2001).
6. Shortt, *Benedict XVI*, pp. 108–10.
7. Jason Berry, *Render Unto Rome: The Secret Life of Money in the Catholic Church* (Crown, 2011).
8. John Plender, reviewing *Render Unto Rome*, TLS (www.the-tls.co.uk, 6 April 2012).
9. Ibid.
10. Joseph Ratzinger, 'Free Expression and Obedience in the Church', in Hugo Rahner (ed.), *The Church: Readings in Theology* (P. J. Kenedy, 1963), p.212.
11. Joseph Ratzinger, *Introduction to Christianity* (Ignatius Press; revised edition, 2004).

12. The comment was made to the journalist Vittorio Messori in the interview later published in Italian as *Rapporto sulla fede*, and in English as *The Ratzinger Report* (Ignatius Press, 1985). A digest of the Italian original, translated and abridged by Elsa Iglich, Fergus Kerr OP, John Orme Mills OP and Robert Ombres OP, was published in the Dominican journal *New Blackfriars* in June 1985. My quotation from *Rapporto sulla fede* is drawn from the *New Blackfriars* version.

13. Ibid.

14. Henry Wansbrough, in Shortt, *Benedict XVI*, p. 7.

15. Tracey Rowland, *Ratzinger's Faith: The Theology of Pope Benedict XVI* (Oxford University Press, 2008); and *Benedict XVI: A Guide for the Perplexed* (Bloomsbury, 2010).

16. David Cameron, *For the Record* (William Collins, 2019), Chapter 17.

17. Linden, *Global Catholicism*, Conclusion.

18. www.togetherforthecommongood.co.uk

19. Jenny Sinclair, 'A synod for the world', *The Tablet* (www.thetablet.co.uk, 23 December, 2021).

20. Jonathan Luxmoore, 'Membership falling in German Churches', *Church Times* (www.churchtimes.co.uk, 14 July 2023). See also https://katholisch. de/startseite for further information on the state of Germany's Catholic community.

21. Bill Huebsch, *Promise and Hope: Pastoral Theology in the Age of Mercy* (Twenty-Third Publications, 2020).

22. David Baddiel, *The God Desire* (TLS Books, 2023).

23. Rupert Shortt, *The Spectator* (www.spectator.co.uk, 8 April 2023).

24. Timothy McDermott, *How to Read Aquinas* (Granta, 2007), p. 95.

25. For examples of fresh but theologically rigorous thinking on sexuality, see James Alison, *Faith Beyond Resentment: Fragments Catholic and Gay* (DLT, 2001); Eugene Rogers, *Theology and Sexuality: Classic and Contemporary Readings* (Wiley-Blackwell, 2001); and Sarah Coakley, *God, Sexuality and the Self: An Essay 'On the Trinity'* (Cambridge University Press, 2013).

26. http://opencinema.net/

27. https://www.expertimpact.com/alumni/airbase-air-base-learning/

28. https://www.bfoundry.org/

29. https://thrivinglambeth.co.uk/

30. https://www.movingbeyond.co.uk/

31. https://www.woodlandsavers.org/

32. Martin Newland, 'The moral case for becoming a foster carer', *The Spectator* (www.spectator.co.uk, 24 June 2023).

33. Samuel Wells Thoughts One Can't Do Without (Juxta Press), 2020, p.15.

Chapter 7: Beyond Establishment

1. Stephen Sykes, in Marsha L. Dutton and Patrick Terrell Gray (eds), *One Lord, One Faith, One Baptism: Studies in Christian Ecclesiality and Ecumenism in Honor of J. Robert Wright* (Eerdmans, 2006).
2. Geoffrey Rowell, Kenneth Stevenson and Rowan Williams (eds), *Love's Redeeming Work: The Anglican Quest for Holiness* (Oxford University Press, 2001).
3. Ibid., p. xxvii–xxviii.
4. Ibid., p. xxx.
5. Ibid., p. xxx.
6. Ibid., p.xxxi.
7. See Shortt, *God's Advocates*, among many other examples of Rowan Williams's influence.
8. Shortt, *Rowan's Rule*, p. 111.
9. Ibid., p. 59.
10. Ibid., p. 60.
11. Shortt, *God's Advocates*, Chapter 6.
12. Wells, *Humbler Faith, Bigger God* – especially Chapter 3.
13. Samuel Wells, *What Anglicans Believe: An Introduction* (Canterbury Press, 2022).
14. Robert Hutton, 'Love and remembrance', *The Critic* (www.thecritic.co.uk, 19 September 2022).
15. Richard Chartres, reviewing *Beyond Establishment*, *Church Times* (www.churchtimes.co.uk, 22 July 2022).
16. Jonathan Chaplin, *Beyond Establishment: Resetting Church–State Relations in England* (SCM, 2022).
17. Anne Atkins, 'Why I have not lost my faith in the Church of England', *Church Times* (www.churchtimes.co.uk, 3 February 2023).
18. Abby Day, *The Religious Lives of Older Laywomen: The Last Active Anglican Generation* (Oxford University Press, 2017).
19. George Carey, *Know the Truth: A Memoir* (HarperCollins, 2004), p. 439.
20. https://www.youtube.com/watch?v=QVVlEBaAmqw
21. Peter Sedgwick, quoted in Shortt, *Rowan's Rule*, p. 315.
22. Ibid., p. 316.
23. *Faith in the City: A Call for Action by Church and Nation* (Church House Publishing, 1985).
24. *Faithful Cities: A Call for Celebration, Vision and Justice* (Church House Publishing, 2006).
25. *Love Matters: Summary Report of the Archbishops' Commission on Families & Households* (Church House Publishing, 2023).

26. Greg Smith, 'Is there still faith in the city, four decades on?', William Temple Foundation website (https://williamtemplefoundation.org.uk/).
27. https://www.message.org.uk/eden/
28. Smith, 'Is there still faith in the city, four decades on?'
29. Tudor Griffiths, interview with the author.
30. Graham Cray, *Mission-Shaped Church: Church Planting and Fresh Expressions of Church in a Changing Context* (Church House Publishing, 2006).
31. Graham Cray, *Church Times* (www.churchtimes.co.uk, 2 November 2006).
32. 'SDF opens a route to faith, says study', *Church Times* (www.church-times.co.uk, 11 March 2022).
33. *Living in Love and Faith: Christian Teaching and Learning about Identity, Sexuality, Relationships and Marriage* (Church House Publishing, 2023).
34. W. M. Jacob, *Religious Vitality in Victorian London* (Oxford University Press, 2021).
35. https://www.faithinvest.org
36. 'Religions unite to respect the earth', *Church Times* (www.churchtimes.co.uk, 31 March 2023).
37. Ibid.
38. Ibid.

Chapter 8: The Pentecostal Whirlwind

1. See David Martin, *Pentecostalism: The World Their Parish* (Wiley, 2001).
2. Asonzeh Ukah, *A New Paradigm of Pentecostal Power: A Study of the Redeemed Christian Church of God in Nigeria* (Africa World Press, 2008).
3. Ogbu Kalu, *African Pentecostalism: An Introduction* (Oxford University Press, 2008).
4. Randall J. Stephens, *The Fire Spreads: Holiness and Pentecostalism in the American South* (Harvard University Press, 2008).
5. David Martin, 'The Pentecostal Christianity practised by the Republican candidate for the vice-presidency is the neglected religious phenomenon of our time', *TLS* (www.the-tls.co.uk, 19 September 2008).
6. Gina Buijs, in conversation with the author.
7. Michael Bergunder, *The South Indian Pentecostal Movement in the Twentieth Century* (Eerdmans, 2008).
8. Martin, 'The Pentecostal Christianity'.
9. Andrew Atherstone, Mark P. Hutchinson and John Maiden (eds), *Transatlantic Charismatic Renewal, c.1950–2000* (Brill, 2021).
10. Matthew McNaught, *Immanuel* (Fitzcarraldo, 2022).

Chapter 9: Artificial and Spiritual Intelligence

1. Robert Runcie, Archbishop's Address to the Headmasters' Conference, 18 September 1990. All quotations are from this talk. It is not currently available online.
2. David Warnes, 'Slough, Reading and Oxford', in *Conference and Common Room*, Vol. 30, No. 3, Autumn 1993. This article also dates from the pre-internet era.
3. Iain McGilchrist, 'Matter Is a Relative Matter', a Lush TV broadcast with Matt Shaw (https://www.youtube.com/watch?v=NZ67R903Row).
4. Shortt, *Outgrowing Dawkins*, p. 56ff.
5. Rowan Williams, *Being Human: Bodies, Minds, Persons* (SPCK, 2018).
6. For an accessible summary of his argument, see Rowan Williams in conversation with the Revd Jordan Hillebert, Llandaff Cathedral, 4 July 2023 (https://www.youtube.com/watch?v=gGYTduSTmb4).
7. *The Mission: An Introduction* – a booklet setting out the aims and values of St Teilo's Church in Wales High School (https://stteilos.com/).
8. Steve Chalke, *A Manifesto for Hope: Ten Principles for Transforming the Lives of Children and Young People* (SPCK, 2023).
9. Ibid., p.35–6.
10. Ibid., pp. 149–50.
11. https://renetwork.co.uk/
12. https://marginalrevolution.com/
13. Tyler Cowen, quoted by Danny Fortson, 'Doom or Boom?', *The Sunday Times* (www.thetimes.co.uk, 29 October 2023).
14. Ibid.
15. Ibid.
16. Ibid.
17. Mustafa Suleyman and Michael Bhaskar, *The Coming Wave: AI, Power and the 21st Century's Greatest Dilemma* (Bodley Head, 2023).
18. Ibid., p. 8 (Kindle edition).
19. Ibid., p. 72 (Kindle edition).
20. Ibid., p. 72 (Kindle edition).
21. Ibid. p. 76 (Kindle edition).
22. BBC News website (https://www.bbc.co.uk/news/live/uk-66108009).
23. 'Married father kills himself after talking to AI chatbox for six weeks about his climate change fears', *Daily Mail* (www.dailymail.co.uk, 30 March 2023).
24. Suleyman and Bhaskar, *The Coming Wave*, p. 284 (Kindle edition).
25. Ibid., p. 202 (Kindle edition).

Chapter 10: Faith Healing

1. Andrew Brown, press review, *Church Times* (www.churchtimes.co.uk, 19 August 2022).
2. Joe Brierley, Jim Linthicum and Andy Petros, 'Should religious beliefs be allowed to stonewall a secular approach to withdrawing and withholding treatment in children?', *Journal of Medical Ethics* (https://pubmed.ncbi.nlm.nih.gov/22465877/ 13 August 2012).
3. David A. Jones, David R. Katz and John Wyatt, 'Doctors, dying children and religious parents: dialogue or demonization?', *Clinical Ethics*, Vol. 8, No. 2, 2013 (https://journals.sagepub.com/home/cet).
4. 'Birth rights', *The Spectator* (www.spectator.co.uk, 17 June 2023).
5. David A. Jones, 'From the Crime of Abortion to the Crime of Expressing Opposition to Abortion', *Zeitschrift für Medizinische Ethik*, 2 June 2023 (https://brill.com/view/journals/zfme/69/2/article-p243_5.xml).
6. Nicholas Reed Langen, 'Flawed ruling on late abortions', *Church Times* (www.churchtimes.co.uk, 20 January 2023).
7. Maggie Fergusson, 'On the side of the angels', *The Tablet* (www.thetablet.co.uk, 24/31 December 2022).
8. John Keown, 'Law, Ethics, and the Beginning and End of Life' (https://www.youtube.com/watch?v=1TZVS6b6BmU).
9. Ibid.
10. Baroness Hollins, House of Lords debate on the Assisted Dying Bill, 22 October 2021 (https://hansard.parliament.uk/).
11. There is further support for this interpretation in the latest Vatican document on the subject: https://www.cbc.ca/news/world/vatican-pope-transgender-baptism-1.7023505
12. David Albert Jones, 'One more way to be human', *The Tablet* (www.thetablet.co.uk, 6 April 2019).
13. Ibid.
14. Shortt, *God's Advocates*, pp. 192–3.
15. 'We the undersigned hold that to fulfil their professional duties to patients, to uphold the integrity of the medical profession, and to avoid harm to society as a whole, physicians must commit themselves to acting ethically in the practice of medicine and must always refrain from actions that they judge to be unethical. The duty of a physician to practise with conscience includes the duty not to act contrary to conscience.

    'A physician who, in good conscience, and in line with a reasonable body of medical opinion, judges a procedure to be harmful, discriminatory, unjust or otherwise unethical must not be placed under a professional, contractual or legal obligation to identify and refer to another healthcare professional who would provide the procedure. This stance is articulated and embodied in the WMA policy on euthanasia and assisted suicide which states that:

'No physician should be forced to participate in euthanasia or assisted suicide, nor should any physician be obliged to make referral decisions to this end.

'There are wider implications of making effective referral compulsory in the context of conscientious objection. For example, if a physician who objects in conscience to a legally-sanctioned medical procedure is obliged to identify and make effective referral to another physician who does not object, then in some jurisdictions a physician who objected to participation in "enhanced interrogation", or to capital punishment, or to force feeding of a prisoner who is on hunger strike, or to "conversion therapy", could be forced to facilitate these procedures by effective referral. However, to require a conscientious objector to facilitate delivery of a procedure to which they have a serious ethical objection is a direct attack on their conscience and moral integrity.

'A principled conscientious objection is always to a procedure and not to a person. Physicians must not refuse to treat a particular patient or group of patients because of beliefs about them unconnected with the medical propriety of the procedure. In particular, physicians must not refuse to treat criminals or enemy combatants or refuse to treat the health consequences of the patient's way of life, choices, or beliefs.

'A physician must ensure that conscientious objection is exercised in a way that takes full account of their duty of care for the life and health of the patient. The physician should also seek to minimise any disruption of patient care. If a clinician cannot in good conscience provide what the patient requests, the physician should, where appropriate, respectfully explain the reasons for the decision and should, where appropriate, inform the patient of other options that are available to them, including the option to seek a transfer of care to some other healthcare professional. However, the physician is not ethically obliged to provide, and must not be coerced into providing, effective referral of a patient for procedures that the physician sincerely and reasonably considers unethical' (https://www.bioethics.org.uk/news-events/news-from-the-centre/open-letter-to-the-world-medical-association-on-conscientious-objection/).

16. 'Spanish bishops resist "secularist" agenda', *Church Times* (www.churchtimes.co.uk, 6 April 2023).

Chapter 11: Being Diverse About Diversity

1. For a sample of the festival programme and its secular bias, see for example, 'Beyond Belief explores modern religion with classical concerts and debate', *Evening Standard* (www.standard.co.uk, 20 January 2017).

2. Damian Thompson, 'Losing their religion', *The Spectator* (www.spectator.co.uk, 23 July 2016).

3. *Beyond Belief*, BBC Radio 4, 16 January 2023 (https://www.bbc.co.uk/programmes/m001h467).

4. Spufford, *Unapologetic*, p. 102.

5. See Shortt, *Outgrowing Dawkins*, Chapter 1.

6. Steve Jones, *The Serpent's Promise: The Bible Retold as Science* (Little, Brown, 2013).

7. A. N. Wilson, *Charles Darwin: Victorian Myth-Maker* (John Murray, 2017).

8. Steve Jones, reviewing A. N. Wilson, *Charles Darwin*, *The Sunday Times* (www.thetimes.co.uk, 10 September 2017).

9. https://religionmediacentre.org.uk/

10. https://www.gov.uk/government/news/government-needs-to-better-understand-faith-independent-review-claim

11. https://trs.ac.uk/

12. Aaqil Ahmed, 'Religious broadcasting in a changing world', *Church Times* (www.churchtimes.co.uk, 17 June 2022).

13. https://religiousfreedomandbusiness.org/1-2-trillion-religious-economy-in-us

14. https://appgfreedomofreligionorbelief.org

15. Roger Scruton, 'Oikophobia', *The Journal of Education*, Vol. 175, No. 2, 1993, pp. 93–8 (https://www.jstor.org/stable/42742290).

16. See A. N. Wilson, 'The hounding of Kate Forbes shows godless squad have won', *The Times* (www.thetimes.co.uk, 25 February 2023).

17. Ibid.

18. Ibid.

19. https://premierchristian.news/en/news/article/christian-scottish-politician-says-constituents-are-telling-her-stories-of-religious-bullying

20. https://www.holyrood.com/news/view. kate-forbes-ispublics-choice-for-first-minister-poll-reveals

21. A 2019 British Religion in Numbers (BRIN) survey has also revealed striking data about the clash of outlook between the predominantly left-leaning clergy and more socially conservative laity in the Church of England (http://www.brin.ac.uk/figures/religion-and-partypreference-in-2019/).

22. https://www.theosthinktank.co.uk/
23. https://www.enterthepitch.com/
24. Ibid.
25. https://www.enterthepitch.com/films/only-child/
26. https://www.thewidowslast.com/
27. https://paulholbrook.co.uk/hollow
28. https://www.enterthepitch.com/watch/till-death-do-us-part/
29. 'From Albert Square to Bethlehem, *Church Times* (www.churchtimes.co.uk, 15 December 2010).

Chapter 12: Reversing Spiritual Climate Change

1. Taylor, *A Secular Age*.
2. See, for example, Ed West, 'Can post-liberalism save the Conservative party?', *The Spectator* (www.spectator.co.uk, 5 October 2023).
3. Robert D. Putnam, *Bowling Alone: The Collapse and Revival of American Community* (Simon &chuster, 2001).
4. Ayaan Hirsi Ali, 'Why I am now a Christian' (https://unherd.com/2023/11/why-i-am-now-a-christian/).
5. Bertrand Russell, *Why I Am Not a Christian, and Other Essays on Religion and Related Subjects* (Simon & Schuster, 1967).
6. David Martin, in Shortt, *God's Advocates*, p. 160.
7. Jacob Phillips, 'Against Christianity's cultured admirers: faith is far more than worldly fulfilment and success', *The Critic* (www.thecritic.co.uk, 17 November 2023).
8. Ibid.
9. Janet Soskice, reviewing John Cottingham, *The Spiritual Dimension*, *TLS* (www.the-tls.co.uk, 30 June 2006).

Index

Reference to endnotes are indicated by n.

Index